THE CARABINIERI COMMAND FOR THE PROTECTION OF CULTURAL PROPERTY

SAVING THE WORLD'S HERITAGE

T0385884

HERITAGE MATTERS

ISSN 1756–4832

Series Editors
Peter G. Stone
Peter Davis
Chris Whitehead

Heritage Matters is a series of edited and single-authored volumes which addresses the whole range of issues that confront the cultural heritage sector as we face the global challenges of the twenty-first century. The series follows the ethos of the International Centre for Cultural and Heritage Studies (ICCHS) at Newcastle University, where these issues are seen as part of an integrated whole, including both cultural and natural agendas, and thus encompasses challenges faced by all types of museums, art galleries, heritage sites and the organisations and individuals that work with, and are affected by them.

Previously published titles are listed at the back of this book

The Carabinieri Command for the Protection of Cultural Property

Saving the World's Heritage

LAURIE RUSH AND
LUISA BENEDETTINI MILLINGTON

THE BOYDELL PRESS

First published 2015
The Boydell Press, Woodbridge
Paperback edition 2019

ISBN 978–1–78327–056–9 hardback
ISBN 978–1–78327–404–8 paperback

The Boydell Press is an imprint of Boydell & Brewer Ltd
PO Box 9, Woodbridge, Suffolk IP12 3DF, UK
and of Boydell & Brewer Inc.
668 Mt Hope Avenue, Rochester, NY 14620–2731, USA
website: www.boydellandbrewer.com

The publisher has no responsibility for the continued existence or accuracy
of URLs for external or third-party internet websites referred to in this book,
and does not guarantee that any content on such websites is,
or will remain, accurate or appropriate

A CIP record for this book is available
from the British Library

This publication is printed on acid-free paper

Contents

Illustrations

Acknowledgments

We would like to begin by thanking the Carabinieri TPC; we are grateful for the support of Briga-dier General Mariano Mossa, Commander of Carabinieri per la Tutela del Patrimonio Culturale, who was enthusiastically receptive to the idea of the book and who wrote such a gracious intro-duction. We appreciate the warmth and encouragement of the former Commander of the CC TPC, General Pasquale Muggeo, and the support of Lieutenant Colonel Roberto Colasanti, who provided us with unwavering assistance from the very beginning and whose continued commit-ment enabled us to carry on and complete this volume. Major Massimo Quagliarella and all of the staff members and officers patiently answered questions and explained their work. Majors Giuseppe Marseglia and Andrea Ilari graciously hosted Laurie at their headquarters and offered detailed information about their work. Thanks to Captains Christian Costantini, Luigi Spadari, Gianluca Ferrari and Marshal Demetrio Cola for their help. Special thanks are due to Lieutenant Fabrizio Rossi; his assistance, expertise and consistent exchange of information on an almost daily basis for the past three years have made possible the birth of a solid friendship.

We are also indebted to Catherine Dauncey, our most capable and patient editor at the International Centre for Cultural and Heritage Studies, Newcastle University, and Professor Peter Stone, OBE, who gave generously of his time and provided comments. Working on this book has been a pleasure and a joy, every step of the way.

Laurie Rush would like to thank the American Academy in Rome and its 2010 Booth Family Rome Prize in Historic Preservation which made this book possible. As with many miracles, many thanks are due, beginning with acknowledging the generosity and kindness of Suzanne Deal Booth. I wish to thank my good friends Kevan Moss and Brian Rose, who encouraged me to apply for the Rome Prize, and my chain of command at Fort Drum who then encouraged me to accept. Special thanks are due to Colonel (retired) James Corriveau, Director of Fort Drum Public Works; James Miller, Chief of the Environmental Division; and Norm McGuire of the Public Works Business Office. Additional gratitude goes to BG Erik Peterson who withdrew the 10th Mountain Division request to serve with the Command Group to Afghanistan when he learned of the opportunity to go to Rome. I will always appreciate the honour of being asked to deploy. Upon arrival in Rome, I learned that I was following in the footsteps of Monuments Fine Arts and Archives Officers who were also fellows of the Academy. It is difficult to describe the privilege of being a part of this piece of history, this extraordinary institution and the opportunity to share a year with the gifted fellows. During the second summer of the book, the Association for Research into Crimes Against Art (ARCA) awarded me the honour of 'Writer in Residence' and special thanks go to Lynda Albertson who was gracious and welcoming and introduced me to General (retired) Pastore of the Carabinieri TPC, who was very helpful and generous in sharing his knowledge and experience. On the home front, Meg Schulz and Heather Wagner watched over the Fort Drum Cultural Resources Program, and my wonderful husband Jack literally kept the home fires burning and used all vacation possible to be with me in Italy. Thanks also to my children who rarely complain about having a mom who almost never calls, and last but certainly not least I am eternally grateful to my brilliant co-author Luisa who made all of the Carabinieri connections and research come to life.

Luisa Benedettini Millington would like to thank Dr Lynne Samuelson, Research Scientist, and Dr Claire Gordon, Senior Research Scientist, for the US Army Natick Soldier Research, Development and Engineering Center (NSRDEC). I met Dr Samuelson back in 2009 at the NEIC (New England Institute of Chemists) award ceremony when I was the recipient of an award for the state of Vermont. She encouraged me to participate in US military archaeological and anthropological projects, a move that led (with the assistance of Dr Gordon) to my cooperation with Laurie. Laurie assigned and assisted me through several different projects dealing with worldwide cultural heritage protection. From the very beginning of our amazing friendship, Laurie has been an invaluable mentor to me in all of our joint projects and I will always treasure her guidance. It has been an incredible honour for me to co-author this book on the Carabinieri TPC – a police force in Italy, my native country – with Laurie. Born and raised in Italy, I had not previously realised that the US Army employs archaeologists and that there is no equivalent of the CC TPC anywhere else in the world. When Laurie asked me to co-author this volume, I first and foremost felt honoured to collaborate on another project with Laurie, to whom I will always be thankful, but I also felt I was taking on the important mission of disseminating the work of the Carabinieri TPC as a model for other police forces in the world.

Reiterated thanks to Lieutenant Colonel Roberto Colasanti, who patiently assisted me with all my requests and visits, providing us with exceptional material and permissions to proceed with our publication on the CC TPC. Thanks again to our now dear friend Lieutenant Fabrizio Rossi, an incredibly passionate expert of art and history, who never stopped supporting our efforts and who graciously conducted any additional work to help us. Thanks to Mrs Melissa Smith who helped with the revision of the initial chapters of this book.

Last but not least, I would like to thank my beloved husband, Bob (creator of some of the drawings in this volume) and son, Franco, who are and always will be my inspiration and who have supported every initiative I have ever taken, even if it meant sacrificing precious family time.

Thank you now from us both to the readers, whom we hope will share our respect and admiration for the Carabinieri Tutela Patrimonio Culturale.

Laurie Rush
Luisa Benedettini Millington

Foreword

GENERAL B MARIANO MOSSA
COMMANDER, CC TPC

It was with pleasure that I accepted the authors' kind invitation to introduce this volume dedicated to the successes of the *Comando Carabinieri per la Tutela del Patrimonio Culturale* (Carabinieri Command for the Protection of Cultural Heritage), of which I am honoured to be Commander.

The commendable project, undertaken with enthusiasm, was to create a book that allows readers to learn about our organisation and our daily commitment to the protection and recovery of cultural heritage, at both national and international levels.

The copious documentation collected between 2011 and 2014 and analysed by Dr Benedettini Millington, and the study visits made by Dr Rush between February and April 2011 to the Operations Department of the Carabinieri TPC, the Data Processing Section that handles the 'Databank of Unlawfully Removed Cultural Property' and to the Nuclei of Florence, Palermo and Monza, provided the essential foundations for this important editorial project.

I carefully read the historical overview presented by the authors – an ideal starting point for understanding the ancient origins of the Italian tradition of protecting works of art and also for understanding the rich and diverse cultural heritage held by Italy for all humanity. The discussion spans ancient to recent history; the significant 'brief' of Leo X of 27 August 1515, wherein he appointed Raffaello (Raphael) Sanzio from Urbino 'Commissioner of Antiquities', with a mandate to prevent the destruction of marble inscriptions; the story of the passionate and generous diplomatic work entrusted by Pius VII to Antonio Canova, through whom we saw the return of exceptional masterpieces, transferred to France following the Napoleonic pillage; and not forgetting the edict issued in 1820 by Cardinal Bartolomeo Pacca, the first example of organic law on the protection of cultural heritage, which introduced the obligations of object documentation and restoration and expansion of the conservation workforce in order to reduce the risk of destruction and dispersal of artistic and archaeological heritage.

It was in this cultural setting that we came to realise the need to establish a specialised police department to protect Italian artistic heritage from criminal attack. The Carabinieri instituted the Command CC TPC on 3 May 1969. The authors exhaustively explain the origins and development of our Command, the most senior of all worldwide specialised police forces engaged in this complex and exciting field.

Special attention is paid to the relevant legislative framework within which the Carabinieri works, from public prosecution to the various central and peripheral components of the Ministry of Heritage and Cultural Activities and Tourism. The volume organically integrates past and present with a meticulous description of field operative experiences. It highlights very effectively the commitment to the fight against illegal excavations and the recovery of masterpieces stolen from museums, churches and private collectors. The *Leonardo* database – the true heart of the Command for the activation and development of investigations in Italy and abroad – is well documented. The description of Operation 'Ancient Babylon', where the Command CC TPC performed a difficult role in Nasiriyah (Iraq), illustrates how the professionalism and experience of the Carabinieri are able to provide concrete answers in situations of crisis and emergency. The monitoring of archaeological sites affected by intense clandestine excavation, the organisation and training of local police to improve a site's security, the census of stolen cultural property and the museum display of recovered objects are still remembered today as examples of activities to protect cultural heritage in crisis areas.

The presentation of the Command CC TPC is completed by the description of the inspections periodically carried out within museums in order to verify the adequacy of security measures against criminal attacks.

The volume extensively explains the educational outreach programmes that have been led by the Command CC TPC over the years. Initiatives such as publications, exhibitions and seminars in schools and universities, as well as interactive games for the younger generation, aim to increase public awareness of the issue of cultural property protection in the hope of encouraging students to become responsible and 'protective' citizens with regard to their own historical and cultural roots.

I am sure this volume will provide US and other readers who are interested in fighting the illicit trade of artworks at the international level with a comprehensive picture of the protection offered to the Italian national cultural heritage by the Command CC TPC.

In order to respond adequately to ever more aggressive crimes and criminals able to transfer stolen assets at an increasing rate, the European Union has funded PSYCHE, a project to upgrade the capabilities of INTERPOL's 'Works Of Art' (WOA) database. The authors fully recognise the importance of this ambitious project that the Command CC TPC (as project leader) will finalise in the coming months. The fast pace of illegal traffic will then be countered by even faster information exchange at international level regarding the stolen items. Thanks to the new implementation by the Command CC TPC, images of sought artworks will be available to view in real time by anyone accessing the database, which has been available to consult online since 2009.

Knowledge of stolen cultural property is a means of preventing and fighting the illicit market. The new application *iTPC*, developed by our technicians, allows anybody to interrogate our archive by sending an image from a tablet or smartphone. The archive contains the most important objects surveyed in the Databank of Unlawfully Removed Cultural Property.

I am grateful for the opportunity not only to share this important technological news, but also to mention the *Handbook on the Protection of Ecclesiastical Cultural Property*, a publication organised by the Command CC TPC delegation of the Ministry of Cultural Heritage and Tourism and strongly supported by the Pontifical Council for Culture. The manual has been distributed to all dioceses of the world. To cover the unique Italian situation, a new publication titled *Guidelines for the Protection of Ecclesiastical Cultural Property* has been created in partnership with the Italian Episcopal Conference to provide practical advice on how to implement more effective defences and protection for the vast wealth of history and art housed in churches.

I extend my best wishes to this editorial initiative in the hope that our organisational model can provide ideas and useful insights into the implementation of the different systems of protection of cultural heritage around the world, strengthening the vital collaboration between police forces and all of those who care about art and culture in their greatest sense.

Prefazione

GENERALE B MARIANO MOSSA
COMANDANTE, CC TPC

Ho accolto con piacere l'invito formulato per redigere la prefazione a questo volume, dedicato al Comando Carabinieri per la Tutela del Patrimonio Culturale (Comando CC TPC) che ho l'onore di comandare.

L'idea, encomiabilmente ed entusiasticamente perseguita, era di realizzare un volume che consentisse ai lettori di conoscere la nostra organizzazione e il nostro impegno quotidiano per la tutela ed il recupero dei beni culturali, in ambito nazionale ed internazionale.

La copiosa documentazione raccolta dal 2011 al 2014 e analizzata dalla Dott.ssa Benedettini Millington nonchè le visite di studio della Dott.ssa Rush, svoltesi da febbraio ad aprile del 2011 al Reparto Operativo del CC TPC, alla Sezione Elaborazione Dati che gestisce la 'Banca dati dei beni culturali illecitamente sottratti' ed ai Nuclei di Firenze, Palermo e Monza,sono la base imprescindibile che qualifica questo importante progetto editoriale.

Ho letto con attenzione la panoramica storica con cui le Autrici hanno inteso iniziare la trattazione: punto di partenza obbligato per comprendere quanto antica sia la tradizione italiana nella tutela delle opere d'arte e del ricchissimo e diversificato patrimonio culturale di cui l'Italia è detentrice per l'intera Umanità. Dalle vicende più remote al significativo '*breve*' di Leone X del 27 Agosto 1515, con cui Raffaello Sanzio da Urbino fu nominato '*Commissario alle Antichità*', con l'incarico di impedire la distruzione dei marmi epigrafici. Ed ancora le vicende dell'appassionato e generoso lavoro diplomatico affidato da Pio VII ad Antonio Canova, al quale dobbiamo il rimpatrio di eccezionali capolavori trasferiti in Francia a seguito delle spoliazioni napoleoniche. Senza dimenticare l'editto emanato nel 1820 dal Cardinale Bartolomeo Pacca: primo dispositivo di legge organica in tema di tutela del patrimonio culturale, che introduceva l'obbligo della catalogazione, del restauro e dell'ampliamento degli organici per l'azione di salvaguardia, al fine di impedire i rischi di distruzione e dispersione delle ricchezze artistiche e dei beni archeologici.

È in questo *humus* culturale che maturò l'esigenza di istituire un servizio di polizia specializzato a tutelare il patrimonio artistico italiano dalle aggressioni criminali. Siamo nel lontano 3 maggio 1969 quando l'Arma dei Carabinieri istituì il Comando CC TPC. Le Autrici espongono esaustivamente le vicende di genesi e sviluppo del nostro Comando, *decano* a livello mondiale di tutti i reparti specializzati, impegnati in questo settore complesso ed appassionante.

Particolare attenzione viene riservata al quadro normativo di riferimento, in cui i Carabinieri operano con la Magistratura ed il supporto degli uffici centrali e periferici del Ministero dei Beni e delle attività Culturali e del Turismo. Il volume, che integra organicamente passato e presente, con una puntuale descrizione delle esperienze operative sul territorio, evidenzia in modo efficace l'impegno nella lotta agli scavi clandestini, nel recupero di capolavori trafugati in danno dei musei, delle chiese e dei collezionisti privati. Ampio spazio è riservato alla banca dati 'Leonardo', cuore pulsante del Comando, con cui si attivano e si sviluppano le indagini in Italia e all'Estero.

Il cenno all'Operazione 'Antica Babilonia', in cui Comando CC TPC ha svolto un difficile compito a Nassiriya in Iraq, descrive come la professionalità e l'esperienza dei Carabinieri siano in grado di fornire risposte concrete in situazioni di crisi ed emergenza. Il monitoraggio dei siti archeologici interessati da un'intensa attività di scavo clandestino, l'organizzazione e la formazione della polizia locale per migliorare la sicurezza dei siti, il censimento dei beni culturali sottratti, la musealizzazione dei reperti recuperati: è stata un'esperienza memorabile, ancora oggi di esempio per le attività di tutela del patrimonio culturale nelle aree di crisi.

La presentazione del Comando CC TPC è completata con la descrizione dei sopralluoghi che periodicamente vengono effettuati nelle sedi museali al fine di verificare l'adeguatezza delle misure di sicurezza contro le aggressioni criminali.

Sono state puntualmente colte e menzionate anche le iniziative, sul piano educativo, che da anni il Comando CC TPC conduce per sensibilizzare l'opinione pubblica alle tematiche di tutela, con pubblicazioni, eventi espositivi e seminari nelle scuole e Università e giochi interattivi per i più piccoli, con l'auspicio che questi ultimi potranno divenire cittadini responsabili e 'gelosi' delle proprie radici storiche e culturali.

Sono certo che questo volume, così come realizzato, fornirà ai lettori degli USA e a quanti, a livello internazionale, sono interessati alle problematiche di contrasto al traffico illecito, un quadro esaustivo della tutela che l'Italia assicura al patrimonio culturale nazionale attraverso il Comando CC TPC.

Per rispondere adeguatamente alle sfide sempre più pressanti di una criminalità che diviene sempre più aggressiva e capace di trasferire i beni trafugati con una velocità sempre maggiore, l'Unione Europea ha finanziato PSYCHE, un progetto finalizzato ad aggiornare le funzionalità della banca dati 'opere d'arte' (WOA) dell'INTERPOL. Le Autrici hanno colto perfettamente l'importanza di questo ambizioso progetto che il Comando CC TPC, quale 'project leader', ultimerà nei prossimi mesi: alla velocità del traffico illecito si contrapporrà la rapidità dello scambio informativo, a livello internazionale, sui beni trafugati. Le immagini delle opere d'arte da ricercare, grazie all'implementazione che sarà realizzata dal Comando CC TPC, potranno essere disponibili in tempo reale e visibili a tutti coloro che accedono a questa banca dati che è consultabile *online* dal 2009.

Conoscenza del patrimonio culturale sottratto, dunque, come mezzo per prevenire e contrastare il mercato illecito. È in questa direzione che si colloca l'applicazione *iTPC* che, sviluppata dai nostri tecnici informatici, consente a chiunque, con il semplice invio di un'immagine da tablet o smart phones, di interrogare un archivio contenente i beni di maggiore rilevanza censiti nella *Banca dati dei beni culturali illecitamente sottratti*.

Sono grato, oltre che per aver riportato questa importante novità informatica, anche per aver inteso menzionare il '*Manuale sulla Tutela dei beni culturali ecclesiastici*': una pubblicazione fortemente voluta dal Pontificio Consiglio della Cultura e realizzata dal Comando CC TPC su delega del Ministero dei Beni e delle Attività Culturali e del Turismo. Il 'Manuale', distribuito a tutte le Diocesi del mondo (per la specifica situazione italiana, è stata realizzata, in collaborazione con la Conferenza Episcopale Italiana, una nuova pubblicazione dal titolo '*Linee Guida per la tutela dei beni culturali ecclesiastici*') contiene consigli pratici per rendere più efficace l'azione di difesa e salvaguardia del vastissimo patrimonio di storia ed arte custodito negli edifici di culto.

Auguri vivissimi dunque a questa iniziativa editoriale, con l'auspicio che il nostro modello organizzativo possa contribuire a fornire idee e spunti utili all'implementazione dei diversi sistemi di tutela del patrimonio culturale nel Mondo, rafforzando l'imprescindibile collaborazione tra forze di polizia e tutti coloro che hanno a cuore l'arte e la cultura nel loro significato più alto.

Abbreviations

AAHM	Asian Academy for Heritage Management
AMGOT	Allied Military Government for the Occupied Territories
ARAR	*Azienda Rilievo Alienazione Residuati*
ARCA	Association for Research into Crimes against Art
ATHAR	Architectural-Archaeological Tangible Heritage in the Arab Region
CC	*Comando Carabinieri*
CEDU	Centre for Human Rights Education
CEPOL	European Police College
CHO	Chief Humanitarian Officer
CNR	Italian National Research Council
CoESPU	Centre of Excellence for Stability Police Units
COINS	Combat Online Illegal Numismatic Sales
CRAST	Centre for Archaeological Research and Excavations of Turin
EAI	Enterprise Application Integration
ESP	Enterprise Search Platform
FPS	Facilities Protection Service
GIASS	*Gruppo d'Intervento di Archeologia Subacquea Sicilia*
GIS	Geographic Information System
ICCD	*Istituto Centrale per il Catalogo e la Documentazione*
ICCROM	International Centre for the Study of the Preservation and Restoration of Cultural Property
ICE	Immigration and Customs Enforcement
ICOM	International Council of Museums
ICOMOS	International Council on Monuments and Sites
IFAR	International Foundation for Art Research
IIHL	International Institute of Humanitarian Law
IILA	*Istituto Italo-Latino Americano*
ITTF	INTERPOL Tracking Task Force
KLPD	*Korps Landelijke Politiediensten*
MFA&A	Monuments and Fine Arts and Archives
MiBAC	*Ministero per i Beni e le Attività Culturali*
MSU	Multinational Specialised Units
NPS	National Park Service
NTPA	*Comando Carabinieri Ministero Pubblica Istruzione – Nucleo Tutela Patrimonio Artistico*
OCBC	*Office central de lutte contre le trafic des biens culturels*
PSYCHE	Protection System for Cultural Heritage
SIM	*Servizio Informazioni Militari*
SOA	Service Oriented Architecture
STAS	*Servizio Tecnico per l'Archeologia Subacquea*
TPC	*Tutela del Patrimonio Culturale*

UNIDROIT	International Institute for the Unification of Private Law
UNODC	United Nations Office on Drugs and Crime
UNTOC	*United Nations Convention against Transnational Organized Crime*
WHC	World Heritage Committee
WOA	Works of Art (INTERPOL Works of Art database)

1

The Carabinieri TPC: an Introduction and Brief History

Perché l'Italia? Why Italy?

The Carabinieri Command for the Protection of Cultural Property – in Italian the *Comando Carabinieri per la Tutela del Patrimonio Culturale* (TPC) – is the most effective military policing force in the world for protecting works of art and archaeological property. There are outstanding officers and programmes elsewhere, but there is no other force that can match the operational organisation, range of expertise, capabilities, nor the record of Carabinieri TPC accomplishment. Given the fact that Italy may be viewed as an open-air museum with perhaps the highest concentration of art and archaeological treasure per square kilometre in the world (CC TPC 2008), it is not surprising that the Italian people would make protection of art and archaeology a national priority. In addition, appreciation of art and beauty is an essential element of Italian culture.

PROTECTION OF HERITAGE, HISTORICAL CONTEXT FOR AN ITALIAN ETHIC

Protection of elements in the Italian landscape dates back at least 2000 years. One of the earliest examples of stewardship in Italian culture was the protection of the sacred forest of Monteluco. The forest is marked by a 3rd-century BC Roman inscription called the Lex Spoletina, which clearly indicates that the forest is protected. Any individual caught illegally harvesting wood from within this sacred forest was required to sacrifice an ox to Jupiter. Only 200 years after the Romans carved and placed the warning of the Lex Spoletina in the forest, Cicero set a legal precedent with the prosecution of Verres, a Roman Senator and Governor of Sicily. The people of Sicily brought suit in the Roman judicial system against Verres, who they accused of illegally appropriating works of art for his personal use. The famous Roman lawyer and orator Cicero agreed with the Sicilians and took the case. Cicero's prosecution of Verres is still referred to as setting the standard for the behaviour of conquering powers where art is concerned, even at a time when warring armies plundered cultural property as part of the spoils of victory. Cicero's prosecution also set guidelines for public versus private appreciation of art.

More recently, in 1646, the Vatican State issued the first relatively modern set of laws governing the protection of cultural property in Italy. At that time, the region we now recognise as the modern State of Italy was governed by a series of independent states and the Vatican owned a large area of central Italy. In 1646, the Vatican issued the law known as the *Editto Sforza*, Sforza's Edict (Surano 2007), which prohibited the removal from Roman ground of any cultural item cited in a list that Pope Aldobrandini had previously issued in 1624. The law was issued in response to the increasing number of art collectors throughout Europe who were under-

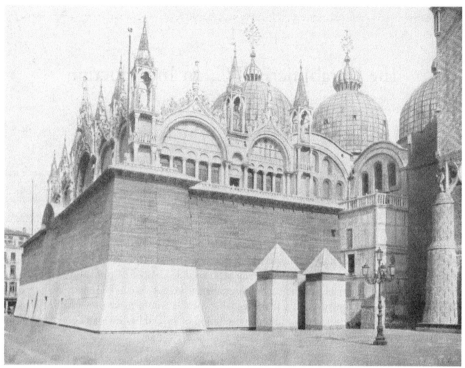

FIG 1.1.   PROTECTION OF THE SOUTHERN SIDE OF SAINT MARK'S, VENICE.

mining Italy's cultural heritage by purchasing art objects, archaeological material, sacred books and manuscripts that had been illegally exported. In addition to the prohibition of excavation for the purpose of removing archaeological material, Sforza's Edict also forbade any exportation of art objects from the region without proper permission or licence.

Approximately 200 years later, Cardinal Pacca, Vatican Secretary of State and Prime Minister to Pope Pius VII, issued a new edict forbidding the export of antique objects and items of archaeological interest from Vatican territory. King Ferdinando I reiterated the same edict for the Kingdom of the Two Sicilies, a region that included the Island of Sicily and the area now known as southern Italy, which was facing the same problem.

In the meantime, the Carabinieri as an armed protective force had come into being in Italy on 13 July 1814, by resolution of King Vittorio Emanuele I. The officers are called Carabinieri because the weapons with which they were initially equipped were carbines. The Carabinieri has an extremely illustrious history. As a fighting force, Carabinieri units distinguished themselves on the battlefields of the Risorgimento or Italian Unification. However, following the Unification of Italy in 1861 (Ministero per i Beni e le Attività Culturali 2011), the new government assigned the protection of Italian cultural heritage to local institutions until the early years of the 20th century when a set of Italian federal laws began to address the problem of the illegal traffic in

Fig 1.2. Protection of the Colleoni statue.

art objects. It is reasonable though to expect that during this time, local units of Carabinieri would have been called upon to enforce art protection laws, investigating thefts of artwork and archaeological objects.

During World War I, the Italians demonstrated their commitment to cultural property protection by designing and constructing structures to protect important monuments (Ojetti 1917) (see Figs 1.1 and 1.2).

These extraordinary measures could be seen throughout northern Italy. From enclosing the Colleone Monument in Venice (ibid) to encasing Trajan's arch in Ancona (Franchi 2010), there were examples of structures and sandbags protecting fountains, towers, domes, columns, altars, pulpits, monuments, statues and arches. Moveable objects were also taken into consideration. Ojetti (1917) shows images of rolled-up paintings from the Doge's Palace, including *Tintoretto's Paradise*, being removed to the countryside for safekeeping, and Franchi (2010) also discusses the remarkable efforts to pack and move irreplaceable treasures to safe places, including the four horses of San Marco in Venice and Titian's *Assunta*. Even though they were not directly involved with heritage protection and stewardship during this phase of history, the Carabinieri, as a military unit, also performed heroically during the War and were awarded the Gold Medal of Military Valour.

FIG 1.3.   PROTECTION OF TRAJAN'S COLUMN, ROME.

By 1939, Italian laws designed to protect cultural heritage had been modified several times and in this year the Italian government decided to assign the protection of Italy's cultural heritage to a department called the 'Direzione Generale Antichità e Belle Arti del Ministero della Pubblica Istruzione' – The General Directorate for Antiquities and Fine Arts of the Ministry of Public Instruction. As it became clear that the art, archaeology, monuments and heritage of Italy would be gravely endangered by the violence of World War II, the Italian people once again proactively began to protect their monuments, just as they had in preparation for World War I. The ingenious brick structure built to protect Trajan's Column (see Fig 1.3) is just one of many examples of Italian engineering skill and extraordinary effort to preserve one of the world's treasures entrusted to them (Cura della Direzione Generale delle Arti 1942).

Along with dozens of other monuments and masterpieces, we owe the safeguarding of this column to the same generation of Italians who protected Da Vinci's *The Last Supper* (*Il Cenacolo*). Their efforts to sandbag and reinforce the wall where Da Vinci painted this masterpiece secured its survival even when the monastery in Milan where it was located was grievously damaged during aerial bombardment (see Fig 1.4a/b).

In addition to the extraordinary considerations required for the protection of monuments and structures in place, the Italians also had to secure extensive public and private collections including art, library and archival materials. As armies crossed the country, many of even the most carefully hidden and secured objects disappeared, carried off by warriors, refugees and miscreants from all sides. However, the most systematic thefts were perpetrated by the Nazis who were actively collecting art from throughout occupied Europe, both for their own private collections and for the extravagant post-war museums they were planning. Detailed accounts of the thefts and the efforts to recover these properties can be found in a range of volumes beginning with Lynn Nicholas' *Rape of Europa* (1995). Although World War II experiences are beginning to elude living memory, the losses and the efforts to recover Italian masterpieces have left indelible impressions throughout Italian society, especially in the arts, archaeology and law enforcement communities.

In response to the thefts and events of World War II, the international community began to address the issue of damage and loss of cultural property during times of war. The first international legal instrument designed to address the issue after World War II was the 1954 *Convention for the Protection of Cultural Property in the Event of Armed Conflict* (The Hague Convention). This Convention obligates the member countries to identify and protect their own cultural property in times of peace and to refrain from deliberately damaging or destroying the cultural property of others during times of war. The Convention was adopted together with its First Protocol which is designed to prevent the export of cultural property from occupied territory and requires the return of any such property. The Convention also proposed marking important buildings and monuments with a blue shield system, designed to be used in a similar fashion to the way the red cross or red crescent symbols are used to identify medical facilities. The Hague Convention also specifies that special units be set up within the military forces to be responsible for the protection of cultural heritage.

In the 1960s, Italy began to recover economically from the devastation of World War II. The new financial growth and emergent prosperity brought with it the unfortunate side effect of an increase in theft and illegal export of art and archaeological objects. This trade was beginning to spin out of control and, in response, the Italian government tasked the General Command of the Carabinieri, *Comando Generale dell'Arma dei Carabinieri*, to form a nucleus of officers specifically

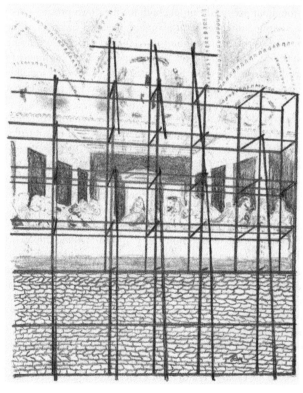

FIG 1.4A AND 1.4B.   THE ITALIANS
PREPARED VERY CAREFULLY
FOR POTENTIAL DAMAGE TO *IL*
CENACOLO (KNOWN IN ENGLISH
AS DA VINCI'S *LAST SUPPER*),
USING SANDBAGS REINFORCED
WITH TIMBER FRAMEWORK.
THESE PREPARATIONS SAVED THE
MASTERPIECE WHILE THE REST
OF THE STRUCTURE WAS ALMOST
DESTROYED.

to protect Italy's cultural, archaeological, palaeontological, artistic and historical heritage (CC TPC 2008). The *pro tempore* Chief of Staff of the Carabinieri Corps, General Arnaldo Ferrara, with support of the Commanding General, Luigi Forlenza, made the decision to form the unit and to attach it to the Ministry of Culture. The first dedicated unit consisted of one Commissioned Officer, One Non-Commissioned Officer and one Carabinieri (Tiberi 2008).

Also during the late 1960s, the Italian government began to anticipate the passage of the 1970 UNESCO *Convention on the Means of Prohibiting and Preventing the Illicit Import, Export and Transfer of Ownership of Cultural Property*. This Convention requires the States Parties to:

> take the necessary measures to prevent museums and institutions from acquiring cultural property originated in another state ... to prohibit the import of cultural property stolen from a museum or a religious or secular public monument or similar institution in another State Party ... to take appropriate steps to recover and return any such cultural property... to ensure the protection of their cultural property against illicit import; export and transfer of ownership.

In addition, this Convention requires the States Parties to:

> set up within their territories one or more national services ..., with a qualified staff sufficient in number for the effective carrying out of these functions... to form laws and regulations designed to secure the protection of the cultural heritage and particularly prevention of the illicit import, export and transfer of ownership of important cultural property. In order to prevent illicit export and to meet the obligations arising from the implementation of the Convention, each State Party to the Convention should, as far as it is able, provide the national services responsible for the protection of its cultural heritage with an adequate budget and, if necessary, should set up a fund for this purpose. (UNESCO 1970)

So it is no coincidence that on 3 May 1969 the *Comando Carabinieri Ministero Pubblica Istruzione – Nucleo Tutela Patrimonio Artistico* (NTPA), translated as the Nucleus for the Protection of Artistic Patrimony of the Carabinieri Command of the Ministry of Public Education, was born. In fact, Italy was the very first country in the world to form such a policing unit, and Carabinieri TPC officers are very proud of the fact that their unit was created prior to the 1970 UNESCO treaty that requires States Parties to set up forces of this nature. On 15 July 1970 it was determined that the functional and operative attributes of the unique Italian force could serve as a model, so during the Fourteenth UNESCO General Conference, held in Paris from 12 October until 14 November of that year, the delegates strongly encouraged the policing agencies of the member states to set up similar specialised teams. Since that time, the Italians have been in a position to assist other nations striving for compliance with the 1970 UNESCO Treaty, or who at the very least are attempting to protect their own cultural patrimony.

On 13 September 1971, upon the decision of the General Headquarters of the Carabinieri, the unit was elevated to the position of having its own headquarters, to be commanded by an officer of colonel rank. Therefore, the following week, on 20 September, the Command was renamed *Comando Carabinieri per la Tutela del Patrimonio Artistico* (CC TPA). At this point, three of its most important activities were coordinated as sections under the command of a Lieutenant Colonel; these sections included Archaeology, Antiquities and Forgeries. On 5 March 1973, the Command (CC TPA) was placed under the jurisdiction of the Inspectorate of Schools and

Special Forces, remaining as a function of the Ministry of Public Education until 10 February 1975. In 1974, the Italians had established the *Ministero per i Beni e le Attività Culturali* – the Ministry for Cultural Heritage and Activities. This ministry assumed all of the responsibilities of the Ministry of Public Education governing antiquities and the arts, academies and libraries, as well as the management of the State Archives that formerly had been under the jurisdiction of the Ministry of Internal Affairs (*Ministero degli Interni*). They also took responsibility for the management of cultural diffusion from the Presidency of the Council of Ministers (*Presidenza del Consiglio dei Ministri*) (CC TPC 2008). As a result, the Carabinieri (CC TPA) then logically fell under the jurisdiction of the New Ministry for Cultural Heritage and Activities, and this relationship was formally established on 10 February 1975 under the leadership of the then Minister of Culture, Giovanni Spadolini. It was during this time that the Command completed one of its first sensational recoveries with the discovery in Switzerland of three paintings stolen from the Ducal Palace in Urbino. The paintings, Piero della Francesca's *Flagellazione* and *Madonna di Senigallia*, and *La Muta* by Raphael, were recovered and are back on display at their original home (Ministry of Cultural Heritage and Activities 2009).

Over the next five years, the Command continued to prove itself through outstanding performance in terms of law enforcement with respect to the arts, and in 1980 it also made the very important step of establishing a databank of stolen artwork, improving its capabilities for recognising and recovering objects. Investment in the Command was also continuing to grow during this time. As of 4 August 1981, the CC TPA force of 43 employees included 4 officials, 19 staff members and 20 officers. In 1985, the Command experienced another organisational change when on 1 July they moved from the combined jurisdiction of the Inspectorate of Schools and Special Forces to the Twelfth Carabinieri Brigade of Rome, assigned to the Special Mobile Division, *Palidoro*.

In 1992, the Ministry for Internal Affairs decided to further increase its investment in preventing and prosecuting crimes against art and officially allocated some of its personnel to the rescue and protection of art work. In order to implement this decision effectively, these functions were then specifically assigned to the Carabinieri CC TPA, augmenting the efforts of the pre-existing CC TPA units. By decree, on 12 February 1992 the Ministry for Internal Affairs designated the unit as a Special Force of the Carabinieri, and on 5 March the Ministry of National Heritage and Culture formalised the functions and duties of the Art Unit under the name of *Comando Carabinieri per la Tutela del Patrimonio Artistico*, or Carabinieri Headquarters for the Protection of Artistic Heritage. At this point, the Command had also recently been elevated to serve under the jurisdiction of a general, with General D Roberto Conforti serving as the first Carabinieri TPA Commander at this rank. Previous commanders were: Colonel Felice Mambor (1969–73); Colonel Pasquale Mazzeo (1973–75); Colonel Pio Alferano (1975–82); Colonel Giuseppe Vitali (1982–83); Colonel Gerardo de Donno (1983–86); Colonel Emidio Napolitano (1986–90); Colonel Antonino Cataldo (1990–91); General D Roberto Conforti (1991–2002); General B Ugo Zottin (2002–07); General B Giovanni Nistri (2007–10); General Pasquale Muggeo (2010–12); and General Mariano Mossa (2012).

As of December 1994, the Carabinieri TPA had grown to become a force of 145 people, composed of 5 Commissioned Officers, 76 Non-Commissioned Officers and 64 Carabinieri, and within the next two years, by Ministerial Decree, regional offices in what were then considered to be the seven highest risk areas were formed with plans to add an additional four offices. The first regional offices included Monza, which had jurisdiction over Lombardy, Piemonte, Valle d'Aosta and Liguria; Venice, which covered the Veneto, Trentino-Alto Adige and Friuli Venezia Giulia; Bologna, which was responsible for Emilia-Romagna and the Marche; Florence, whose district included Tuscany and Umbria; Naples, governing Campania and Calabria; Bari, with responsibility over Puglia and Basilicata; and Palermo, covering Sicily. In addition to the regional offices, the central nucleus in Rome also governed issues in Lazio, Sardinia, Abruzzo and Molise. By 1998, the four additional planned regional offices were placed in Turin, Genoa, Cosenza and Sassari. The following chart (see Fig 1.5) illustrates the organisation of the TPC as of 2012.

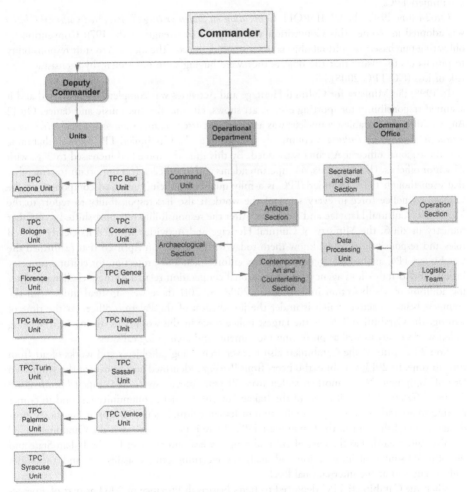

FIG 1.5. STRUCTURE AND ORGANISATION OF *COMANDO CARABINIERI PER LA TUTELA DEL PATRIMONIO CULTURALE* (CC TPC).

The European Union (EU), during the course of confederation, was also concerned about cultural property being put at risk, as the union made passage and the transportation of goods from state to state much easier. EU Council Regulation No 3911/92 of December 1992 was designed to harmonise export controls out of the European states. It also provided a structure for member states to work together in terms of sharing information and standardising customs practices. In 1993, the Council also passed a Council Directive requiring the return of cultural objects illegally removed from the territory of a member state. The European council regulations and directives further strengthened the law enforcement tools available to the emerging Carabinieri TPC.

On 24 June 1995, the UNIDROIT *Convention on Stolen or Illegally Exported Cultural Objects* was adopted in Rome. This Convention was designed to strengthen the 1970 Convention by obligating purchasers of cultural objects to return said objects. The idea was to shift responsibility to purchasers to ensure that the objects they were buying were not stolen, by increasing their risk of loss (CC TPC 2008).

In 1998, the Ministry for Cultural Heritage and Activities was completely reorganised and it assumed responsibility for sporting events, art shows, cinema, theatre, music and dance. On 12 August 2001, the Carabinieri nucleus was assigned its current name, *Comando Carabinieri per la Tutela del Patrimonio Culturale*, commonly referred to as the Carabinieri TPC, and in that same year the regional office at Ancona was added. By this time the force had increased to 278, with 25 senior officials, 117 inspectors, 45 superintendents and 91 officers. It is important to remember that even though the Carabinieri TPC is a fully qualified policing unit and component of the Carabinieri police force in every sense of the word, it also has responsibility to report to the Ministry of Cultural Heritage and Activities. After the responsibility for sport shifted to another ministry in 2006, the Ministry of Cultural Heritage and Activities assumed its clearly defined roles and responsibilities as we know them today with a decree on April 26 that reaffirmed the Carabinieri TPC as the lead agency for all law enforcement and protection for cultural property in Italy and as Italy's lead agency for international cooperation related to these challenges. After the addition of a sub-section in Siracusa in 2008, by 2011 there were 13 field units, with the youngest being Siracusa, which is under the jurisdiction of the Palermo office. At the time of writing, the Carabinieri TPC is the largest police force in the world specialising in recovering stolen works of art as well as protecting monuments and archaeological sites.

Non-TPC units of the Carabinieri also recover archaeological objects and works of art from time to time. In 2013, Carabinieri officers from Piacenza identified and recovered the sculptured face of Agrippina, Nero's mother, stolen over 30 years previously from Pompeii (*asca.it* 2012; *Montreal Gazette* 2012). All facets of the Italian law enforcement community respond to crimes relating to art and archaeology – a reflection of Italian cultural values in supporting the extraordinary accomplishments of the Carabinieri TPC. There is no question that the Carabinieri TPC is universally regarded as the core of cultural property law enforcement for the Italian State and the ultimate source of information and analysis concerning crimes against art and antiquities within Italy and at the international level.

When the Carabinieri TPC deployed to Iraq's Nasiriyah Province in 2003 as part of a peace-keeping mission, their operations and success in the area of heritage preservation demonstrated their unique capabilities to the entire world. As advisers and subject matter experts study this Carabinieri mission, the overall organisation of the Carabinieri TPC and its distinguished officers, it quickly becomes clear that the Carabinieri TPC should serve as an example and model for developing similar capabilities in departments and ministries of defence of other nations. By the same token, the Italian preservation ethic is also worthy of worldwide emulation. As one learns more about the Carabinieri TPC and the Italian approach to cultural heritage, it becomes increasingly clear that TPC enforcement efforts are ultimately driven by the Italian belief that good stewardship requires: protection of resources *in situ*; preventative and security measures to protect art and archaeology; return of stolen objects to their countries and/or communities of origin; international cooperation; mediation of competing interests; and a willingness to negotiate loans and agreements for sharing of cultural heritage between communities and countries.

ORGANISATION

Following the development of the regional offices, the Carabinieri can be considered to have two basic structural components: the regional jurisdictions and the central headquarters functions. The central headquarters, based in Rome, includes, in addition to Command leadership, jurisdiction over Lazio and the Abruzzo, the Archaeology Unit, the databank, the photography laboratory and a facility for emergency conservation and temporary storage of recovered objects. The Command in Rome, located on the north side of Piazza Sant'Ignazio, is in an historic baroque palace built by Filippo Raguzzini (1680–1771) in 1723. The Brigadier General or Commander's office is located here, as is the Vice Commander, who is a Colonel and is in charge of all of the sections. There is also some administrative support located at Sant'Ignazio and, in the lobby, an exhibition of recovered objects. The remaining functions in Rome are located in a renovated franciscan monastery which is a secure facility in the neighbourhood of Trastevere, across the Tiber. This building was also used by the Bersaglieri Corps of the Italian Army as barracks during the 19th and 20th centuries and it is still named after the founder of the Corps, General La Marmora. Because of the function of the Carabinieri TPC and its relationship with the Ministry of Culture, the regional command headquarters are also located in historic structures and are a source of great pride for all of the commands.

RESPONSIBILITY

As one might imagine, in a country such as Italy, the responsibility for the protection of art and antiquities is enormous. It is even more daunting given the fact that, according to Italian Law since 1909, all evidence of antiquity found in the landscape is considered as property to be held in trust for all Italian people by the Italian government. So, for example, if one were to discover a tiny Etruscan bronze figure while digging in a privately owned garden, the figure would belong to the Italian government and should be reported, if not surrendered, to the Superintendency for the region where the discovery was made. The resulting enforcement tasks seem even more overwhelming when considered as specific and comprehensive responsibilities that include investigating all crimes and violations of the law that affect cultural patrimony while coordinating with the judicial system. These crimes include, but are not limited to:

- Theft and/or receipt of stolen objects of art;
- Damage to monuments and archaeological deposits;
- Forging or altering paintings, graphic art, sculpture, objects and artefacts of antiquity;

- Black marketeering and/or smuggling works of art;
- Extortion and money laundering concerning works of art.

In order to meet these goals effectively, the Carabinieri TPC works to protect the countryside, coordinates with other law enforcement elements of the Carabinieri and other Italian policing agencies and is responsive to the law enforcement needs of all aspects of the Ministry of Culture sector including museums, libraries and archives. To protect archaeological sites on both land and sea, cooperation with the airborne, mounted and underwater units of the Carabinieri has been extremely effective. Recognising that it is usually easier to protect cultural property than it is to recover stolen and looted objects, the Carabinieri TPC has also become extremely proactive in terms of education and security efforts for any entity that holds a collection or a valuable object, whether it is a private individual, government agency or an ecclesiastical diocese. These efforts are beginning to be reflected by positive changes in theft statistics coming in from some of the regions.

For its outstanding efforts in protecting the cultural property of the Italian State, the Carabinieri TPC has been awarded five gold medals (Ministry of Cultural Heritage and Activities 2009), including:

- First Class Certificate conferred with Republic Presidential Decree dated 1st of June 1981, 'By marking the glowing and glorious tradition, with indefectible commitment, tenacious abnegation and high degree of technical qualification, offered a constant and valuable contribution to the safeguard of national heritage, also consenting to recover; in Italian territory and abroad, stolen works of art of extraordinary historical and cultural value'.
- First Class Certificate conferred with Republic Presidential Decree dated 20th of May 1986, 'Renewed its most noble traditions in the protection of national artistic heritage achieving, with its professionalism, dedication and tenacity of its officers to the recovery of many works of art, including masterpieces of inestimable value'. National and Foreign Territory, 1981–1985.
- First Class Certificate conferred with Republic Presidential Decree dated 2nd of January 1995, 'The Carabinieri Corps, marking the glowing and glorious tradition, with incessant commitment, tenacious abnegation and high professionalism, offered a constant and precious contribution for the safeguard of the national artistic heritage, accomplishing significant results in the fight against the organized crime devoted to the illicit traffic of works of art. The recovery in Italian territory and abroad of numerous stolen works of art of incommensurable artistic, historical and cultural value, consolidated, in a decisive manner, the image and the prestige of the Institution in international ambit too.' National and Foreign Territory, 1986–1994.
- First Class Certificate conferred with Republic Presidential Decree dated 17th of May 2005, 'During a decade, being compact in its articulated presence on the territory and marking the glowing and glorious tradition, the Carabinieri Corps gave continued proof of remarkable professionalism and laudable commitment in the protection of national cultural heritage, recovering in Italy and abroad, a large quantity of stolen works of priceless historical and artistic value. Such brilliant results, achieved thanks to the perfect synergy between the special Department of the Carabinieri dedicated to the protection of cultural heritage and territorial Unites, which have crossed the national borders, obtaining

the grateful admiration of citizens and institutions. The unceasing activity of Carabinieri in the sector has contributed to render public awareness more sensitive to the respect of cultural and artistic values – patrimony essential for humanity – and to consolidate the image of Italy and the Carabinieri also in international ambit.' National and Foreign Territory, 1995–2004.

- First Class Certificate conferred with Republic Presidential Decree dated 30th of May 2008, 'For the incisiveness and variety of interventions performed by the Carabinieri Corps in protecting and safeguarding the national cultural heritage, in excellent operational synergy between the different specialized territorial units and in complete unity of intent with the government structures, through meticulous reconstruction of historical and judicial events, contributed significantly to the repatriation of archaeological artifacts of invaluable historic-artistic importance illegally exported abroad, raising unanimous, unconditioned praise from the highest public offices of State for the meritorious work done in securing the knowledge and the conscience of its past and the collective identity for future generations'. National and Foreign Territory, 2006–2007.

- Gold medal awarded by the President of the Republic of Italy, Giorgio Napolitano, on 25th of March 2013, upon proposal of the Minister of Culture, conferred to the Carabinieri for the Protection of Cultural Heritage, Benefactors of School, Art and Culture, for the merits acquired in over forty years of protection of Italy's national heritage.

It is abundantly clear that the efforts of the Carabinieri TPC are recognised and appreciated by the president and government of Italy on behalf of the Italian people, in addition to the genuine appreciation of the Italian people themselves.

2

Headquarters, the Databank and
Operative Department in Rome

The structure of the Carabinieri TPC begins with a headquarters in Rome, along with the databank and the Operative Department which is divided into Archaeology, Antiques and Forgery Units. The main headquarters are located in Piazza Sant'Ignazio, in a palace designed and built by Filippo Raguzzini (1727–28), while the databank and Operative Department are located in a renovated monastery complex called Caserma La Marmora, on the west side of the Tiber in Trastevere. The Rome headquarters and Operative Department are complemented by the regional offices that have varying sets of priorities and corresponding expertise as required by the differing challenges of the regions. This organisational structure, with resources and assets in a central location supplemented by regional field offices with local knowledge, forms an extremely effective foundation for comprehensive law enforcement related to the arts and archaeology. In addition to the databank, the Rome operative unit also offers 'in-house' forensic analysis to complement its liaison services to universities for additional forensics, artistic, archaeological and other specialised expertise. The Rome-based units also coordinate technological support for investigations such as wire-tapping and mobile phone call interceptions.

Militarised policing, partnered with the requirement to be responsive to the needs of the Ministry of Culture, results in a level of professionalism that is very difficult to duplicate in any other context. Essentially the Carabinieri TPC offers the best of both the academic and law enforcement worlds, with outstanding subject matter expertise combined with investigation experience. Field officers and the operations units collect information from all over Italy and organise that information into the databank, from where it can be readily retrieved and analysed, providing the Carabinieri with an extremely powerful base of information at their fingertips to support reconnaissance, as well as prosecution and recovery efforts.

THE DATABANK

One of the signature programmes of the Carabinieri TPC is the databank, or Banca Dati *Leonardo*. One of the earliest efforts in the world to use computer technology to trace stolen works of art, the databank remains up to date and is one of the most important assets available to Italians and the international community for the recovery of art and cultural property. A visit to the databank unit reveals the tremendous sophistication of the system and the extraordinary expertise of the officers who work with it on a daily basis.

Banca Dati *Leonardo* is a state-of-the-art Oracle enterprise system. The organisation of the database is an information tree that begins with the general category of an object at the macro level such as sculpture, textile, painting, or ceramic vessel. Each of these categories can be broken down further. For instance, textiles can be broken down into object types such as carpets, tapestries, quilts, coverlets and clothing. The carpet category can be further divided into fibre types such as wool, silk and cotton. In addition, carpets can be distinguished by design and the designs can be further divided by descriptors such as plain, figures, designs, medallions, or prayer rug. Designs could be even further broken down into descriptors such as repeated or border.

Banca Dati *Leonardo* can also be interacted with by field officers using mobile handheld units. As a result, an officer in the field can take a digital photo for comparison with photos from the databank and download information while analysing an object or work of art in real time. The database platform is multilingual and can provide document management while interfacing with other forms of police investigation software. As a result, an officer in the field can initiate reports remotely via electronic means working directly with analysts based in Rome at the database unit. Banca Dati *Leonardo* can also interface with other police and international databases, making it an even more effective tool and adding to its power. The Carabinieri TPC database system also has a Geographic Information System (GIS) with Oracle Spatial and Oracle map viewer components, so that patterns of illegal activity on the ground can be tracked and analysed. The database is based on six different interacting softwares: Oracle web, application and database; Java 2 Enterprise; SOA (Service Oriented Architecture); EAI (Enterprise Application Integration); ESP (Enterprise Search Platform) and Architettura Hardware Itanium 2. Together these softwares allow flexibility for multiple search and simultaneous applications (Tiberi 2008).

Just as documentation can serve as a deterrent against the deliberate destruction of cultural property in a contested landscape, it also serves as a critical component of an effective security system. If a quality image with precise measurements and detailed descriptions exists, it is much easier to identify and recover a work of art should it reappear for sale on the art market. If a potential thief is aware of the existence of documentation of this nature, he or she may choose to attempt to steal a less 'visible' object instead.

Unfortunately, until recently, the existence of inventory information that would meet law enforcement standard was very unusual. Still today items go missing about which there exists minimal information. The databank is set up to gather as much information as possible; not just details of the lost object but also about events surrounding the loss of the object. For example, if a family had a painting of a landscape with an ancient Roman bridge stolen from their home, they would phone the police or the Carabinieri. Since the theft involved a work of art, the investigation would eventually be referred to the Carabinieri TPC. However, in the meantime, understanding that the original responding police may not have the expertise of the TPC, the databank questions are designed for use by a non-specialist to elicit as much useful and specific information as possible for submission to the databank. Officers would begin by asking if the family had a photo of the lost painting. Even if efforts had not been made to document the object, sometimes through patient questioning it might perhaps be remembered that on a previous holiday the family posed in front of the painting for a photo, and so the investigation begins. With or without a photo, the victims of the theft will be asked to remember every possible detail. Were there animals in the image? What did the bridge look like? Do they know which Roman bridge it might have been? Do they know the name of the artist? Was the painting in oil, watercolour, on canvas, paper, wood panel? Approximately how big was the painting? All of these details will be entered into the database system so that if a landscape painting of a Roman bridge appears for sale at an auction house or on the internet, it can be flagged as a possible match for the missing painting. The more descriptors that can be entered into the databank, the greater the probability of an eventual match and recovery. At this point in the investigation, the Carabi-

Fig 2.1. Operator of the Data Processing Section of the Carabinieri TPC Command consulting the *Leonardo* databank, the world's most important databank of unlawfully removed cultural property.

nieri completes specific forms designed to document every possible aspect of the criminal act (theft, armed robbery, misappropriation etc). Data retrieved from the police/Carabinieri report, including details obtained in conversation with the person who reported the theft, place the location of the theft (region, province, municipality, address) and *modus operandi* are then added to the forms. Each stolen object is described in a separate form and details such as type of object, material and technique, dimensions, author, signature, title, weight, insurance, monetary value and photo(s) are added following the guidelines of the 'Object ID'.

Banca Dati *Leonardo* uses multi-language research software to match specific words or technical terminology and it is also able to match photos or parts of photos for colour, contrast, shape and texture. The databank can also match art crimes on a regional and geographical scale, looking for patterns of criminal behaviour, preferential routes used by art criminals, common denominators and other details that provide an enormous amount of information to detectives investigating art crimes. In order to circumvent these searching and matching capabilities, some art thieves and criminal dealers will cut apart a canvas or a work of art and sell the fragments separately so that the resulting items that come up for sale only represent portions of the original. In such cases, the expertise of the art historians on the databank staff is critical. For example, in the case of a large canvas with worshipping figures looking into the heavens, if the angels have been removed and possibly even replaced by a sky with clouds, it will be obvious to the experienced eye that a key component of the original is missing. The painting will no longer make sense, because people do not generally look up in awe at an empty sky. As a result, if found, the damaged painting can still potentially be matched with its original database entry information because the Carabinieri analyst will know to add the missing angels back into the search criteria. An example is the *Madonna del Rosario*, a large canvas stolen from a church (Manola and Ragusa 2012), which the criminals had cut into sections. Operatives at the databank who recovered a suspicious fragment noticed that the figures were all looking down and to the left in admiration. When checking against images in the databank, it became clear that the original painting was an adoration and that the figures had been cut away from the image of the Christ Child. To date, only four fragments of the painting have been recovered. It is difficult to describe the emotional response that many experience when they encounter a moving work of religious art that has been wilfully cut into pieces by criminals for the sake of monetary profit.

Along similar lines, thieves might perhaps paint out an element of a piece, such as a campanile in the background of a Madonna and Child. A good art historian may recognise that the perspective and composition of the image is not quite right and begin to speculate and search for the missing components. In situations such as these, a quality photograph of the original work of art is extremely helpful, as the remaining foreground and images could still be identified. The database system proves its worth in these situations because it has the capability of comparing portions of photos and fragments of works of art against objects of questionable origin.

At times the contest between law enforcement and the criminal element of society could be characterised as an arms race. As law enforcement capabilities improve, criminals attempt to develop new and creative ways to confound or evade these capabilities. Just as art thieves began to cut paintings apart to confound database matching systems, forgers began to graft their fake efforts onto actual ancient bases when they discovered that the Carabinieri could identify fake antiquities by carefully sampling and dating the bases of the objects.

As difficult as the documentation of two-dimensional works of art may be, working with objects offers an even more complex set of challenges. During a tour of Banca Dati *Leonardo*, one of the Carabinieri officers offered a kylix as an example. A kylix is a relatively small Greek bowl, an object that might very easily be looted from an archaeological site or stolen from a collection. If photographed from above, it looks just like a plate. As a result, any kylix that is entered into the databank must also be cross-referenced with plates and entered into the 'plate' category. For an object, it is optimal to have as many photos as possible from as many angles as possible. In the case of a column capital, for instance, if the only photos available prior to the loss were from one side of the column and the recovery photo is from a different side, omitting the carvings, an attempt to match would fail. This column capital from the Collegiata di Santa Maria Assunta di Lugnano in Teverina offers a perfect example. On one facet, we see the figure with the serpents, while on another we see a rendering of the Last Supper (see Fig 2.2).

Banca Dati *Leonardo* is also a critical tool for recovering library books, manuscripts and archival materials, even if they have been missing for 20 years or more. One of the most spectacular recent recoveries was a Venetian edition of *De Architectura* by Vitruvio, a 16th-century volume, stolen along with other books from the library of the Archdiocese of Montreal (Tabita 2012). This book was from the original collection of Ludovico II del Torres, Archbishop of Montreal from 1573–84. Officers at the databank spotted the volume when it was put up for sale by an auction house. They tracked the book to the owner in Bologna and seized it from

FIG 2.2.   COLUMN CAPITAL,
COLLEGIATA DI SANTA MARIA
ASSUNTA, LUGNANO IN
TEVERINA, UMBRIA.

his home. The courts found the owner guilty, even though he claimed that he had inherited the book from his deceased father. The Carabinieri TPC was able to return the book to the archives. *De Architectura*, by Vitruvio, is of special interest to book lovers because it features not only illustrations by Andrea Palladio but also commentary by Daniele Matteo Alvise Barbar, Cardinal of Aquila, humanist and scholar of philosophy, mathematics and optics (1514–1570).

For different object materials, different characteristics and variations will assist tremendously in the matching process. With stone, sometimes matching the veins in marble or grain in other forms of stone will provide a key. For example, imagine a situation where the column pictured below (see Fig 2.3) has been stolen and cut into two sections. If both sections were recovered, there would be no question about the veins matching up in this distinctive marble, demonstrating beyond doubt that both sections belonged to the same original piece.

Furthermore, this principle works for other types of objects such as amphorae and large ceramic vessels that are without decoration, as well as imperfections and patterns of imperfections that can identify a specific vessel. For pieces of bucchero ware – distinctive black glazed pottery which might also be undecorated – the glazes will be the most important attribute, performing a similar function to the grain in wood or marble.

Within the databank, some additional descriptors are unrelated to the inherent attributes of the objects themselves. Such additional information can, however, include the potential market value of objects, as well as their historical value. One of the great strengths of Banca Dati *Leonardo* is the events category. If a group of objects are stolen at one time, even if they are all very different, they are linked by the fact that they were part of a group stolen by the same thief or thieves from the same place at the same time. This information can be critical for an investigation because if just one of the objects from the group is found, then the new information can potentially be used to trace the other objects. Another advantage of a databank system is that no matter how long an object has been missing, should the object reappear the corresponding data and documentation can be retrieved instantly.

The ability to track events is absolutely critical for archaeological looting and investigations into the activities of the *tombaroli*, the Italian term for grave robbers and a term often generically applied to looters of ancient tombs and archaeological sites in Italy. If fresh and detailed evidence of looting at an archaeological site is gathered, expert knowledge concerning that site can be used to match previously unknown objects appearing on the market with the location of the theft. Technological improvements in trace element analysis also mean that objects looted from the earth may now be matched to the soils where they were originally found – a sort of geo-chemical version of DNA.

Every day, databank operatives search the internet for evidence of objects documented in Banca Dati *Leonardo*. The tremendous power of the database structure and the information stored there increases the likelihood of a match, if a stolen object surfaces on the art market. In addition to internet auction and sales sites, galleries, dealers and auction houses from around the world yield information about stolen objects. In terms of internet sales, the officers who work on the internet every day can begin to identify patterns of behaviour in terms of individuals, aliases and computer addresses. Sometimes these data, when combined, can lead to the identity of the criminal(s) and the operative unit can, as it was euphemistically described to the authors, 'pay that person a visit'. Statistical analysis of sales and looting events can also provide guidance for efficient mobilisation of the operative units, because the patterns identified offer predictive power in terms of where future events are likely to occur.

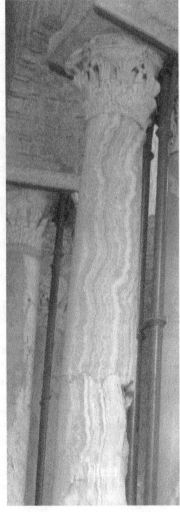

Fig 2.3. Ancient columns of the baptistery of Santa Maria Maggiore of Nocera Superiore. The columns' distinctive grain illustrates how such pattern detail can aid authorities in reuniting broken antiquities.

In order to monitor e-commerce more efficiently, the Carabinieri took the unprecedented step of signing an agreement with *eBay* to gain access to the identity of vendors of objects with a suspicious origin such as archaeological objects, ancient coins, religious objects, manuscripts and archive documents and antique books.

Information in the databank can also be easily retrieved for the purposes of publicising the search for a stolen artwork. The databank publishes annual bulletins of stolen objects, titled *Arte in Ostaggio – Bollettino delle opere d'arte trafugate* (Art Held Hostage – Stolen Artworks Bulletin), in Italian and in English, including photos and descriptions (author or school, title, technique, dimensions and Carabinieri's database file number) of objects of artistic and/or historical relevance. Also, members of the public may search the public portions of the databank, available on the internet, thereby adding to the pairs of eyes which become increasingly familiar with the missing objects. This increased familiarity also increases the odds of a stolen object being recognised when it is encountered.

On one occasion, a Carabinieri officer on holiday in New York City spotted a statue from the database on display in the window of a Manhattan sales gallery. Non-commissioned officer Michele Speranza was walking down Madison Avenue when a marble torso caught his eye. The statue had been stolen in 1988 from a small museum in Terracina, Italy, a seaside town south of Rome. Because he had seen images of the statue in the databank, the torso looked familiar. Officer Speranza took a photo of the statue with his mobile phone and decided to check on his tentative identification when he returned to Rome. In addition to the Terracina marble, it transpired that the gallery also contained a bronze statue of Zeus that had been stolen from the National Museum in Rome in 1980. As Officer Speranza had been able to make a positive identification leading to proof that two objects stolen from Italian museums were up for sale in New York City, the Carabinieri was able to partner US Customs and Immigration in taking custody of the objects and initiating the repatriation process. On 19 November 2010, the Carabinieri held a press conference announcing the return of the two statues (see Fig 2.4), whose combined market value was estimated to be US $1 million (*Art Daily* 2010).

Another recent recovery and repatriation illustrates the power of Banca Dati *Leonardo*. On 1 October 1978, thieves stole two wooden statues depicting saints Dominic and Catherine from the Church of St Oswald in Baselga di Piné, in the province of Trento. Fortunately, church officials were able to provide the police station at Baselga di Piné with photographs and detailed documentation for the two objects. The police, in turn, forwarded the information to the Carabinieri TPC, so that it could be entered into the databank in Rome. As a result, during the summer of 2012 when the Carabinieri TPC of Venice decided to photograph items on display in an antique shop in Pordenone, 286km away from the original location of the theft, the force was able to match its photos of the two statues with the database information. This connection prompted a careful investigation with cooperation between the databank unit in Rome, the Carabinieri TPC in Venice, the Carabinieri TPC in Trento and the Baselga di Piné police. As a result, two individuals were charged with receiving stolen property. Even more importantly, after restitution of the objects to the province of Trento, the Carabinieri TPC was able to return the two sacred objects to the church where they belonged (*Messaggero Veneto* 2012).

Churches are especially vulnerable to theft of art and ecclesiastical objects. In order to fulfil their mission as places of sanctity and prayer, these items are often left unprotected and open to visitors and parishioners; such easy access makes them a target for criminals. Only a small percentage of items stolen from churches are ever recovered. Often the objects are very small,

FIG 2.4.   FRIDAY 19 NOVEMBER 2010: ITALIAN CARABINIERI MARSHAL ASSISTANT DEPUTY OFFICER OF
PUBLIC SAFETY, MICHELE SPERANZA, STANDS NEXT TO A BRONZE STATUE OF THE GREEK GOD ZEUS AND A
MARBLE FEMALE TORSO, BOTH DATING FROM THE END OF THE 1ST-2ND CENTURY AD.

have not been thoroughly inventoried or documented and can be easily stolen, hidden and
removed. Carabinieri TPC outreach programmes for improving ecclesiastical security will be
discussed in greater detail later in the book.

THE ARCHAEOLOGY UNIT

Protecting archaeological deposits and artefacts throughout all of Italy is a task worthy of the
heroes of ancient mythology. To provide a sense of the magnitude of this task and the accomplishments of the Carabinieri TPC, note that the force has recovered over 390,000 archaeological
artefacts as of January 2011 (Manola and Ragusa 2012). Even though all regional units are responsible for the protection of archaeological sites within their jurisdictions, there is also a central

archaeology unit, based in Rome. A significant component of the archaeology unit's success has been its ability to work cooperatively with other units of the Carabinieri, as well as with local police, academic archaeologists and institutions of higher learning, including the Italian National Research Council (CNR). These partnerships are effective in protecting known archaeological sites and for contributing to new archaeological discoveries. It is not unusual for local *tombaroli* to systematically loot archaeological sites that are unknown to science. In cases where police action results in the discovery of an archaeological site previously unknown to archaeologists, the relationship between the Carabinieri and the CNR ensures that sites discovered in this way are added to the comprehensive archaeological maps of Italian land.

One reason why criminals find the looting of archaeological sites to be a lucrative undertaking is that, if a valuable object is recovered from the soil, there is no previous record of the object's existence. As a result, the item will not appear on any list of stolen objects. It will not feature in the Carabinieri database, the INTERPOL list of stolen objects, IFAR, the Art Loss Register, Art Recovery International or any other recognised source that would identify it as stolen, should it appear on the art market. Unfortunately, hundreds of people are willing to pay thousands – if not millions – of dollars for objects that have been torn from archaeological deposits and smuggled to countries where collectors eagerly await. Therefore, an organisation which has a recovery record encompassing hundreds of thousands of objects deserves careful examination by other law enforcement organisations. The methods of the Carabinieri TPC include (but are not limited to) vigilant and regular reconnaissance, access to the very best subject matter expertise and comprehensive investigative capabilities.

Italy has at least 6000 known archaeological sites within its territorial boundaries, both on land and under water, and these known sites represent only a small percentage of the country's archaeological wealth. With so many sites to monitor and protect, observation begins in the air. At least once a month, the operative units use helicopter surveillance to monitor known archaeologically sensitive areas (see Fig 2.5). Where the officers in the helicopter recognise signs of illegal excavation, they follow through with field reconnaissance. The Carabinieri TPC prides itself on its ability to access even the most remote locations. Archaeological investigations may require hiking into remote mountains and forests, or even cooperation with mounted police such as the 4° Reggimento Carabinieri a Cavallo.

The Italian partnership between law enforcement and the academy works both ways. Archaeologists routinely fly on the Carabinieri surveillance missions and it is not unusual for new sites to be discovered from this aerial platform. Just as archaeologists are beginning to discover new sites using analysis of aerial and satellite imagery on a global basis, Italian archaeologists have the opportunity to routinely survey the landscape from the air by participating in the reconnaissance flights. One example of the benefits of this type of partnership was the discovery of a previously unknown necropolis. From the helicopter, the variation in vegetation density and colour showed a characteristic pattern of tombs (Manola and Ragusa 2012), an observation that was subsequently confirmed by ground investigation. Patrizia Tartara of the CNR also illustrates this type of discovery in her 2008 article (Tartara 2008). The Carabinieri TPC coordinated an opportunity for her to fly over the study area with the Carabinieri Helicopter Group of Pratica di Mare, based near Rome. She combined her images and observations from these flights with British Royal Air Force (RAF) images taken during World War II reconnaissance. Her research resulted in the discovery and documentation of a series of archaeological settlements and necropolises following the sheep migration route out of the Campo Imperatore in the high elevation plains

Fig 2.5. A Carabinieri helicopter on patrol. Aerial patrols assist in the identification of looting and enable officers and archaeologists to monitor protected areas.

of the Abruzzo. She notes in her summary that the work is of value not just for the discovery of the sites themselves but also as a model for using partnership with law enforcement for productive archaeological research.

The academic partnership continues to contribute at the collections and market level. When a previously unknown object appears at an international auction house or in a museum collection, experienced and knowledgeable archaeologists can often accurately identify the region, if not the precise archaeological site, from where the object is most likely to have originated. This expertise, when made available to law enforcement, provides the Italians with the capability to put a sensitive area with looting potential under surveillance. The Etruscan tombs at Cerveteri, a UNESCO World Heritage Site, offer an example. The extraordinary vases, objects, offerings and tomb furniture make Etruscan tombs valuable to archaeologists and heritage professionals, as well as to thieves. However, Etruscan objects from these tombs are extremely distinctive and experts can identify objects as looted from certain features, even if they have not been previously recorded as stolen. Located less than 30 miles from Rome, the area is still quite rural and members of the local community have extensive and detailed knowledge of the tombs. As a result, episodes of looting in and around Cerveteri have the potential to occur on a regular basis. Regular reconnaissance offers multiple methods for tracking theft from archaeological sites. Current looting can be

FIG 2.6.   ATLETA DI FANO, A GREEK BRONZE RECOVERED BY AN
ITALIAN FISHERMAN AND SMUGGLED TO THE US FOR SALE TO THE
GETTY, EXEMPLIFIES BOTH A RARE OBJECT OF ANTIQUITY COVETED
BY COLLECTORS WORLDWIDE AND THE COMPLEXITY OF LEGAL CASES
SURROUNDING SUCH OBJECTS WHEN THEY ARE ACQUIRED UNDER
ILLEGAL OR QUESTIONABLE CIRCUMSTANCES.

identified in several ways: from the air, if new excavations are noted during aerial surveillance; from the ground, during routine patrols or if concern is expressed by archaeologists working in a given area; and from the marketplace, if new and distinctive objects begin to appear for sale on the internet or in marketplaces such as Porta Portese in Rome.

Looting of archaeological materials does not stop at the shoreline. The Carabinieri TPC also has an underwater diving unit for the protection of submerged archaeological resources. Italy is surrounded by the Mediterranean, Adriatic, Ligurian, Ionian and Tyrrhenian seas, and is a region where maritime technology has played a vital role for at least 10,000 years (Ammerman 2010). When we consider the quantities of seafaring vessels over many thousands of years, combined with storms, conflicts and other events affecting maritime transport, there is no question that the sea floor within Italian territorial boundaries is rich with shipwrecks and related archaeological features. Sometimes fishermen even recover statues and other objects in their nets off the coasts of Italy.

In addition, geological activity, erosion, flooding and other earth-changing processes have altered the shorelines over the centuries. As a result, harbour, shoreline villas and other settlement deposits can be found in submerged contexts. Bodies of fresh water may also yield archaeological material. From shipwrecks and sunken river ports to ritual objects thrown into tiny Italian lakes, concerns for archaeological material extend to all bodies of water in Italy. The Carabinieri TPC recognises that it is also responsible for these elements of Italian heritage and takes these responsibilities seriously. It cooperates with established underwater archaeological services such as the Technical Service for Underwater Archaeology (*Servizio Tecnico per l'Archeologia Subacquea* (STAS)), a branch of the Ministry of Culture and governing authority for all Italian underwater archaeological sites, with the exception of Sicily, which is governed by the *Gruppo d'Intervento di Archeologia Subacquea Sicilia* (GIASS). The TPC also cooperates with the Italian National Centre for Underwater Archaeology (*Centro Nazionale Archeologia Subacquea*) and various regional archaeological superintendencies such as Ostia Antica, the ancient port of Rome, on underwater issues.

One example of the complexity and protection challenges surrounding submerged deposits is the Getty bronze called the 'Victorious Youth', or 'Atleta di Fano' (see Fig 2.6).

An Italian fisherman originally recovered this statue of an athlete in 1964. It is an extraordinary object. Archaeologists and art historians believe that the statue may have ended up on the ocean floor following the sinking of an ancient Roman ship that may have been bringing objects back to Italy from Greece as spoils of war. Some art historians believe the artist might have been Lysippus, personal sculptor to Alexander the Great. The fisherman reportedly hid the statue by burying it, while arranging to sell the object on the black market. The statue appeared in London in 1970, and in 1974 the Italians attempted unsuccessfully to recover it from Germany, where it was being restored. The Getty Museum purchased it in 1976 after the death of John Paul Getty, who was opposed to purchasing the statue if its ownership was in doubt. The true ownership is still in question and, as recently as May 2012, Italian courts ruled that the exportation of the statue from Italy was illegal and that the object should be returned to Italy. Jason Felch (2012) has followed the story in great detail for the *LA Times*.

The Antiques Unit

Just as the officers who work at the databank inspect the internet on a daily basis for evidence of stolen or illicit objects for sale, officers of the TPC also attend antique and art markets with the same goal. It is not as unusual as a law-abiding citizen might think for the TPC to encounter stolen paintings, sculptures and other works of art in otherwise legitimate fora such as international art sales, flea markets and established auction houses. Sometimes stolen objects even show up in museum exhibitions. In one case, an extremely vigilant Carabinieri officer, who may well have a photographic memory, was browsing through an exhibit catalogue, probably for the 1990 exhibition of paintings by Giambattista Tiepolo at the Niedersachsisches Landesmuseum in Hannover, Germany. In the catalogue he noticed a painting that he remembered as having been stolen from a private home in Paris. The painting had been stolen in 1979 and the theft was promptly reported to the police in Paris, who failed to forward the information to INTERPOL. Many years later, in 2001, the owners contacted the Carabinieri TPC asking for further help, claiming that the painting had previously been declared a cultural asset of special importance to the State of Italy. The observant Carabinieri officer initiated an investigation, adding images of the painting to the databank and verifying that the painting was indeed the stolen item in question. In fact, the exhibit label in Hannover actually listed the painting as being from the collection of the family who had reported it stolen. Despite the clear and damning evidence presented by the Italians, the museum claimed to have purchased the painting in good faith in 1985 (Cremers 2008) and won its first court challenge in 2007. However, during the subsequent trial in the regional court of appeal, details of the Hannover curators' efforts to smuggle the painting into Germany in a van between two bookcases were revealed (Von Perfall 2010). The appellate court ruled in 2010 that the painting be repatriated to its rightful owners, the heirs of Paola Modiano Ferrari di Valbona, ending the painting's 31-year odyssey (Rossi 2011a).

The Forgery Unit

Every year, forged works of art cost collectors and museums around the world hundreds of thousands, if not millions, of dollars. Contemporary works of art are at greatest risk of forgery and some of the most talented forgers in the world happen to be Italian. One reason why forgery, the creation of fakes or art fraud, is a critical element of law enforcement is that trade in forged works of art is often embedded in schemes for laundering money from illegal activities such as the drug trade. A hypothetical example may be useful to illustrate this relationship. Imagine a drug dealer named John Doe who has just made €100,000 in an illegal transaction. If he puts the money in a bank account or spends it on expensive items, it will immediately attract the attention of the police and tax authorities. Instead, John calls his friend Joe Smith, an art forger, and pays him €100 to create a fake contemporary painting. John then sells the painting, possibly even to himself, for €100,000, which he then declares to the authorities as profit from a wise art investment. In Italian law, forgeries are governed under Article 178, Legislative Decree 42/04, Code of Cultural Heritage and Landscape.

The forgery unit in Rome, like other centrally located operative units, helps to coordinate investigations at the regional office level. Issues related to forgery tend to emerge most often in the operative units based in urban areas such as Monza, Florence, Bologna and Rome. It is difficult to estimate what impact the presence of a law enforcement agency with forgery expertise is having on the contemporary art market. There is no question, though, that the market is becoming more restrained as criminal dealers are brought to justice, law suits increase and curators, authenticators and collectors begin to exercise much more caution (*The Economist* 2012).

At a June 2012 conference in Basel, the Carabinieri TPC stated that an estimated 84% of contemporary works of art for sale on the international market are fake (Cortellessa 2012). Colonel Luigi Cortellessa, Deputy Commander of the Carabinieri TPC, showed delegates a series of images of fraudulent art recovered by the Carabinieri over the course of two years (2010–2011). The forgeries represented mostly paintings but also included sculptures and antiquities such as the reproduction of Etruscan and Apulian vases and amphorae. The Colonel outlined proactive efforts for counteracting this form of illegal activity, including: monitoring the contemporary art market more closely to identify fraudulent objects; closer tracking of individuals and associations previously known to have created or sold fake works of art; increasing prosecution of dealers and galleries who knowingly handle and sell fakes; and making use of information from individuals who turn to the Carabinieri and other law enforcement agencies for help after purchasing a forged work of art. The operative unit also emphasises scientific analysis and subject matter expert cooperation for the identification of forgeries.

Carabinieri TPC and the Rule of Law

The cases of the Madison Avenue statues, the religious objects from St Oswald in Baselga di Piné, the Atleta di Fano and the stolen Tiepolo all illustrate the critical importance of highly qualified law experts serving as officers within the Carabinieri TPC. The most detailed database in the world combined with the most vigilant field officers would not be able to save a single artefact or work of art without the support of an experienced and competent pool of prosecutors who take the cases to court, convict thieves and argue the cases for recovery and repatriation. In the first two cases, the presence of police reports for the original thefts were critical in making the case that the objects, once discovered and identified, had in fact been stolen. In the case of the Madison Avenue statues, since the stolen statues had been smuggled into the United States, cooperation with customs authorities was required in order for the objects to be legally removed from the gallery and returned to Italy. The Atleta di Fano case illustrates the complexities that arise when an archaeological object is removed from its original context and appears on the market. In such cases, there may not be any police reports associated with the theft and the objects, if previously unknown, cannot be entered into the databank. The ownership of Atleta di Fano has now been the subject of legal challenge for over 40 years. The case of the Tiepolo also illustrates that legal teams need to be patient and persistent. Even though the Italians lost in court the first time, they won on appeal, and the painting was recovered.

The time factor contributes to the legal challenges. Crimes against archaeological sites and evidence of objects having been looted are often discovered only many years after the crime is committed. A common pattern of behaviour is for looters to hide stolen property and place it on the market only when the statute of limitations on the theft has expired. In some cases, the statute of limitations begins when the object is stolen, rather than when the crime is discovered. The famous prosecution in Rome of Marion True, Curator of the Getty Museum, ended when the statute of limitations expired on the crimes against Italian cultural property of which she was accused (Bianchi 2010).

Another complication is the creative and wide-ranging forms that art crime can take. In addition to the looting of archaeological sites and theft of works of art, other illegal methods of acquiring objects abound. American museums have hidden the purchase of stolen objects by classifying them as donations from wealthy patrons. Auction houses and dealers falsify object history and provenance records at an international level in order to enter stolen objects in the international marketplace. Offering falsely inflated values for art objects and artefacts also makes these objects attractive for money laundering. Forged art, in addition to being used to cheat collectors, can also be recycled to help criminals hide illegal sources of funds.

For the legal process to be effective there must be laws protecting cultural objects. In Italy, all objects and features of cultural patrimony buried in the soil or found submerged belong to the State – even those objects and features found on private property. If a thorough investigation by the Carabinieri TPC can demonstrate that an object was removed from Italian soil then a Public Prosecutor informed by Carabinieri can begin to make a case in the courts for its recovery. When an object is smuggled out of Italy, the legal case becomes immediately more complicated, because the legal cooperation of the nation where the object appears is required for resolution.

LEGAL PRECEDENTS

The 2003 conviction in New York of Frederick Schultz for conspiring to deal in stolen antiquities helped to lay some of the legal ground rules for the repatriation of stolen objects from the United States to their countries of origin. The Schultz conviction demonstrated that the US was capable of evaluating cultural patrimony laws and that US courts determined that property stolen from a foreign country should be treated no differently to property stolen from a foreign museum or a private home (Ferri 2009, 206). A similar legal decision in the Supreme Court of Appeals of England and Wales in the case of the Republic of Iran vs Barakat Galleries Ltd in 2007 had a similar effect on the potential for law enforcement and antiquities in the United Kingdom.

MULTILATERAL TREATIES

For the most part, the Italians rely on five multilateral treaties, two normative acts within the European Union and bilateral agreements. The five multilateral treaties are:

- UNESCO *Convention on the Means of Prohibiting and Preventing the Illicit Import, Export and Transfer of Ownership of Cultural Property 1970*. It is this convention that the Italians anticipated with the creation of the original Carabinieri TPC in 1969. This convention also makes 1970 the critical date for import of a cultural object.
- The International Institute for the Unification of Private Law *Convention on Stolen or Illegally Exported Cultural Objects* (UNIDROIT) 1995.
- The First Protocol of the 1954 *Convention for the Protection of Cultural Property in the Event of Armed Conflict* (The Hague Convention).
- The 2000 *United Nations Convention against Transnational Organized Crime* (UNTOC), often referred to as the Palermo Convention.
- The 2001 UNESCO *Convention on the Protection of the Underwater Cultural Heritage*.

The 1954 Hague Convention and its protocols are clearly designed to apply to situations involving conflict and conflict zones. In terms of the Carabinieri, the components that clearly apply are the requirement to safeguard and respect cultural property during both international and non-international armed conflicts and the requirement to set up special units within military forces that will be responsible for safeguarding cultural property.

The 1970 UNESCO and the 1995 UNIDROIT treaties are the ones that often apply to ongoing international criminal investigations. The 1970 UNESCO treaty requires States Parties to prevent museums within their territories from acquiring cultural property which has been illegally exported; to prohibit import of cultural property stolen from a museum or public institution after entry into force of the Convention; and at the request of the State of origin, to recover and return any such cultural property stolen and imported. The UNIDROIT Convention is designed to complement the 1970 UNESCO Convention. Its most important feature is the articulation of the principle that anyone with a stolen item in his/her possession must return the object. This principle shifts responsibility for confirming the provenance of an object to the potential buyer. UNIDROIT also sets standards for the tracing and return of illegally exported cultural objects. For the contracting parties, objects stolen in one state and smuggled into another must be returned. The party obligated to return an object may be reimbursed if he/she can demonstrate due diligence prior to the purchase.

The Carabinieri TPC has also found the 2000 Palermo Convention to be especially useful in terms of prosecuting major organised criminal efforts involving crimes affecting the cultural property of Italy. For UNTOC to apply, the crime has to be transnational and perpetrated by an organised group. The crime must also be serious, involving penalties of at least four years' imprisonment. In addition to crimes such as human trafficking and terrorism, the agreement is also specifically intended to address money laundering, corruption, illicit trafficking in endangered species and offences against cultural heritage (United Nations 2004, 2). Palermo offers an additional tool for prosecution, especially in cases where antiquities of great value have been looted and smuggled abroad and in cases of conspiracy involving art forgery and money laundering.

The Italians played a significant role in mediating the negotiations for adoption of the UNESCO *Convention on the Protection of the Underwater Cultural Heritage*. This convention is supplemented by a regional agreement for strengthening cooperation for protection of underwater heritage in the Mediterranean based on rights and obligations agreed upon by nations meeting in Siracusa, Sicily, in 2003.

The two European Council (EC) regulations that apply are:

- EC Council Regulation No 3911/92 of 9 December 1992 on the export of cultural goods.
- EC Council Directive 93/7/EEC of 15 March 1993 on the return of cultural objects unlawfully removed from the territory of a Member State.

The EC instruments are more specific, defining categories of cultural objects and financial thresholds that apply to each category. They render the European Union (EU) export controls, including the export licence process, uniform. The regulations also provide for mutual assistance between the member nations (CC TPC 2008).

Bilateral agreements are those between two countries that restrict import of cultural objects from one country to another. Under Article 9 of the 1970 UNESCO Convention, one country may petition another to restrict import of classes of objects that are at risk. Two key bilateral agreements that apply to Italian cultural heritage are a Memorandum of Understanding between the US and Italy, signed in 2001 and renewed in 2006 and 2011, and a Memorandum of Understanding signed between Italy and Switzerland in 2006. The agreement between the US and Italy restricts the import of pre-classical, classical, and imperial Roman archaeological material from Italy into the US (Agreement 2001).

The US–Italian agreement also illustrates the importance of bilateral cooperation as it articulates the anticipated efforts from both sides to protect Italian cultural heritage. As the US promises to restrict the import of these objects and to return any objects of this type that find their way into the US illegally, the Italians also agree to play their part by: prosecuting looters more promptly and with greater penalties; regulating the use of metal detectors; providing additional training for the officers of the Carabinieri TPC; intensifying TPC investigations of international smuggling; and encouraging other nations in the region to increase cultural heritage law enforcement efforts.

The importance of international treaties, agreements between countries and legal instruments can be illustrated by the case of the Sabratha head. The thieves who stole the Sabratha head in Libya in 1990 waited until the Gaddafi government was no longer in power before putting the object up for sale. Even though a police report clearly demonstrated that the object had been stolen from a museum in Sabratha, the absence of a functioning Libyan government gave the thieves the confidence they needed to post the object up for sale using the internationally known Christie's auction house in London. When an Italian citizen purchased the object, the Carabinieri was then given the opportunity to make the case that the object was stolen. The Carabinieri's action pressured Christie's to refund the purchase price and Generale di Brigata Pasquale Muggeo returned the Sabratha head to the Libyan people in 2012 (Gill 2012).

According to one of the leading members of the Carabinieri TPC legal team, when it comes to working in other countries, challenges for the Italians ironically include the fact that a force like the Carabinieri TPC is so unusual. As a result, often no counterpart force exists. Because the US does not have a police force dedicated exclusively to art crime, or even a ministry of culture, the Italians, depending on the case, might need to partner with US Customs and Immigration, members of the FBI Art Crime Team, the US military, the US State Department, or even the US Postal Service. Officers in the Monza regional office also point out the challenges of working with different states within the United States. The networking and partnership challenges become enormous; essentially the complexity is multiplied by a factor of 50. When multiple policing organisations and government departments are potentially working on similar issues, it can be extremely difficult to coordinate policies, practices and combined operations. The resulting challenges for networking and coordination and the absence of counterpart agencies in other countries mean that fewer ongoing informal conversations and communications occur at international and interdepartmental levels, leaving few opportunities to build long-lasting collegial relationships between officers of the Carabinieri and their potential colleagues abroad.

By providing professional support to the Prosecutors, according to Italian Penal Procedure regulations, the Carabinieri has also become expert in submitting letters of rogatory to members of the judiciary in other countries. A letter of rogatory – the term for a request for judicial assistance from another country – may include assistance in collecting both material and witness evidence. This method makes it possible for courts from another jurisdiction to take action against criminals who are suspected to be complicit in crimes against Italian cultural property.

Absences in the law represent another challenge. Some countries have not signed the major international conventions or agreements and bilateral agreements may be lacking. Some countries do not have legislation that prohibits excavation of archaeological material. Experienced criminals will focus on looting, smuggling and black-market activities in areas they know have the weakest legal guidelines. To add further complication, even countries with robust legislation and enforcement will offer variations in domestic law. For example, in the US it is illegal to collect palaeontological materials on federal land, but it is legal to collect and own fossils from private land. In Italy, all fossils collected from the soil belong to the people of Italy. Therefore, if a fossil from the US shows up for sale in Italy, and a complaint is made, the Italians would have to work with US authorities to determine the original source of the object. A recent case handled by the regional unit in Monza illustrates the challenge from the other direction. A palaeontological specimen stolen from unique fossil beds in the region of Livorno appeared for sale in the US. In order to recover the item, the Italians had to demonstrate that the fossil had come from Italian soil and had an opportunity to educate their US counterparts about Italian cultural property law. Even more complicated situations can arise when there is incompatibility or a lack of legislation from country to country concerning other types of crimes, such as money laundering and forgery.

Variation can also exist within domestic laws governing search and seizure. For example, Italian law permits the Carabinieri to share information about telephone card holders with INTERPOL, while other nations may prohibit the sharing of this type of information without a warrant. This type of discontinuity adds time and complexity to investigations in progress. Domestic laws also vary in terms of the rules for monitoring internet sites where stolen works of art and/ or antiquities may turn up for sale. Carabinieri officers consistently advocate for strengthening surveillance at international border locations and negotiating permissions to pursue criminals across international boundaries.

Different methods of tracking theft and crimes against art pose another challenge when working in a transnational setting. Italy is again unusual because it has the Banca Dati *Leonardo* and stores all of its crimes against art in this unique database entity. Most other law enforcement organisations include stolen artwork and other art crimes as a component of larger stolen property database systems. Art objects are often treated like any other item of stolen property rather than being considered in a separate category, as is the case in Italy. The Carabinieri TPC has worked proactively with INTERPOL and its database to help with this problem and has ongoing working relationships with other organisations dedicated to tracking stolen art. To further increase the effectiveness of the database, the Carabinieri offer export offices and art trade associations free access to the information. Such access means that there is no excuse for a stolen object in the database to be legally declared for export or to make it to an auction house for sale.

In autumn 2011, Generale di Brigata Pasquale Muggeo also announced an Italian proposal to the European Commission for approval and financing for PSYCHE (Protection System for Cultural Heritage), which would help to merge Banca Dati *Leonardo* with the current INTERPOL WOA (Works of Art) database and other national database systems for tracking stolen art and artefacts. The PSYCHE initiative is moving forward with approval and funding from the European Commission. Generale Mariano Mossa addressed the General Assembly of INTERPOL in autumn 2012 in order to further discuss the initiative (Mossa 2012). Initial implementation will make Banca Dati *Leonardo* seamlessly interactive with the INTERPOL stolen art database and eventually it will work compatibly with law enforcement databases in 15 member countries, including Austria, Belgium, Bulgaria, Cyprus, Estonia, France, Germany, Greece, Hungary, Malta, the Netherlands, Slovakia, Slovenia, Spain and Sweden.

Since 9 August 2009, the INTERPOL stolen art database has been available for online consultation to its 199 member countries and to the general public (collectors, art dealers, museums, customs, auction houses, scholars, universities and lawyers). Access to the INTERPOL database is granted after completion of the password-request form available at: http://www.interpol.int/Forms/WorksOfArtDatabase. Upon obtaining a password, the General Secretariat will then allow access to object-related information and quality images stored in the WOA database, thus contributing to due diligence and making the database available as stated in article 4, paragraph 4 of the UNIDROIT 1995 Convention:

> In determining whether the possessor exercised due diligence, regard shall be had to all the circumstances of the acquisition, including the character of the parties, the price paid, whether the possessor consulted any reasonably accessible register of stolen cultural objects, and any other relevant information and documentation which it could reasonably have obtained, and whether the possessor consulted accessible agencies or took any other step that a reasonable person would have taken in the circumstances.

As this information is subject to accurate 'quality control' and for that reason is ready to be taken into court, where there is a hint of an object being recognised as stolen, contact can be established with the Works of Art Unit at the General Secretariat or the National Central Bureaus of INTERPOL to take action according to legislation in force, thus activating the Carabinieri (or other specialised services, if established), to speed procedures for restitution and/or repatriation.

The Carabinieri TPC legal team has also identified best practices for art law enforcement at the international level.

- One measure is to study and compare procedures and methods practised by art law enforcement agencies or officers in other countries.
- It is important to encourage the exchange of information from art crime databases between countries.
- As a related measure, law enforcement agencies need to acquire and understand the technical specifications of other nations' database systems in order to make data sharing as efficient, accurate and rapid as possible.
- It is critical for law enforcement agencies to partner with non-governmental and academic organisations that specialise in fighting art crime and in the protection of cultural heritage, such as the Association for Research into Crimes against Art (ARCA) and the new centre for studying the illicit trade in antiquities at the University of Glasgow, Scotland.
- International law enforcement agencies must work together to identify pathways and routes used by criminals to smuggle works of art and artefacts across international boundaries. These agencies also need to work together to identify locations and individuals who store and hide objects in addition to providing fake identifications, provenances and who initiate sales.
- International forces need to work together to analyse events in which criminal organisations and masterminds commit art crimes in order to establish patterns and to identify key criminal individuals.
- Smuggling and enforcement agents need to study and identify all the different methods that are used to conceal artefacts and works of art in order to cross international borders.
- Summaries of foreign laws that govern the protection of cultural heritage and repatriation of works of art to the country of origin would expedite the legal process for any enforcement lawyer working on cases in international settings.

THE MINISTRY OF CULTURE COMMITTEE FOR REPATRIATION NEGOTIATIONS

Once the Carabinieri TPC has made a strong legal case demonstrating that a foreign entity has a stolen work of art or antiquity of Italian origin in its collection, the Italian Ministry of Culture is empowered to begin negotiations for repatriation. One of the underlying principles guiding the Italians during the course of the process is the belief that the value of heritage is unrelated to the number of dollars, euros or pounds that may be exchanged for an object in the marketplace. Even though the Italians are known for the successful repatriation of their own heritage back to Italy, officers of the Carabinieri TPC would be the first to point out that the TPC and the Italian legal system work hard to ensure the return to its proper home of any object that enters their sphere of influence, no matter where in the world that home may be.

When mediating and negotiating repatriation, the Italians emphasise proactive cultural property protection measures (Cappitelli 2009, 14), such as information and education plans, up-to-date management of national inventories, definition of security programmes and procedures for sites, museums, sacred, public and private collections, international cooperation, agreements for loans and travelling exhibitions of objects, permissions for international research on Italian soil and measures that encourage wider participation by civil society. In considering repatriation from this perspective, Italian efforts for global training and its leading role in law enforcement cooperation, like the sharing of database information, makes all activities completely consistent with *in situ* preservation and working to bring objects back to their places of origin. The terms of repatriation of objects back to Italy from the Metropolitan Museum of Art in New York City, the Getty in Los Angeles and the Tokyo Fuji Art Museum reflect the proactive Italian approach. In all three cases there will be loans of comparable items back to the repatriating country and exhibitions of the recovered objects throughout Italy associated with the repatriations. The philosophy behind using repatriation to stimulate new contexts for cultural exchange reflects the concept that an institution which has legal access to unique and valuable objects has no motive to purchase illegal objects in the future.

The Italians have been working patiently and diplomatically on establishing agreements with both the Japanese and Chinese with the goal of strengthening collaboration on protection and preservation of the world's cultural heritage, along with assistance in the management of galleries and museums (Scott 2008, 880–1). In 2008, the Italians and Japanese signed an 'agreement' intended to lead to a Memorandum of Understanding related to shared preservation goals. The Italians and Chinese actually signed an official Memorandum of Agreement which, in addition to promoting the exchange of information concerning restoration and preservation, would also establish a centre for the protection of cultural heritage, to be located in Beijing. The Italians are hoping to share their restoration technologies to assist in the preservation of works of art and heritage in Chinese collections and to emerge as a global 'point of reference' for preservation expertise.

In summary, the combination of Ministry of Culture partnership, legal expertise, the extraordinary Banca Dati *Leonardo* and the robust headquarters units for archaeology, antiques and forgery provide strength at the core of the Carabinieri TPC and indeed strength at the core of Italian influence for preservation efforts worldwide.

3

Carabinieri Public Outreach and Education

The Carabinieri TPC has long recognised that it is much easier to prevent the theft of valuable works of art and antiquities than it is to recover those same objects. As a result, the force has developed a robust educational, outreach and security programme that applies across Italy and internationally. The goals of the Carabinieri outreach programme include educating the public about the importance of heritage *in situ* and why archaeological sites should be protected from looting. The idea is that a better informed public will be less likely to purchase looted antiquities and archaeological objects, especially ancient coins which will in turn decrease the incentive and market for looting. Specialised outreach is also available for owners of works of art or collections of objects in order to help the owner(s) improve the security of those items.

Carabinieri outreach initiatives begin with educating children and extend to include security inspections for museums, ecclesiastical collections and churches; visits to private collections with recommendations for improved security; visits to proposed sites of exhibitions; and direct public interaction with the database – not just to familiarise the public with lost art but also to ensure that the database structure can be used to document private collections. Along with representatives of the higher headquarters, nuclei of the Carabinieri TPC routinely offer outreach through public presentations, participating in cultural events and celebrations, visiting school groups, delivering conference papers and even hosting gatherings of academicians and officials to discuss achievements, improvements and potential collaborations for law enforcement in the arts. The Carabinieri also issues bulletins of missing objects and contributes to Italian society by organising exhibitions of objects recovered over the course of time. In the summer of 2012, UNESCO hosted an exhibition in Paris of recovered objects which featured the Carabinieri TPC and shared its accomplishments with the world. The Carabinieri TPC also proactively offers training courses to law enforcement counterparts all over the world. International agencies such as UNESCO often call upon the Carabinieri TPC to share its expertise and representatives of policing agencies have a standing invitation to travel to Rome to learn from the TPC at its headquarters. Carabinieri TPC officers also find it very productive to travel to foreign countries to coach, train and encourage their counterparts.

VIRTUAL EDUCATION FOR CHILDREN

The Carabinieri website offers a video game for children that provides an introduction to the TPC and some of the force's accomplishments. In the game, a virtual child enters a reproduction of the headquarters at Piazza Sant'Ignazio, where an enthusiastic officer welcomes him/her. The child enters the lift and gets to select any of the different floors, each of which offers a different set of lessons. On the ground floor, one learns about the gold medal awards, the flag of the unit and finds links to the series of Carabinieri historic calendars. There are also options to visit the databank and, on level three, the operative units include forgeries, archaeology and antiquities.

In the antiques section, the player has the chance to learn about very important works of art that the Carabinieri TPC has recovered and returned to the people of Italy. The descriptions and explanations are all offered at introductory and greater levels of detail, so the game is filled with information. The recovered objects are carefully selected not only for their artistic significance but also for the extra lessons in law enforcement that they illustrate. For example, the wood panel painting *The Sacred Family with Saint John* by Giovanni Antonio Bazzi, nicknamed '*Il Sodoma*', stolen from the Civic Museum paintings collection in Montepulciano in 1970, was recovered in 1991. Italian art historian Federico Zeri identified the object in Paris and informed the Italian ambassador. The Carabinieri used the information from the databank, including the original police report, to provide documentation to the French that the object had indeed been stolen. In cooperation with their French counterparts, the OCBC (*Office central de lutte contre le trafic des biens culturels* – central office for the fight against the trafficking of cultural property), the Carabinieri was able to make the case for repatriation, which took place on 19 February 1992. The return was celebrated as a solemn and joyous occasion. This example skilfully introduces a series of important lessons: first, with the database in place, stolen art can be identified many years after it disappeared; second, informed citizens can contribute to the recovery process; and third, international cooperation is crucial for the recovery of art and antiquities in a world where thieves work hard to move stolen objects across international boundaries.

The virtual visit to the archaeology section also focuses on repatriated objects, featuring Tyche and the bronze Nike, returned from the Getty, the Vibia Sabina, returned from the Museum of Fine Arts Boston, and the Euphronios krater, returned from the Metropolitan Museum of Art and now proudly on permanent display at the National Etruscan Museum Villa Giulia in Rome. These repatriations represent the successful Carabinieri investigation of high profile purchases of stolen objects by these major US museums, an accomplishment that has dramatically changed the dynamics of modern museum collecting practices around the world. In addition, the successful repatriation of looted objects to Italy and other countries of origin has provided an example and model for other countries and communities which still have objects on display or in storage in overseas museums.

The fraud and forgery section features an extremely impressive animated laser beam illuminating a painting. In fact it represents a raman spectrometer – a photonic tool for analysing pigment components – one of the many highly technological tools at the disposal of the Carabinieri Fraud Section. The virtual headquarters visit concludes with a discussion of Carabinieri, UNESCO and UNIDROIT international response and peacekeeping activities. As the player concludes the visit, there is an excellent review of the structure and actions of the force, emphasising vigilance, excellence in investigation and a comprehensive responsibility to protect cultural property.

EDUCATIONAL PROGRAMMING

The Naples TPC unit runs an ambitious school programme that is a great example of the type of community outreach offered by the regional TPC offices to young people. The Captain of the Naples unit, along with the Captain of the territorial unit in Benevento and in cooperation with the Carabinieri of Cerreto Sannita, attended a college located in the community of Telese Terme to deliver a presentation on the importance of law enforcement to the life and future of a healthy community. To an audience of approximately 100 students and the faculty, the officers discussed the dangers of alcohol and drug abuse, impaired driving and Saturday night binge drinking. The TPC officers gave an introduction on the specialised work of the cultural heritage units, including discussion of art crime investigations and identification of forgeries (*il Quaderno.it* 2013).

CARABINIERI TPC WEBSITE

The video game is only one small component of the Carabinieri TPC website which is designed to not only provide an introduction to the history and capabilities of the force but also to engage members of the public with the database and maximise their exposure to images and descriptions of missing objects. The website also provides precise instructions for situations where members of the public might encounter stolen art, notice evidence of illegal archaeological excavations, purchase a forged work of art or discover an important archaeological site.

The Carabinieri is understandably proud of the objects it has recovered and returned to private owners, their countries of origin or the people of Italy. The website includes a Virtual Museum of the Carabinieri TPC. Once inside, the visitor can tour rooms of objects recovered by units in Rome, Florence and Naples, as well as examples of forged works of art.

One of the most useful pages is the 'Object ID'. Clicking on the Object ID link immediately brings up a guide for documenting art objects. These forms can be downloaded and printed so that any owner of a work of art or valuable cultural property can complete the form, add images and establish, in essence, a catalogue of their own collection. Then in the case of loss, the Carabinieri, or any other law enforcement agency, will have all of the information they need, in a format they are familiar with, to begin their investigation and recovery.

The Carabinieri TPC partnered with the Getty Information Institute in the preparation of the Object ID form because the Getty had long since adopted a similar form for distribution to private institutions for a more efficient and expedited inventory called 'Document of Work of Art'. The copyright for the Object ID was later passed to UNESCO, but the Carabinieri adopted the same type of form called 'Document of Work of Art – Object ID', recommending its use. The Carabinieri has also made this form readily available on its corporate website for anyone to download (individuals, collectors, etc).

Other options on the website include a direct link to profiles of missing Italian objects of great importance. The Italians also offer direct links to databases of objects missing from the National Museum of Iraq since the 2003 looting, as well as to objects missing after the fall of the Gaddafi regime in Libya.

Another aspect of public outreach is educational information designed to help members of the public to avoid purchasing stolen or forged objects. The website has multiple pages devoted to both subjects. Advice for purchasing an item of cultural property encourages research into the background of the object. Also, according to article #64 of Italian law, Decree #42/2004, all objects should come with provenance history, including photographs. The seller needs to provide a certificate of authenticity that includes information about the origin of the object, a photograph and his or her signature. The Carabinieri warn of purchases where the price seems too low or where the transaction seems too casual. They also emphasise that a purchase of this nature should never be made in cash, so that there are records of the financial transaction. The Carabinieri reminds owners of valuable works of art or artefacts to use the Object ID, as mentioned above, and to store the resulting documentation, including images, in a location separate from

the objects. The section on forged objects also includes useful advice, emphasising the importance of clear identification on whether the object is a copy or an original. The Carabinieri TPC
has established an institutional *Decalogue against 'the Unconscious Purchase' of Contemporary Art*
which they have publicised and shared with other organisations, including The Italian National
Commission for UNESCO. The Decalogue offers the following useful advice:

- enquire about the artistic journey of the author and the artist credited in the references (monographs, catalogues and directories);
- follow the market trend, quotes and estimates to date;
- avoid incompetent intermediaries;
- contact only sellers with a good reputation and of good standing, who contacted or purchased the art work directly from the artist himself;
- enquire about the market and prices and updated estimates;
- be wary of 'deals', and avoid buying the work at a lower price than the current estimate;
- verify that the work is accompanied by certificates of authenticity and provenance;
- distrust certificates provided by people who have no expertise in the arts and seek advice from institutions, the author's archives and academic experts;
- before concluding the purchase, verify the authenticity of the certificate by contacting the artist himself or the person legally authorised to be archiving/cataloguing data or photo-graphs of his or her work;
- check the exact correspondence between the work reproduced in the photograph authen-ticated by the seller and the work that you are buying;
- at the time of purchase ask for a copy of the declaration of authenticity and provenance of the work signed by the seller, together with the tax records of the amount paid.

(Carabinieri.it 2013)

The website warns potential purchasers about the presence of forged artwork within the market,
a phenomenon which has increased steadily since the 1960s.

The website also includes guidance for individuals who have had artwork stolen, who
encounter illegal archaeological excavations or who fortuitously discover an archaeological site.
In the case of theft, the best case scenario is that the victim will have completed their Object ID
form and will have a good quality photograph (or more than one) of the missing object. In any
case, the theft should be reported immediately to the nearest Carabinieri office. From that point,
the Carabinieri will enter the information into the databank. Illegal excavations also need to be
reported to the Carabinieri right away. In the case of an archaeological discovery, care should be
taken to secure or stabilise exposed objects or features. The discovery must be reported to the
Superintendent of Archaeology for the area, or the Mayor, within 24 hours.

The Carabinieri TPC publishes an annual bulletin of stolen art. The eight most recent bulletins are available for download on the public Carabinieri Corps website, along with a bulletin
that summarises recent recoveries. The bulletins are titled '*Arte in Ostaggio – Bollettino delle Opere
d'Arte Trafugate*', or 'Art held Hostage, Stolen Art Bulletin'. The summary sections of the bulletin
are available in Italian and English. The *Bollettino* also expresses an interesting philosophy in
terms of art that has been stolen. In the words of the Carabinieri:

We believe that what has been stolen must not be considered as lost forever. On the contrary,
we regard it as held hostage by offenders who can and must be defeated by Italian and

international police forces, together with the Ministry of Culture, art dealers and all citizens.

(Carabinieri TPC 2011)

INTERNET VISIBILITY

Even casual 'surfing' reveals the presence of the Carabinieri TPC on the internet. Facebook pages share images of recovered objects in addition to images from events such as a reception welcoming the Italian delegation to UNESCO, and images from the 2012 Recovered Treasures exhibition in Paris. In January 2014, a quick Google search resulted in ten direct links to videos featuring interviews with Carabinieri officers and newsworthy accomplishments such as the recovery of valuable works of art and antiquities. One video is a professionally produced introduction to the responsibilities and activities of the TPC with narration in English.

iTPC

The Carabinieri Command is also particularly active in promoting awareness initiatives aimed at encouraging citizen participation in the protection of cultural heritage. Acknowledging widespread smartphone use, the Carabinieri created an application called *iTPC* for new generation phones and tablets. Through this app citizens may directly access the CC TPC website and databank from virtually anywhere. The ability to instantaneously compare artworks on the market with the CC TPC databank of stolen objects is an invaluable tool in the fight against art crime. This innovative app offers users the opportunity to contribute to the search for wanted artworks while at the same time opening up the CC TPC databank to a larger audience of contributors. Making use of citizens' input is one of the century's greatest innovations (citizen geo-caching is another example that utilises the public's input to increase mapping resolution of remote, non-accessible geographical areas) and will increase surveillance of illicit art trafficking.

EXHIBITIONS

In summer 2012, at the UNESCO headquarters in Paris, an exhibition called *Recovered Treasures* opened, with the subtitle 'International cooperation in the fight against illicit trafficking of cultural property: successes of the Italian Carabinieri'. The exhibition was scheduled to coincide with a series of meetings at UNESCO focusing on the challenges of illicit trade in cultural property. In fact the official opening of the exhibition was on 19 June 2012 and coincided with the First Meeting of the special Committee to review the Practical Operation of the 1995 UNIDROIT *Convention on Stolen or Illegally Exported Cultural Objects*. The exhibition featured 31 objects, each of which had been recovered by the Carabinieri with cooperation from other countries, including the US, Switzerland, Greece, Ecuador and France. The 31 objects included:

- The incunabulum of Christopher Columbus' description of discovering the New World. Stolen: civic library, Fermo, Italy, 1986; recovered: Sotheby's, New York, 1992.
- Folios from an illuminated choir book, an antiphonary and a psalter. Stolen: the Convent of Santa Maria in Aracoeli, Rome, 1986; recovered: flea market Bollate, Milan, 1987.
- Thirteen of the 337 archaeological objects recovered during 'Operation Andromeda, 2008–2010' (see Fig 3.1), an investigation of a Japanese dealer and Swiss businessman with a

Geneva warehouse filled with stolen objects. The objects included an Apulian hydria or water jar, an Attic red-figure krater, an Apulian funerary krater, an Apulian funerary hydria, an Apulian red-figure loutrophoros or ritual water vase, an Apulian red-figure amphora, two round white marble oscillum with carved satyrs that once decorated a public building, an Attic red-figure kylix or drinking cup, a red-figure bell-krater, an Apulian red-figure dish, an Apulian red-figure fish plate and a Paestan red-figure fish plate (see Fig 3.2).

- A kalyx krater with the Kidnapping of Europa, originally looted from a site near Sant'Agata dei Goti (Benevento), recovered in 2005 from a museum in California that had purchased it illegally in 1981.
- Two fragments of medieval frescos from the Grotta delle Fornelle, an archaeological area in Pignataro Maggiore near Caserta where, in 1982, thieves removed a series of frescos from a stone church using power saws. Athenian police recovered these two examples from a dealer's villa and, in cooperation with the Carabinieri, repatriated the frescos to Italy in 2009.
- Two paintings stolen during remodelling at the Capitoline gallery in 1999 and recovered that same year: Guercino, Saint John the Baptist and Ludovico Carracci, Holy Family with Saints Francis and Catherine of Alexandria.
- Two altar panels from the cathedral of San Secondiano in Chiusi. Stolen in 1994; recovered in the UK in 2011. Of the 13 panels stolen, the Carabinieri has recovered seven.
- An ivory crucifix containing a relic of Saint Sabinus. Stolen from the Cathedral of San Sabino in Canosa di Puglia, in the province of Bari, in 1983. The *Office central de lutte contre le trafic des biens culturels*, the French counterparts of the TPC, noticed the object on the French art market in 2008. The French immediately contacted the TPC via INTERPOL and the two forces worked together to identify and arrest the woman who was planning to smuggle and deliver the object.
- Five objects of pre-Columbian art looted from Ecuador and discovered by Carabinieri monitoring the internet in 2011. The objects were repatriated directly to the Ecuadorian ambassador to Italy.

In addition to illustrating the importance of international law enforcement for recovering stolen art and archaeological materials, the objects were also selected to demonstrate the wide spectrum of art forms that the Carabinieri is responsible for protecting. The objects included paintings on canvas by the early baroque painters Guercino and Carracci. Violence and destruction often associated with theft were exemplified by the inclusion of 15th-century wooden altar panels painted by Bernardino Fungai. Thieves removed these panels from the cathedral of San Secondiano in Chiusi in 1994 using chainsaws. 'The Kidnapping of Europa', a vase from the ancient Roman city of Paestum, was one of the looted archaeological objects. Additional objects included two portions of a medieval fresco, a 12th-century ivory crucifix stolen in 1983 from the Cathedral of San Sabino in the southern town of Canosa di Puglia, several pages of illuminated manuscripts and a 1493 incunabulum[1] of a letter written by Christopher Columbus describing his discovery of the New World, translated into Latin.

The catalogue of the exhibition is a beautifully designed full-colour book featuring striking photographs of the objects accompanied by discussions of significance and recovery in three languages: English, French and Italian. A sense of the importance of the exhibition and the issue

---

[1] An incunabulum is a book printed (rather than handwritten) prior to 1501.

FIG 3.1. ROME, 16 JULY 2010. OPERATION ANDROMEDA: EXHIBIT AT THE COLOSSEUM OF 337 ARCHAEOLOGICAL FINDS FROM LAZIO, PUGLIA, SARDINIA AND MAGNA GRAECIA, DATED BETWEEN 8TH CENTURY BC AND 4TH CENTURY AD, REPATRIATED FROM GENEVA (SWITZERLAND) BY THE CC TPC.

is reinforced by introductory comments contributed to the catalogue by Irina Bokova, Director General of UNESCO; Giulio Terzi di Sant'Agata, Minister of Foreign Affairs, Republic of Italy; Lorenzo Ornaghi, Minister for Cultural Heritage and Activities, Republic of Italy; and Brigadier General Pasquale Muggeo, former Commander of the Carabinieri Department for the Protection of Cultural Heritage. Minister Ornaghi reminds the audience that, in the spirit of the Italian belief that cultural heritage belongs to the whole world, the Carabinieri TPC has been instrumental in returning works of art to Portugal, Bulgaria, Mexico, Spain, Peru, France, Costa Rica, Romania and Libya (Ornaghi 2012). All of the contributing authors also emphasise the Carabinieri's role in promoting international cooperation for the recovery and preservation of heritage and its accomplishments as an embodiment of the principles and goals of the UNESCO 1970 Convention.

Although the UNESCO venue in Paris was a first for a Carabinieri TPC exhibition, the force uses the exhibition medium as an important means of communicating to the public its capabilities and accomplishments. The TPC regularly organises exhibitions of recovered works of art for display in national and regional venues. The shows are often accompanied by beautifully presented interpretive catalogues. For example, in 2009 there was a series of exhibitions titled '*L'Arma per l'Arte*', or 'Carabinieri for Art'. The exhibition at Pitti Palace, Florence, from

FIG 3.2.   APULIAN RED-FIGURE HYDRIA, 4TH CENTURY BC, RECOVERED ALONG
WITH 336 OTHER ARCHAEOLOGICAL OBJECTS IN JUNE 2010 FROM A PRIVATE
WAREHOUSE IN VADUZ (FL), LIECHTENSTEIN.

November 2009 to April 2010 focused on objects of recovered ecclesiastical art, while a comparable exhibition in Naples from May to September featured recovered archaeological objects.
The Ministry of Culture, together with the Carabinieri, published the accompanying catalogues
'*L'Arma per l'Arte: Aspetti del Sacro Ritrovati*', and '*L'Arma per l'Arte: Archeologia che ritorna*'. The
catalogues feature photographs of the objects along with dual catalogue entries. One discussion
describes the theft, aspects of the investigation and recovery while the other offers an academic
perspective on the history and significance of the object with detailed references.

In the spring of 2011 the Carabinieri TPC hosted an exhibition of recovered objects in the
exhibition hall on the upper floor of Castel Sant'Angelo. The Emperor Hadrian originally built
the structure, which dates back to the 1st century AD, as a mausoleum for his remains and those
of his family members. The location, along the Tiber, was one of the most select in the city and
a similar mausoleum, built for Emperor Augustus, still stands on the other side of the river. The
story of the castle over the years mirrors the history of the city of Rome. Visigoths sacked the
mausoleum in 410 and architectural elements were borrowed and reused in constructing the
nearby St Peter's Basilica in the Vatican. Given its strategic position and incorporation into the
Aurelian walls of Rome, the structure was rebuilt into a fortification and became a papal fortress,

residence and prison. Castel Sant'Angelo is now a national museum and one of the most important monuments of the City of Rome. The castle's selection for a major exhibition of artefacts recovered by the Carabinieri TPC reflects the importance of the force and its role in protecting the arts for the people of Italy. Furthermore, the Castel Sant'Angelo's popularity as a tourist site meant that thousands of international visitors to the City of Rome had the opportunity to view this special exhibition.

Exhibitions of recovered objects can also be extremely significant at the regional level. On 14 December 2012 an exhibition of recovered antiquities opened in the city of Latina at the Museum Duilio Cambellotti. Dignitaries who participated in the opening included: Giovanni Di Giorgi, Mayor of Latina; General Ignazio Mariano Mossa, Commander of the Carabinieri TPC; Captain Massimo Maresca, Commander of the Archaeology Section of the Carabinieri TPC based in Rome; Colonel Giovanni De Chiara, Commander of the Provincial Police of Latina; Dr Elena Calandra, Superintendent of National Heritage and Culture; and Dr Francesco Di Mario, Regional Superintendent for Archaeology of the Ministry of Culture.

Once a year, during the month of April, the Italian Ministry of Culture sponsors Culture Week. During this special week, museums often reduce or waive admission fees and extend opening hours. Culture Week offers an excellent opportunity for TPC offices across the country to organise and host special exhibitions, events and educational programming. In 2012, the Bologna TPC hosted a one-day exhibition of recovered objects at the Museum Morandi of Bologna with promotion from the Museum of Modern Art of Bologna. The exhibition, *I Capolavori Ritrovati (Recovered Masterpieces): Morandi, Chagall, Picasso*, was free to the public.

This exhibition focused on three masterpieces. One was a recovered painting by Chagall. Another was a fake Morandi, fashioned after a famous Italian printmaker from Bologna who specialised in still life. The third work of art was a Picasso fake. In addition to the exhibition, the Director of the Museum, Gianfranco Maraniello, together with Captain Ciro Imperato, the Commander of the Bologna TPC, gave a presentation explaining the importance of the TPC and its work. They discussed the scientific methods used to determine when a work of art is fraudulent and they also told the stories of each of the objects. Prior to being recovered by the Bologna TPC, the fake Morandi had twice been sold as authentic. The Chagall was seized in Rome as part of a settlement for embezzlement but, instead of being returned to its rightful owner, it was handed over to an exhibition and then sold to a third party. The Picasso might be the most amazing of the three. A complete fake with significant differences from the original, it was on its way to Paris with completely fabricated authentication where criminals were planning to sell it for €2.5 million (Adnkronos 2012).

PUBLICATIONS

Exhibition catalogues are only one type of Carabinieri TPC publication. In 2009, the TPC published an introduction to the unit titled *Ministero per i Beni e le Attività Culturali; Comando Carabinieri Tutela Patrimonio Culturale*. This full-colour document gives a brief history of the force with introductions to its capabilities, including a discussion of the databank, outreach initiatives and current priorities. The book also includes a summary of significant awards received by the force, as mentioned in Chapter 1.

A major portion of the document is devoted to a small anthology of images: full-colour reproductions of images of works of art that have been returned to the Italian people by the

TPC accompanied by descriptions and specific information about their loss as well as their recovery. The book also introduces all of the regional offices, including contact information, and reproduces the Object ID forms for easy utilisation. Other publications include the annual Carabinieri historical calendar which has become a collectable object throughout Italy. Regional offices can also produce their own publications. The Palermo office has a portfolio of artistic black and white photos featuring Carabinieri officers, in addition to a set of postcards featuring the 'most wanted' missing works of art, designed for distribution to the wider public.

PUBLIC PRESENTATIONS

Carabinieri officers recognise that educating future generations is an important element of crime prevention. Italian school groups often visit the operative unit in Rome and regional headquarters to meet the officers and learn about their activities first-hand. Educational films available both in Italian and English describe TPC activities and capabilities, accompanied by dramatic footage. Carabinieri officers also have educational partnerships with foreign university programmes in Rome, such as John Cabot and Villanova Universities. ICCROM, the International Centre for the Study of the Preservation and Restoration of Cultural Property, relies on the Carabinieri as an educational resource for their foreign students and cultural resource conservation programmes. Carabinieri officers also provide introductory and specialised slide presentations and courses for international conferences and programmes related to law enforcement and the protection of cultural property at venues such as UNESCO and the International Institute of Humanitarian Law in San Remo, Italy. Presentations by representatives of the Carabinieri TPC typically introduce the force's range of capabilities and include discussion of their methods and accomplishments.

From time to time the TPC hosts major conferences, encouraging participation from law enforcement and heritage protection counterparts from all over the world. One example was a conference on illicit trafficking hosted by General Conforti in 2001, with over 80 participants representing 19 countries and at least 4 international organisations (CC TPC 2002). TPC conferences can also result from agreements and collaboration with international and other organisations. In 2012, as part of the 14th week of a culture programme promoted by the Ministry of Culture, the International Council of Museums (ICOM) chapter in the Italian Marche and the Museum Sector of the Ministry of Culture for the Marche region worked with the Ancona TPC nucleus to host a day-long seminar focusing on museum security. The event offered a technical security update for all types of museum employees with discussion of regulatory requirements, structural challenges and solutions, setting priorities and analysis of case studies (*vivereancona. it* 2012).

PUBLIC OUTREACH FOR IMPROVED SECURITY

There is no doubt that it is much easier to prevent an object from being stolen than it is to recover an object following its theft. The Carabinieri has therefore established proactive programmes to encourage collection inventories in addition to security inspections for ecclesiastical, museum and private collections. Security initiatives for ecclesiastical collections have led to the publication of a manual titled *Manuale per la Tutela dei Beni Ecclesiastici*, in cooperation with the Pontifical

Council of Culture,[2] and to an agreement with Italian bishops to work together with the Carabinieri to protect sacred objects. A key component of this agreement is that the Carabinieri now have access to BeWeB (ecclesiastical objects catalogue, available from: http://www.chiesacattolica.it/beweb/UI/page.jsp?action=home), the database of the Italian Bishops Conference. As the agreement is implemented, there are a series of protective measures that the Church can apply at diocesan and parish levels. Carabinieri officers are more than willing to inspect churches to identify objects that may be vulnerable to theft. They encourage the inventory of ecclesiastical objects with images and identify security weaknesses within church property. When visiting churches with officers of the Carabinieri TPC, it is clear that officers are immediately recognised and welcomed – as witnessed by the author (Rush) during a tour of Milan Cathedral with the then Captain and head of the Monza nucleus, Andrea Ilari, on 5 April 2011. As the 'Recovered Treasures' catalogue points out, the theft of ecclesiastical objects is a crime on two levels (Muller 2012). Not only do these thefts represent losses of cultural property, they also deny the use of these objects for sacred purposes.

In response to continued theft of ecclesiastical property throughout Italy, in the spring of 2013 the Carabinieri TPC published a handbook for protection of ecclesiastical property in English and Italian (Carabinieri.it 2013). The handbook begins with an introduction to the Carabinieri TPC and its capabilities, including the databank. The handbook then provides essential and basic information for protecting works of art and sacred objects in the Church's possession. It provides a general introduction to the nature of ecclesiastical property, recommendations for cataloguing and documenting ecclesiastical objects and information on assessing risk to objects located in sacred spaces. It also stresses the importance of regular inventory, especially during periods of change in leadership, and offers recommendations on security for churches, including the use of volunteers to help monitor sanctuary spaces, visitors and moveable objects. The manual also provides technical advice in terms of security systems and appropriate environments for sensitive objects, and concludes by outlining what to do in the case of a theft (Carabinieri Service for the Protection of Cultural Property 2013).

The Carabinieri authors of the ecclesiastical handbook are able to apply their years of experience as they describe risk assessment and make their recommendations. The Italian experience has been that churches are most vulnerable when open to the public without trusted individuals present, when the leadership of a Catholic community is changing, during the course of renovations or repairs and when breaking and entering is made easier in the absence of a security system. The recommendations for improved security are eminently practical, with suggestions for securing valuable, moveable objects, the installation of improved illumination (and possibly cameras) and the paying of particular attention to access points, upgrading locks and alarms on doors and windows. In some cases, the Carabinieri might even recommend the creation of replica objects for public placement in the church so that the original valuable relics and works of art can be held in a secure space. The document also discusses the installation of highly technical intrusion detection and alarm systems, ideally directly linked to local law enforcement authorities (ibid) (see Fig 3.3).

---

2   See: http://www.beniculturali.it/mibac/multimedia/MiBAC/documents/1361956415878_Manuale_sulla_tutela
    _dei_beni_culturali_ecclesiastici.pdf [25 November 2014]

FIG 3.3.   CHURCH PROPERTY STOLEN BETWEEN 2006 AND 2008 FROM VARIOUS CHURCHES OF UMBRIA
AND RECOVERED IN 2009 FROM A PRIVATE HOME IN THE PROVINCE OF ROME.

THE MEANING OF LOSS

It is difficult to describe the personal and community impacts when irreplaceable cultural property is lost. Professor Mimmo Savino, President of the Pro Loco (local) association of Giugliano,
organised a photographic exhibition of works of art stolen from the churches and public spaces
of the community of Giugliano. As the journalist (*InterNapoli.it* 2013) who covered the exhibition for the Neapolitan press points out, when art is stolen, everyone is diminished. The location
for the exhibition was the base of the Santa Sofia bell tower, where three stones were stolen on
the night of 31 May 1994. Art theft has continued to plague the community ever since, with
paintings and objects disappearing from churches, palaces and public spaces. Some of the stolen
art has significant market value, including paintings by Paolo de Matteis, Angiolillo Arcuccio,
Pietro Negroni, Giuseppe Marullo and Pacecco De Rosa. By collecting and exhibiting black and
white photos of all of the stolen works of art in a public space, Professor Savino hopes to bring
the lost works back into the living memory of the community.

THE MEANING OF OBJECT RECOVERY

Just as a community that has experienced a theft gains appreciation of the significance of loss,
perhaps only the victim of a theft can truly appreciate what it means to experience the restitution

of a valued or sacred object. However, as one reads accounts of the restitution of stolen objects to members of local communities and churches, there can be no doubt that the successes of the Carabinieri TPC represent contributions that are way beyond measure. Take, for example, the return of *Madonna con Bambino* (Mother Mary with Child), a 14th-century statue made of wood, to the Church of the Sacred Heart of Castel dell'Aquila (Eagle's Castle) near Orvieto, in the province of Umbria. The sacred statue had been stolen six years previously. Clearly the statue would have monetary value as a work of art on the illegal market, but its true value is, of course, as a sacred object belonging to the Church and its community.

Although the newspaper account does not describe the Carabinieri investigation that recovered the object, it refers to the work of the TPC as 'brilliant' (*Terni Magazine* 2012). The ceremony conducted as the statue was returned also reflects the true value of the object and the community's appreciation for the actions of the Carabinieri TPC. The parish priest presided over the special ceremony as part of the festival of St James, patron saint of Castel dell'Aquila. Officers of the Carabinieri TPC, envoys of the Superintendence of the Ministry of Culture, members of the Parish Council and representatives of the diocese were all invited as participants. As part of the ceremony, a delegation received the statue at the border of the parish and began a torchlight procession to the church where Bishop Tuzia Benedict presided over a liturgy of the word and a prayer vigil. The parish also plans to increase security to protect the object in the future.

Emotions also run high regarding the theft of ecclesiastical objects when there is concern that the objects are being stolen not for the black market but for alternative and dark forms of ritual behaviour. A news report from Lamezia Terme (2012) described two thefts in one day. First, a wooden cross over one metre tall was unscrewed from its base and stolen from a wooded shrine near a grotto dedicated to Our Lady near the village of St Mina. On the same day, thieves stole several gold-plated objects plus an image of the Virgin and earrings in brass and silver from her statue at the Church of Our Lady of Graces, in the district of Bella of Lamezia Terme. The priest who discovered the theft also noted that the sacred host had been thrown to the floor and that the thieves had left the sanctuary in disarray. The fact that the stolen objects had almost no market value and the clear contempt shown to a Christian sanctuary and Christian symbols caused grave concern regarding the motive for the theft and the thieves' intended use of the stolen objects. Clearly, the recovery and repatriation of sacred objects in a situation such as this would provide great relief to the congregation and community.

Celebrations of repatriation are also opportunities for the Carabinieri TPC officers to remind members of the public about the nature and importance of their work. On Saturday 28 September 2013, in honour of European Heritage Days and in partnership with the Superintendent for Culture, History, the Arts and Ethnography of Salerno and Avellino, the Commander of the Naples TPC formally returned the restored 14th-century painting *Madonna con Bambino e Santi* by Pavanino of Palermo. The painting had been stolen from the Church of San Biagio in Eboli in 1990 and was recovered by the TPC from Switzerland. This recovery provided an opportunity for the TPC and the Superintendent to demonstrate that law enforcement works effectively not only together with the Ministry of Culture but also with police forces both within and outside Italy. The Commander and the Superintendent also used the event to exhibit additional works of art and antiquities from the region that had also been stolen and recovered (*Salernonotizie.it* 2013).

FIG 3.4. AGRIGENTO,
TEMPIO DI ERACLE, '*UNA
CULTURA PER LA LEGALITÀ
DELLE ANTICHE RADICI*'.

THE WORK OF THE CARABINIERI AND MEANING FOR LOCAL ARTISTS

One perspective on the work of the Carabinieri that is not often considered is the meaning of their work for living artists. Jo Going, a prominent US artist from Alaska, expressed it well: 'You mean people like you work to protect my art? How do we thank you?' (Going 2011, *pers comm*). The Italian contemporary artist Marco Lodola, from Pavia, found a way to thank the officers of the Monza TPC (*Il Cittadino mb* 2009). In 2009, as part of the Carabinieri TPC's 40th anniversary celebrations, Lodola created two sculptures and donated them to the Monza office at Villa Reale. With his work having been targeted by forgers, he appreciated the importance of the Carabinieri's role in protecting the integrity of his true works of art and in preventing his work from becoming a focus for fraud, financial speculation, illegal trade and money laundering. Lodola was especially appreciative because he is an artist who wants his work to be popular and appreciated by all, not just by elite collectors. He is even quoted as saying 'Dovendo scegliere se fare una mostra in una galleria o in un supermercato sceglierei il supermercato…' ('if I had the choice of creating an exhibition in a gallery or in a supermarket, I would choose the supermarket'). One of Lodola's acrylic glass sculptures depicts a life-size Carabinieri officer in full uniform; the other is a stylised version of the traditional tall hat worn by Carabinieri officers. The gift was greatly appreciated by the then Captain Andrea Ilari of Monza and his team, and they celebrated the donation with a ceremony featuring the sculptures.

PARTNERSHIP WITH THE ARTS FOR OUTREACH

When we consider the Carabinieri TPC's contributions to the art community, it is not surprising that one way in which artists show their appreciation is by collaborating with the Carabinieri for public relations purposes. In Agrigento in 2003, the regional archaeological museum featured *Obiettivamente: i Carabinieri e la Sicilia nella Fotografia d'Autore*, or 'Objective: the Sicilian Carabinieri in Commissioned Photographs'. As described by Fabio Granata, Sicily's Regional Councillor for the Ministry of Culture, Environment and Public Instruction, the purpose of this photographic exhibition was to demonstrate the respect, trust and appreciation felt by the Sicilian people for their Carabinieri force (Granata 2003). The compelling black and white photographs were taken by Letizia Battaglia, Giuseppe Leone, Melo Minnella, Angelo Pitrone (see Fig 3.4), Letterio Pomara and Shobha – all well-known and highly respected photographers with links to Sicily.

During the summer of 2013, the Giffoni Film Festival (or 'Gff'), one of the world's leading children's film festivals, included a partnership project designed to teach children about the work of the Carabinieri TPC and the importance of preserving cultural heritage for all Italian people. Partnering with the regional Carabinieri of Salerno and the Carabinieri TPC nucleus of Naples, the Gff invited the Commanders of the Naples TPC and the Provincial Carabinieri of Salerno to discuss heritage protection as an educational programme for their young audience and made sure that the Italian press covered the event. The Commanders, along with the artistic director of the Gff, made the point that heritage is Italy's richest economic resource. They also wanted the young people to understand the important work done by the TPC and by the Carabinieri overall in recovering stolen artworks and antiquities and they reminded their audience that the Carabinieri's job is not just to recover these objects but, more importantly, to return them to the Italian people (D'Arco 2013).

4

Central Italy and the Adriatic: Lazio, Florence, Bologna and Ancona

Introduction

This chapter reviews Carabinieri TPC operations at the regional level and offers an opportunity to examine cultural property protection responsibilities and priorities, as they vary owing to regional culture and types of resources.

Fig 4.1.   Map showing regional offices of the Carabinieri per la Tutela del Patrimonio Culturale. R.O. signifies Operative Department.

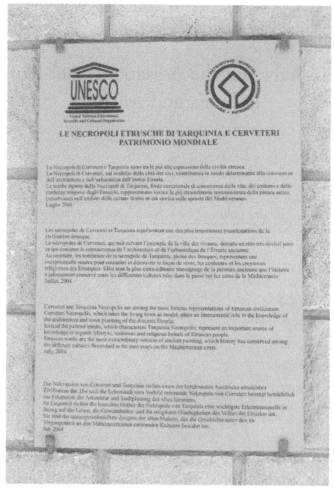

Fig 4.2. Declaration of UNESCO World Heritage Status, Tarquinia.

Rome as a Regional Office

The TPC headquarters in Rome serves as the *de facto* regional office for the provinces of Lazio and Abruzzo and is also in charge of carrying out investigations of particular importance throughout the Italian territory. A particular challenge associated with the Lazio province is the protection of portions of ancient Etruscan land, including the necropoli of Banditaccia at Cerveteri and Monterozzi at Tarquinia, both properties on the UNESCO World Heritage List (see Fig 4.2).

Both modern communities lay foundations, literally and figuratively, on those of their Etruscan ancestors and have, for generations, had knowledge of the ancient tombs and treasures. Wealthy Etruscans wanted to be sure that they would enter eternity in comfort. Etruscan families built elaborate tombs, sometimes with multiple rooms, featuring wall paintings and filled with extraordinary objects. Remains of family members were placed in elegantly carved sarcophagi. The Sarcophagus of the Spouses, from the Etruscan tombs at Cerveteri and now on exhibit at Villa Giulia in Rome, is one of the most moving and well-known objects from all of antiquity. In addition to sarcophagi, Etruscan tombs featured a wide range of objects considered useful in the afterlife: weapons, chariots, works of art, statuettes, items for personal grooming, home furnishings and even stylised hands and spheres, combined to make human images that also resided in the tombs. One result of these practices was that the ancient Etruscans left the countryside filled with remarkable structures full of unbelievable quantities of treasure.

Unfortunately, along with a heritage ethic, *tombaroli* and a culture of looting also emerged throughout the region. As the two communities of Tarquinia and Cerveteri have responded in different ways to the buried resources surrounding them, they offer contrasting examples that help us to understand the factors that contribute to preservation success. Marín-Aguilera (2012, 572–5) points out that the city of Tarquinia developed a tourism economy based on the heritage. The original walled city and its medieval quarters welcome tourists in great number to museums, shops and restaurants. Even more importantly for archaeological preservation, the protected perimeter of Monterozzi includes all of the known tombs. Selected tombs are accessible to visitors who purchase tickets (see Fig 4.3) and these paying customers arrive by the busload – an economic incentive for the entire community to ensure preservation. City planners also take heritage into consideration when issuing new building permits.

Cerveteri focuses its tourism efforts on modern development of its Mediterranean coastline and beaches. Fewer tourists seem to find their way up the hill to the necropolis, even though the community is a short bus ride from the cruise ship port of Civitavecchia, which handles millions of tourists annually. For decades, if not hundreds of years, some local families in Cerveteri have supported themselves by looting the Etruscan tombs and ancient neighbourhoods of the original Etruscan city. Even though the tombs at Cerveteri are also on the World Heritage List, are extremely impressive and available to visit upon payment of an admission fee, the casual tourist finds Tarquinia to be more welcoming and tends to visit that community for longer. Marín-Aguilera (2012, 572) attributes some of the differences to the politics of Cerveteri. She feels that some community leaders in Cerveteri view the tombs and presence of the ancient city as an encumbrance to development, rather than as an asset. To further complicate the goal of protecting the tombs, over 400 hectares of known tumuli were left outside of the boundary of Banditaccia (see Fig 4.4). In 2012, at least one concerned journalist (Rizzo 2012) reported that young people of Cerveteri may have been increasing looting activity with a goal of compromising the site's World Heritage status. It is possible that some entrepreneurs in the municipality are under the impression that the loss of UNESCO designation would make protected land available for construction and development. Rizzo (2012) also pointed out that the unstable political situation in Cerveteri has made it more difficult for the community to support consistency in law enforcement.

The concept of controlling such large acreages so rich in archaeological remains is difficult to grasp; one Italian law enforcement officer described the situation as 'relentless' (Carroll 2002). In the same article, appearing in the British newspaper *The Guardian*, Carroll quoted a police commander: 'The only way to stop those guys is to hide a man behind a bush every night...' (ibid). Interviews with current and former *tombaroli* provide insight into the personalities and skills that the TPC and other law enforcement officers are up against. Pietro Casasanta, referred

FIG 4.3.   *IN SITU* PRESERVATION, TARQUINIA.

FIG 4.4. OVERGROWN TOMB AT BANDITACCIA, CERVETERI.

FIG 4.5.   CLANDESTINE EXCAVATION DISCOVERED IN THE ARCHAEOLOGICAL AREA OF CERVETERI.

to by one journalist (David 2007) as 'prince of the tombaroli', discussed his career. Casasanta grew up in the region around Anguillara, a town along the shores of Lake Bracciano, a volcanic crater lake north of Rome. The area is incredibly wealthy in Etruscan and Roman archaeological remains, with many still waiting to be discovered by the wider scientific community. As recently as 2010, one of the original sources of a major Roman aqueduct, Aqua Traiana, was discovered in the vicinity of Bracciano.

When he was 14 years old Casasanta became interested in the archaeology of the region while following a local land surveyor. Casasanta was fascinated by the fragments of pottery and sculpture they encountered in the soil and he quickly learned to read the land, from both the air and the ground. He used clues such as variations in vegetation to reveal the locations of ancient walls, methods identical to those used by scientific archaeologists. In fact, he used some of his profits from his sales of artefacts as a young man to purchase books about archaeology. Casasanta made amazing discoveries during the course of his illicit career. In 1994, he discovered a 4th-century BC ivory mask of Apollo with a possible attribution to Phidias, the greatest of the ancient Greek sculptors (Todeschini and Watson 2003). The object may, in fact, be one of the most unique and important works of art from ancient antiquity. When his buyer refused to pay the agreed $10 million, Casasanta went to the police. The object was recovered in London in 2003 from notorious dealer Robin Symes, and is now in the National Museum in Rome. Authorities caught

Casasanta again in 1992 when one of his employees turned him in following his discovery of the Capitoline Triad, the only known intact sculpture depicting Jupiter, Juno and Minerva together, at a site called L'Inviolata, a temple cult settlement where Casasanta claims he found 63 statues, 25 of them life-size. The sculpture is now part of the collection of the national archaeological museum at Palestrina. Recovery of the Capitoline Triad is still a point of great pride for the Cara- binieri TPC (Rossi 2011b). Casasanta describes his feelings for archaeology and his discoveries by comparing it to 'falling in love with a woman'. Even a jail term did not initially discourage him from looting. Cecilia Todeschini (2011) also remembers conversations with *tombaroli* during which they professed love for the objects and the history they were systematically destroying (see Fig 4.5).

It is clear, when comparing Cerveteri to Tarquinia, and when thinking of a looter using a bulldozer on a Roman villa in broad daylight, that a major component of successful site protec- tion is a shared community preservation ethic. One way this ethic can be expressed is through the formation of archaeological preservation groups. In 1960, in Tarquinia, a small group of people banded together to form *l'Unione Archeologica dell'Etruria*, the Etruscan Archaeological Union. This group has sponsored education and awareness initiatives to teach community members about the Etruscan heritage of Tarquinia and its importance. Group members have discovered important archaeological sites in their community, such as the ancient harbours of Cerveteri and Tarquinia; the group established a journal and their success inspired the development of a similar group in Cerveteri called *Gruppo Archeologico del Territorio Cerite* (Archaeological Group of the Territory of Cerveteri). As of 2012, there are some additional signs of hope in Cerveteri as additional groups of volunteers, including the *Archeo Theatron, Mare Vivo* and *Italia Nostra*, have begun to work together with the Carabinieri TPC to clear the vegetation from the tombs, thus reducing cover for looting activities, exposing evidence of looting and making the sites more appealing to visitors (Rizzo 2012).

In Tarquinia, one of the most important accomplishments of the Etruscan Archaeological Union was to prevent construction of new homes on the sites of the ancient harbours they had discovered. Involvement in project planning and monitoring ground-disturbing undertakings are both critical components of a successful landscape preservation strategy. Carabinieri TPC, concerned members of the community, the Ministry of Culture and the Archaeological Super- intendents of the Ministry of Culture all work together throughout Italy to meet this goal (see Fig 4.6).

OPERATION IPHIGENIA

The recovery of the contents of an extended series of tombs in Perugia also illustrates the impor- tance of archaeological survey and evaluation of the landscape prior to new construction in the archaeologically sensitive areas of Etruria. In the summer of 2013, the Carabinieri TPC held a press conference to announce the results of Operation Iphigenia: the recovery of 23 funerary urns made of white travertine from Perugia belonging to the Cacni family complex along with over 3000 artefacts (Povoledo 2013). Ten years ago, a group of construction workers entrusted with work on a villa near Perugia discovered a series of Etruscan tumuli belonging to the extended Cacni family. Instead of reporting the tombs to the Carabinieri TPC or the Ministry, as is required by law, the workers decided to keep the objects they had discovered and, to avoid detec- tion, attempted to introduce them gradually onto the black market. Fortunately, the vigilance

FIG 4.6.   THE PLACEMENT OF THESE ETRUSCAN TOMBS AT BANDITACCIA ILLUSTRATES HOW THEY ARE HIDDEN IN THE LANDSCAPE AND HOW EASILY THEY COULD BE DISCOVERED DURING THE COURSE OF A CONSTRUCTION PROJECT.

of the Carabinieri resulted in detection as ancient Etruscan sarcophagi began to enter the Italian black market. Over the course of nine years, the thieves managed to sell only 7 of 23 urns, and the eighth attempt was enough to tip off the TPC. An individual well known to TPC officers in Rome was found attempting to sell the eighth sarcophagus by shopping around a photo of it and showing a small travertine head in his possession that had been removed from the item. After consulting with an expert at the University of Rome Tor Vergata, who recognised the artefact as typical of Etruscan tombs in the area of Perugia, the Carabinieri TPC was able to narrow down the region that had produced the item. Working with the Superintendent for Archaeological Objects of Umbria, they were able to begin surveillance to figure out precisely where the archaeological materials were coming from. In February 2013, Perugian Prosecutor Paolo Abritti approved increased surveillance of a group of construction workers who in fact turned out to be the very individuals who had discovered the series of extended family tombs and failed to report the find. Five of these individuals were charged with illegal excavations, in addition to the crime of selling cultural goods belonging to the people of Italy (*The History Blog* 2013). The TPC has also been able to recover all of the urns that were sold illegally (see Fig 4.7).

On a more positive note, once the Carabinieri TPC had identified the criminals who in turn revealed the location of the tombs, the discovery became a significant contribution to scientific

FIG 4.7.   OPERATION IPHIGENIA, MARCH 2013. RECOVERY OF 23 ETRUSCAN TRAVERTINE URNS IN THE
PROVINCE OF PERUGIA.

understanding of the Perugia region Etruscans. The Cacni were an aristocratic family dating to
the 2nd and 3rd centuries BC and were known to have established alliances with Rome as the
Empire began to expand into Etruria. In addition to the sarcophagi, bronze weapons, statues –
some of which had originally been covered in gold – and a rare bronze kottabos, their tombs
contained a vessel used in ancient Greek drinking games where guests competed by throwing
wine residue at targets. There were numerous ceramic vessels and the Carabinieri named the
investigation Operation Iphigenia, because some of the vessels portrayed the Greek myth of
this daughter of King Agamemnon, destined to be sacrificed. Some of the vessels also featured
images of fighting centaurs and bull fights. The tombs of the Cacni are especially important to
science due to the family's role in negotiating new relationships between the Romans and the
Etruscans during this lesser understood time period (Corvino 2013). In addition, the tombs may
have continued to be used in more recent times since some of the artefacts also dated from the
medieval period. Some consider these tombs to be the most important Etruscan find in over 30
years, since the discovery of the Cai Cutu tomb in 1982, also in Perugia (*The History Blog* 2013).
Italian archaeologists are optimistic that this discovery may lead them to additional tombs and
significant archaeological sites in the area.

THE ABRUZZO

As mentioned above, regional responsibilities of the Rome office extend as far east as the Abruzzo,
the spectacular mountainous area east of Rome that stretches to the Adriatic. Again, one of the
secrets of effective site protection in this far flung, rugged and rural area is cooperation with the
archaeological superintendence, as well as with regional and local police forces and concerned
citizens. In one case the TPC Archaeological Unit in Rome, in partnership with the Archaeological Superintendence for the Abruzzo from the Ministry of Culture, along with the members

of the local community of Tagliacozzo were able to apprehend and charge two individuals found using heavy equipment to damage a 13th-century abbey (*Marsicalive* 2012); they were even removing stones from the interior of the structure. The site, Santa Maria della Vittoria, was built in 1274 by Carlo D'Angiò (Charles of Anjou) to commemorate his victory over Corradino di Svevia (Conrad Hohenstaufen, Duke of Swabia) in the Battle of Tagliacozzo. Not only is the abbey an excellent example of French Cistercian architecture in Italy, it also commemorates an historically important battle where the Hohenstaufens lost their power in northern Italy.

The Operational Unit and Challenges in Urban Rome

The Rome-based units also need to meet the challenges of art crime in urban Rome. In early March 2012 the Operative Unit identified and recovered a series of 37 paintings that had been stolen from a wealthy home in the Parioli neighbourhood over 40 years before. The recovery began when a TPC officer spotted four of the missing paintings for sale in an auction catalogue. As the officers tracked down the seller, they discovered that not only had she claimed to own the four paintings she had put up for sale but she was also proudly exhibiting an additional seven paintings from the theft on the walls of her home, located in the same neighbourhood where the theft occurred. The TPC also discovered that she had an additional home outside the city where they found a further 26 paintings. The identity of the original thief is still unknown, but the woman was charged with receiving stolen property. The paintings included works by famous painters including van Dyck, Poussin, Berlinghieri, Guido Reni and possibly a Rubens; their recovery is one of the greatest in TPC history. The paintings were returned to the heirs of the original owners, who had not seen the works of art since they were small children (Kington 2012).

Florence

The privilege of a visit to the regional TPC office in Florence quickly confirms that the challenges facing the TPC units based in central Italy are in essence a microcosm of the challenges facing the nation at large. In contrast to the need to emphasise efforts to prevent archaeological looting in the south and forgery, theft and money laundering in the north, the officers in the central region face the full range of art crimes on a daily basis.

The Carabinieri TPC nucleus headquarters in Florence is located at Palazzo Pitti, the Renaissance home of the Medici and the Grand Dukes of Tuscany. The palace is home to extensive museum collections and the Boboli Gardens, in addition to hosting the offices of the Ministry of Culture and the Carabinieri TPC. The Carabinieri offices are on an upper floor of the palace, with a balcony that offers a spectacular view overlooking the towers, roofs and domes of Florence in nearly every direction, not to mention the hills beyond. The view offers a fitting daily reminder of the combined heritage of Tuscany and Umbria that it is the TPC's responsibility to protect. Even brief consideration of the extraordinary wealth of art and archaeology in the city of Florence alone – not to mention Siena, Pisa, Lucca, Perugia and Assisi, in addition to the walled villages, palazzos, castles, villas and churches of the Tuscan and Umbrian countryside – demonstrates a staggering responsibility. Florence is an example of how the nuclei must continuously balance the needs of protecting art, archaeology and ecclesiastical objects while also interdicting fraud and forgery.

Summary TPC accomplishments in the Tuscany and Umbria regions for 2012 illustrate the need for art protection and the TPC response. Officers from the Florence TPC recovered 55 stolen works of art with a value of €2.8 million. Recovered works of art included a painting by contemporary artist Lucio Fontana. The painting was stolen in Brescia and recovered in Florence, with an estimated value of €2 million. Additional recovered works were a 16th-century wooden panel with a figure of Santa Caterina attributed to Alessandro Allori, nephew of Bronzino and an Italian portrait painter in his own right and a member of the Florentine Mannerist school, and a Guerini painting, tempera on a wood panel with a gold background that had been stolen from the Brera Art Gallery in Milan. In addition to the paintings, the Florence TPC traced and seized 29 forged works of art. If these objects had not been seized, criminals would have attempted to sell them to unsuspecting art collectors for prices in the region of €25,000 per object.

The Florence TPC recognises that security education and prevention programmes may be one of the most powerful weapons in their arsenal. In 2011 Captain Costantini outlined to the author (Rush) the outreach programme designed both for individuals and institutions (Costantini 2011, *pers comm*). The Florence outreach programme emphasises documentation and cataloguing, inventory, environmental and security standards for storage and exhibition and guidelines to advise individuals on making considered purchases of artworks and cultural objects. The 2012 statistics for the Florence unit indicate that they are achieving some success with their proactive outreach and education methods. From 2011 to 2012 thefts of work of art decreased by 8%, from 125 to 115, while the number of solved crimes increased, from 906 to 972 (*Firenze Today* 2013). In addition, officers from the Florence TPC nucleus performed 50 security inspections for museums, libraries and archives and inspected over 50 archaeological sites (including underwater sites) and nearly 300 shops, markets, fairs and private collections.

A case from autumn 2013 illustrates the importance of inventory and documentation in the protection of art collections (Forbes 2014). When Dario Matteoni took over the position of Director at the Museo Nazionale San Matteo di Pisa, he immediately initiated a comprehensive inventory of the Museum's collections. As the inventory unfolded, it became clear that 12 master-pieces were missing. He was able to determine that the paintings in question had been sent to a restorer in Lucca in 2002 and had never been returned. In December 2013 the Museum filed a lawsuit against the restorer, an act that empowered officers of the Carabinieri TPC to become involved. The Carabinieri initiated its investigation in January 2014 and, within six months, all 12 paintings had been located. Six had been sold and were in the hands of foreign dealers. These paintings were immediately confiscated and returned to the Museum. Four were still in the custody of the restorer, who returned them. The Carabinieri tracked the remaining two master-pieces to French museums that had no idea the paintings had been stolen when they purchased them. Because the paintings had not been reported as missing for over 11 years, even diligent research of stolen art databases would not have readily identified the transaction as illegal. As of June 2014, negotiations for their repatriation are in progress.

Clearly, value can be considered in measures other than money. When we think about non-monetary worth, the value of recovered objects offers another dimension to appreciating the importance of the work of the Florence TPC. Some objects are not only of significant market value but are also historically important, such as eight pages of manuscript attributed to Dante Alighieri, containing his verses of Paradise, and three pages attributed to Giovanni Boccaccio, a 14th-century Italian poet and scholar, with verses of 'The Nymphs of Fiesole', considered by some to be his greatest poem. Another example includes the return of a 16th-century religious manuscript to the library of the Benedictine Abbey of Vallombrosa, an institution dating back to 1038. The object had been missing for 20 years before it was discovered for sale in an antiquities market. The successful discovery, seizure and return of the manuscript was also the result of a long-established partnership between investigators working for the libraries and archives sector of the government of Tuscany and the Florence TPC nucleus (*Valdarnopost* 2012).

A case of counterfeit stamps and postcards illustrates the wide range of crimes that the Florence unit finds itself up against. Members of the Federation of Italian Philatelic Societies, an organisation of Italian stamp-collecting organisations, started to become suspicious of stamps and postcards being offered for sale on the internet from a source in the city of Trento and reported their suspicions to officers of the Florence TPC. Officers were able to obtain a search warrant for the house of an accountant, where they found a quantity of antique stamps, prints and postcards, all counterfeit. The collection included over a million counterfeit stamps which, had they been authentic, would have been worth over €20 million. In addition to the accountant from Trento, also involved were five stamp dealers and a Florentine banker. Beside the counterfeit stamps, the forgers began with early 20th-century postcards and correspondence, including letters to the American consulate in Florence. They embellished these items with counterfeit stamps and postmarks using contemporary typewriters and inks, also found and seized as evidence during the search. On average, using these counterfeiting techniques, a piece of correspondence worth €30 could be sold to an unsuspecting collector for as much as €600 (*Trentino Corriere* 2012).

Bologna

The Bologna TPC's office is located in the heart of the city, on the second floor of the Palazzo Pepoli Campogrande. This palace is actually one half of a two-palace complex constructed by the Pepoli family, who took power in Bologna in 1334. They built the first Pepoli Palace in the very centre of the city at that time, now known as Palazzo Pepoli Vecchio. When Count Odoardo Pepoli was granted the title of senator in 1653, he began the construction of a new palace for his family, just across from Palazzo Pepoli Vecchio. The design of his palace stresses the triumph of a noble house and decorations within the palace feature major Bolognese artists of the second half of the 17th century. The palace was completed at the end of the century by his heirs, Hercules and Alexander Pepoli. Two famous architects of the time, Francesco Albertoni (1645–1708) and Giuseppe Antonio Torri (1655–1708), contributed to the design and construction of the building. It took the last 30 years of the 17th century to complete the rich interior decoration of the vaults and the lounges, including the staircase frescos that illustrate the glorious medieval history of the Pepoli family (Arma dei Carabinieri 2010).

The building is also home to the Pinacoteca di Bologna and the picture gallery Zambeccari, one of the most important collections in Bologna, which features leading artists of the region, including Ludovico Carracci, il Guercino, Albani and Crespi. The TPC office shares the second floor of the palace with the Photographic Archives of the Superintendence for the Historical, Artistic and Ethno-anthropological Heritage, which includes a rich iconographic documentation of the historical provinces of Bologna, Ferrara, Forli, Cesena, Ravenna and Rimini. It goes without saying that working within such a distinguished palace must be inspiring for those officers whose mission it is to protect heritage. Even though the office is based in the centre of a major Italian city, officers of the Bologna TPC respond to a full range of cultural property challenges, ranging from major cases of fraud to thefts from tiny rural churches.

One example of art and finance fraud encountered in the urban environment of Bologna involved an individual who was shopping at galleries and doing business with art dealers throughout the central area of the city. He would show interest in a particular object or painting and then pay for it with a fraudulent cheque. By the time the owner or merchant realised that the cheque was worthless and offered no clue to the forger's true identity, the individual was long gone. In fact, it turned out that the thief was using false ID cards that were the product of previous robberies. However, the TPC, working together with the Bologna police, were able to identify a pattern that finally enabled them to trace the individual, who was subsequently sentenced to jail in Rimini. Unfortunately, this individual was not an art collector. As a result, along, probably, with all of the other objects he 'purchased' with bad cheques, the artworks disappeared onto the black market and have not as yet been recovered by the TPC. The missing works also include lithographs by Giorgio De Chirico, Guttuso and Leonardo Cremonini (*BolognaToday* 2013) – all very important contemporary Italian artists.

A case from 2012 in the Emilia-Romagna region of Bologna also illustrates how quickly cases can become complicated. An architect from Reggio Emilia, near Bologna, commissioned the theft of a series of five paintings and eight antique firearms from the church of San Martino (dating as far back as 1451) in Velva, a tiny hamlet just outside Genoa, located in the Italian region of Liguria, north of Tuscany. The thief, a 60-year-old from the Ligurian area, stole the objects and the architect was charged with receiving stolen property and illegal possession of ammunition. In a situation that is not atypical, we see a case crossing regional boundaries, the theft of multiple types of object at one time, potential problems as questions arise about true responsibility for the crime and additional complications due to the involvement of firearms and ammunition (*Myreggionline* 2012). Whether or not the architect is guilty, a very disturbing trend can be noted in which architects and landscape and interior designers incorporate antiquities and stolen works of art into plans for homes belonging to wealthy clients. At the Association for Research into Crimes against Art (ARCA) conference in 2012, Dr Kathryn McDonnell, a Classicist from the University of California, Los Angeles (UCLA) reported on her experience as a consultant for US West Coast Immigration and Customs Enforcement (ICE) agents. The agents became suspicious of a shipment of objects identified as landscaping supplies that turned out to be looted antiquities. The statues and architectural pieces were intended for delivery to high-end West Coast designers and architects (McDonnell 2012).

The Bologna TPC is also challenged by ecclesiastical thefts, sometimes in very rural areas of Emilia-Romagna. In Cantalupo, a very small village between Argenta and Boccaleone, thieves stole from the church a painting of the Madonna, two statues, two offering boxes and an ancient rosary. Vandals had victimised the church once before by inscribing the devil's symbol of 666 on its walls (*La Nuova Ferrara* 2012). Thefts and damage to a tiny rural church – especially one that prided itself on its genuine holy relics – are crimes of a very personal nature within a small community.

Sometimes it is easy to forget that musical instruments are works of art in and of themselves. Captain Imperato and his team recovered a violin, valued at over €200,000, from a restoration workshop in Bologna. The violin, made by Ansaldo Poggi in 1924, had been reported stolen six years prior to its recovery. Ansaldo Poggi is regarded as perhaps the greatest violin-maker of the 20th century, with 322 instruments to his credit. Poggi made violins for Mistaslav Rostropovich, Isaac Stern and Yehudi Menuhin, amongst others; a pedigree that demonstrates the significance of a lost Poggi violin. Once officers from the Bologna TPC confirmed the violin's presence in

FIG 4.8.   A 2008 CARABINIERI TPC INVESTIGATION LED TO THE SEIZURE OF 200 CONTEMPORARY HAND-CRAFTED VIOLINS, SOLD AS PRODUCED BY FAMOUS VIOLIN-MAKERS OF THE 1700s AND 1800s.

the workshop, they were able to interrupt an attempt to sell the instrument on the black market and hold the three individuals responsible (*La Repubblica Bologna.it* 2014).

Antique violins have always been sought after by art collectors; in 2008 the Carabinieri TPC discovered a clandestine market of contemporary hand-crafted violins being sold as created by famous violin-makers of the 1700s and 1800s, such as Amati, Guarneri and Guadagnini (see Fig 4.8).

Theft and black market activity taking place in and around Bologna also results in damage to archaeological sites, near and far. In one case, an individual from Parma put a terracotta female head on the market, claiming that he had owned it for over 30 years and that it legally belonged to him. When the sculpture of the woman was subjected to scientific analysis, it quickly became evident that the object had been removed from the soil less than ten years earlier (Alderman 2012). Since objects of this type are usually found further south in areas such as Lazio, archaeologists partnering the Bologna TPC recognise that future soil analysis may yield valuable information about the true geographic origin of the object.

According to the Activity Summary of the Bologna TPC nucleus for 2011, the majority of stolen objects in the Emilia-Romagna region are paintings, wooden sculptures from churches, archival and library materials. In 2011 this nucleus extended its theft prevention programme to protect artwork displayed to the public, such as sacred objects and antique documents in

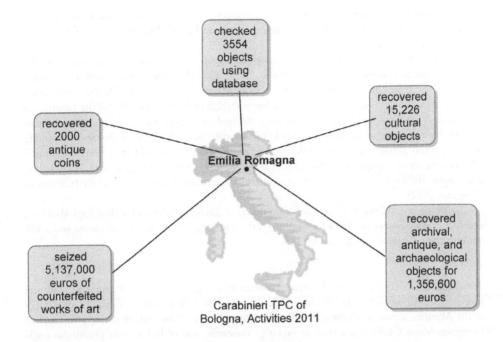

checked
3554
objects
using
database

recovered
15,226
cultural
objects

recovered
2000
antique
coins

Emilia Romagna

recovered
archival,
antique, and
archaeological
objects for
1,356,600
euros

seized
5,137,000
euros of
counterfeited
works of art

Carabinieri TPC of
Bologna, Activities 2011

FIG 4.9. SUMMARY OF THE BOLOGNA TPC'S OPERATIONAL ACTIVITIES IN 2011.

rural churches. They also completed 40 inspections of museums, libraries and archives (+52.5% compared to 2010); 34 inspections of archaeological areas (+5.8%); 12 visits to areas protected by landscape constraints (+25%); 231 inspections of antique shops (+41%); and 68 inspections of antique fairs and modern markets. This number was down 45% owing to the economic situation; ie fewer events were held owing to an insufficient number of exhibitors (*Il Resto del Carlino* 2012).

The Bologna TPC nucleus reported a 25.2% decrease in thefts of works of art for 2011; in fact, only 77 thefts were recorded, with mainly churches and public and private institutions being targeted. The worst affected provinces appeared to be Parma and Bologna, where rural thefts focus on mostly private collectors and churches of the hinterland. Some of the rural thefts may also have been associated with 'Il Mercante in Fiera', the large fair or open market that takes place in the province of Parma.

The Activity Summary for 2011 shows 15,226 recovered works of art, archival materials and antiquities, up 97% compared with 2010 and with a total value of €1,356,600, in addition to €5,173,000 worth of fakes and forged works of art (ibid). Among the objects recovered, the Bologna TPC nucleus reported three oil-on-canvas paintings (two from the 18th century by painters Francesco Lorenzi and Francesco Conti and one from the 17th century representing *Madonna, Bambino e Santi* (*Madonna and Child with Saints*)); two 16th-century oil-on-copper paintings attributed to Annibale and Ludovico Carracci; and two 16th-century sketches (*bozzetti*) of altarpieces, stolen in France and subsequently reported by INTERPOL as the subject of an international search (ibid).

In 2011 the Carabinieri of Bologna continued to focus its investigations on the fake artworks market; counterfeit works of De Pisis, Picasso, Lomi, Cascella, Arman and others were among the pieces seized in 2011. An unwitting buyer from Modena purchased the De Pisis counterfeit painting after seeing it for sale on television for €40,000; the Carabinieri found the painting in his home. A fake sculpted bust of a woman, attributed to Picasso, was sold to an art gallery in Paris by Italo Spagna, an art dealer already known to the Carabinieri TPC of Bologna for having been previously implicated in the bankruptcy of the historic Marescalchi art gallery. Carabinieri officers were able to intercept the fake object and seize it in a private storage unit in Milan before it left Italy. The French art gallery was completely unaware that the work was a fake (*Corriere di Bologna.it* 2012).

The Bologna TPC nucleus' constant monitoring of illicit trafficking of archaeological objects also led to the recovery in 2011 of a fossil from the Mesozoic era in the city of Parma and 2000 antique coins (*Il Resto del Carlino* 2012).

ANCONA

The Ancona TPC is located in the Palazzo Bonarelli and is responsible for protecting cultural property in a region of Italy known as the Marche, which stretches from the Adriatic Coast north of the Abruzzo, across to Umbria. The Palazzo Bonarelli is an 18th-century palace attributed to Francesco Maria Ciaffaroni, a student of Luigi Vanvitelli, one of Italy's most prominent engineers and architects of the 18th century. This unit of the TPC also celebrated Culture Week but, rather than feature an exhibition, they hosted an educational seminar in partnership with the Regional Directorate for the Cultural Heritage and Landscape of Marche and coordinated with the International Council of Museums (ICOM), Marche. The seminar covered risk management, technical updates on security measures and the roles of all staff members in protecting the collections for which they are responsible (*vivereancona.it* 2012).

Following the Carabinieri model of cooperation, the Ancona TPC has worked successfully with policing units at a very local level to investigate and solve crimes involving works of art and antiquities. In a case from July 2013 the Ancona TPC, in collaboration with Carabinieri units from Sant'Angelo in Vado, Piobbico and Arcevia, arrested three Neapolitans responsible for invading homes across five rural communities. The thieves' greatest mistake was specialising in the theft of antique furnishings, as this led to TPC involvement. Another key to the successful investigation and prosecution was the fact that the Chief of the Carabinieri unit for Piobbico had noticed the three Neapolitans in the community, realised that they did not have a good reason for being there and notified the Carabinieri TPC in Ancona. Thanks to this coordinated effort, when the dispersed and local units compared evidence, they were able to detect a pattern and realised that the crimes were part of a series of thefts that had occurred over the course of more than a year. The stolen goods were valued at over €230,000 (*tele2000.it* 2013). The investigation led not only to the arrest and incarceration of the three thieves, who turned out to be from Arzano, a rural village just east of Naples, but also to the identification of the fence who was taking receipt of the stolen goods for resale.

5

Activities in the North: Genova, Monza, Torino and Venezia

Carabinieri TPC offices in the North include the Genoa, Monza, Turin and Venice nuclei. The landscape of the northern regions of Italy is immensely varied: from the Italian main plain (Pianura Padana) to the Alps; from large glacial and alpine lakes to the Adriatic Sea; and, of course, many islands. These regions offer spectacular landscapes, as well as profound geographic and historical differences. In the 14th and 15th centuries a series of important independent city-states emerged in the region, among which Genoa, Florence, Milan and Venice became the most powerful. As the city-states declined, Spanish, French and Austrian rulers began to govern the region, creating kingdoms. One kingdom, the Piemonte (Piedmont), was under the control of the Austrian monarchy for centuries. It took many hundreds of years and several wars of independence for these regions to be freed and to become part of the Kingdom of Italy, which was formally born in 1861.

The long history of foreign domination and the relatively recent unification of modern Italy mean that the region is characterised by incredible cultural diversity. Communities along the north-eastern borders can be bilingual, with residents speaking both German and Italian – a reflection of the strength of the shared heritage and traditions. It is not uncommon to travel through the Trentino-Alto Adige region near the Dolomites and realise that the population speaks mainly German rather than Italian. Such diversity leads to an incredible variety of artistic and cultural wealth, making the work of the Carabinieri TPC even harder. The offices in the North have to be prepared for cultural diversity and geographical challenges, as well as overseeing Milan and its surroundings – the largest industrially developed region of Italian territory.

The city of Milan has seen tremendous industrial growth in the last century, expanding outward and engulfing neighbouring cities such as Monza and Segrate. A portion of Segrate has been developed to meet the need for new homes, thus creating what is now known as Milano 2. The population of the Lombardy region where Milan is located reached approximately 3 million in 2012, the second most populated region in Italy, after Rome (*Comuni-Italiani.it* 2012).

MONZA

The Monza Carabinieri TPC office, just north of Milan, is located in its own wing of the historic palace of Villa Reale. Known in English as the Royal Villa of Monza, the structure was originally built for Archduke Ferdinand of Austria by Giuseppe Piermarini, known also for the Teatro alla Scala, between 1777 and 1780, when the northern Italian province of Lombardy was part of the Austrian Empire. It is located on the banks of the River Lambro and the palace grounds are now one of the largest public parks in Europe. In fine weather, the park is filled with families strolling, picnicking and playing sport. The famous Formula One circuit at Monza lies within the

FIG 5.1. 'MADONNA IN GLORY', OIL ON BOARD, 18TH CENTURY. STOLEN IN 1998 FROM THE CHURCH OF SANTA MARIA IN THE PROVINCE OF VARESE AND RECOVERED IN 2003 FROM A PRIVATE HOME IN MACERATA.

original grounds of the villa, built into one of the woodland areas of the park. The Monza office is responsible for the region of Lombardy; no small responsibility considering its proximity to the financial capital of Milan. The region has been described as 'one of the world's crossroads of stolen works of art' (Rossetti 2009). In the spring of 2011, the first thing one would notice upon entering the TPC Captain's office at Villa Reale was a most impressive stack of fake Domenico 'Mimmo' Rotella decollages. A visit to the team at Monza offers a reflection of the Carabinieri TPC structure of complementary skills, backgrounds, experience and dynamic personalities. Interviews with team members combined with a review of recent press releases yield a range of successful enforcement actions, ranging from identification and seizure of an illegally excavated fossil panther to the exposure and prosecution of an international ring of money laundering counterfeiters.

In 2009, in cooperation with the government of Lombardy (and especially the Councillor for Art, Identity and Autonomy, Massimo Zanello), the Monza office published a book titled *Recuperi d'Arte in Lombardia* (*Recovering Art in Lombardy*). The book describes the challenges faced by the nucleus as well as many success stories. Some of the most important objects recovered by the team at Monza and featured in the book include the reredos of the Choir of the Basilica of

Saint Ambrose, *Madonna and Child with St John the Baptist* by Lucas Cranach the Elder and *The Graces* by Antonio Canova. Many of the most valuable objects had been stolen from churches, so their recovery took on even greater meaning (see Fig 5.1). The book makes the point that when art is stolen from public and ecclesiastical collections to be sold to individual collectors, the opportunity to enjoy and appreciate those works of art is also stolen. Stolen art held in private collections exists only for the pleasure of one person and perhaps his or her family and close friends. The importance of the relationship between the TPC nucleus at Monza and the ecclesiastical Community of Lombardy was further illustrated by the presence at the book presentation of the Archbishop of Milan along with the diocese's Vicar of Culture. The clerics also used the opportunity to announce the launch of their project to catalogue over 500,000 works of art and objects in the collections of the diocese with the assistance of the Carabinieri (Rossetti 2009).

In 2013, Major Andrea Ilari reported on 'Operazione Reliquia' ('Operation Relic'), an investigation designed to focus on sacred objects stolen from churches throughout Lombardy (*La Repubblica Milano.it* 2013). Operation Relic began in January 2013 when the Monza Carabinieri TPC identified on an online auction site numerous missing objects from local churches. Following two months of investigations, the Monza nucleus was able to arrest a 30-year-old man who had committed the thefts between July 2012 and January 2013. The thief had kept accurate notes of all the thefts, targetting monstrances, wooden statuettes and especially reliquaries (hence the name of the operation), small items he thought he could easily sell online. The thief posted the sacred items online and waited for an accomplice who specialised in buying/selling cult objects to officially purchase them. Once they had made the connection, the thief would bring the stolen objects to the accomplice in Tuscany. The accomplice would then sell the stolen relics for up to three times the amount he had paid. The Carabinieri arrested the thief at Milan Central railway station, where he was found to be carrying a bag containing numerous stolen sacred objects, ready to board a train for Tuscany. The Carabinieri recovered other sacred objects from the thief's home. The monetary value of the 57 recovered objects was estimated at around €30,000 (Sala 2013) but their value to the parishes is incalculable.

Major Ilari also reported that ecclesiastical thefts in the Lombardy region had remained stable from 2011–2012, but was pleased to report that the theft of religious objects had decreased in 2013. The Monza TPC had also noticed a change in pattern concerning this type of theft. In 2013, the crime had shifted to what the Captain described as predatory. Thieves were taking advantage of lax security to help themselves to available objects that they were, in turn, hoping to sell. This predatory nature was even reflected in the opportunistic patterns of seasonality, with the majority of the losses occurring between summer and autumn. This type of crime is in contrast to organised theft or theft on commission, where a collector hires a thief to steal and provide a specific object. Unfortunately, the internet offers continuous opportunity for thieves to sell objects to unscrupulous customers, but overall the statistics were encouraging. In order to keep the public informed, the Monza TPC (2013) also prepared a slide presentation featuring some of the missing religious objects, with images and detailed information concerning the thefts, and made it available on the internet for broad visibility and distribution.

Policing agencies are sometimes put in the very awkward position of needing to provide law enforcement in cases where a government representative has committed a crime. In 2012, the Monza TPC participated in securing the arrest of Luigi Germani, an accountant responsible for the funds of the Ministry of Culture for the province of Lazio (*Milano.corriere.it* 2012). Germani was caught attempting to escape to Switzerland in a rented van after having stolen €5 million

Fig 5.2.   Still life, oil on board, 18th century. Stolen in 2004 from a public gallery in Slovenia and recovered in 2011 from a private home in the province of Como.

that he had acquired by falsifying money orders and evading the computerised accounting system of the Ministry. He had also attempted to hide some of the stolen funds in fraudulent companies together with an accomplice, Mr Leonardo Vassallo, a principal of one of the fake companies. Working with the Prosecutor of Milan, the Monza TPC and the Milan Radiomobile nucleus began to track Mr Germani and Mr Vassallo and, after receiving a tip-off that Germani was making his move to leave the country, found him in the van that had been hired by Vassallo. Germani even attempted to show the police false identification in order to evade arrest.

The Monza office is often successful because its officers work effectively with other Italian and international policing units. For example, in 2011 they partnered with the regional Carabinieri of Como to identify, investigate and arrest a 63-year-old man at the centre of a major ring for trafficking stolen art and antiquities. The investigation identified an additional 12 criminals and recovered approximately 70 works of art worth half a million euro. The criminals were mostly using the art to decorate their homes and villas (see Fig 5.2). In addition, the ring was handling antiquities stolen from homes and churches in Comasco, Lecchese and Bergamo, along with 31 archaeological objects looted from Puglia (Rosa 2011).

At the international level, the Monza nucleus worked in cooperation with the Procurator of Milan and the French Brigade of Research and Financial Investigation on 'Operation Ottocento', to identify and intercept a citizen of the Republic of Georgia who had organised a ring of thieves specialising in stealing paintings from apartments in northern and central Italy. The investigation led the TPC to Paris where officers found €2 million worth of important 18th-century Italian paintings stolen from a home in Milan, torn out of their frames on the floor of a hotel room and ready to be sold on the black market (Sala 2009).

GENOVA (GENOA)

The Carabinieri nucleus at Genoa is located in the monumental complex of Sant'Ignazio, almost at the summit of Carignano Hill and behind the ancient church of Santa Maria in Via Lata. The complex dates from pre-1659, when records indicate that it was purchased by the Jesuits. The complex was utilised by the Jesuits for over 100 years, until 1773; thereafter the Nuns of Saint Mary Magdalene resided there. In 1798 the complex was converted into military quarters and it currently hosts the important State Archives.

TPC officers of the Genoa nucleus do not shy away from major challenges. Among their recent accomplishments (2013) is a series of raids on members of a criminal organisation accused of both forgery and receiving stolen art. This enforcement action was taken in a number of cities across northern Italy and resulted in the recovery of over US $10 million worth of art (Ministero dei Beni Culturali 2013b).

In December 2013, through a complex investigation called 'Operation Art Gallery' coordinated by Captain Salvatore Lutzu, his officers were able to seize 181 fake paintings with a market value of €10 million. This operation revealed a highly structured criminal organisation whose leaders were able to channel counterfeit works of art into the legitimate market for contemporary art by creating fraudulent certificates of authenticity.

The counterfeit works emulated De Chirico, Dorazio, Angeli, Nitsch, Kounellis, Prini, Boetti, Calzolari, Vasarely and Mambor paintings. Interestingly, amongst those arrested were some professional artists who had spent time with the above-mentioned painters in order to learn about their techniques and style of execution. The criminal organisation also possessed numerous original works, used to help the forgers perfect their techniques, to the point where the forgers working for the organisation had become extremely skilled. The forgeries were good enough to go undetected by many experts' evaluations and in some cases they even fooled the scholarly foundations of reference associated with the original artists.

During the search of the organisation's laboratory, numerous pieces destined to become components of forgeries were seized: masks, cutouts, paper, cloth, arrays of letters, numbers, symbols, stamps and so on. The Genoa Carabinieri also found an archive containing various forms of documentation (newspaper clippings, articles and catalogues) and sheets of glossy paper featuring reproduced signatures of the original artists. The criminals had been accumulating the materials for years and spent countless hours studying and practising the technical execution of the artists they were to counterfeit (Ministero dei Beni Culturali 2013b).

Given its location along the Riviera and the traditions of the community as a port, it is not surprising that the Genoa TPC also faces challenges in terms of the preservation and enforcement of protection of underwater archaeological sites, features and artefacts. Sometimes the criminal makes law enforcement slightly easier. In one case from 2013, a former councillor and coral diver aptly named Giovambattista Pesce ('pesce' translates as 'fish' in English) was discovered to have in his personal possession Roman amphorae stolen from a shipwreck in the shallow waters of the Tyrrhenian Sea, not far from the port of Genoa, dating to the 1st century BC (*Lettera 43*

FIG 5.3.   SURVEYS ON THE WRECK OF A ROMAN SHIP, INSIDE THE MARINE ARCHAEOLOGICAL SITE IN THE HARBOUR OF ALBENGA, NEAR SAVONA, ITALY.

2013). The TPC had originally grown suspicious when an anonymous source reported seeing a picture of a looted amphora on social media. Adding to the evidence, an alert Carabinieri corporal noticed another suspicious object when Mr Pesce asked police to come to his house to investigate a theft from his safe. In 2008 the Carabinieri TPC had discovered two Roman ships loaded with amphorae in relatively shallow water (see Fig 5.3). They used mosaic photos of the ships to document the wrecks, including the associated objects on the sea floor.

The TPC were able to use these images to reconstruct the thefts and build a criminal case against Mr Pesce. Even though he denied their involvement, the police found amphorae fragments in the home of his children and so the investigation was extended to his wife and family members. In addition, a friend of Mr Pesce voluntarily returned a looted amphora to the TPC. The TPC also seized a laptop computer containing images of the underwater thefts in progress and confiscated Mr Pesce's scuba equipment.

TORINO (TURIN)

The Turin Carabinieri TPC office is located in a palace called 'Casa Spalla' in the Royal Palace complex. The structure dates back to 1563, when the capital of the Duchy of Chambery was transferred to Turin. The palace complex, located on Via XX Settembre, looks out over an archaeological district that includes the ancient Roman Theatre and Palatine Towers or city gates (of 'Augusta Taurinorum'). The Turin TPC is responsible for a region in the far north-west of

Italy, comprising the Piemonte and the Valle D'Aosta and surrounded by the French and Swiss Alps. The Turin nucleus faces many challenges similar to those of other regions.

In 2013, officers of the Turin TPC worked with professors and international legal experts to recover 11 pages of illuminated manuscript originally stolen in 1990 from the ecclesiastical archives of the Archbishop of Turin (Pescara 2013). The case illustrates a series of common challenges: inadequate security for churches and ecclesiastical collections combined with the absence of detailed inventory and documentation of losses.

The manuscripts were not reported missing until 1996, six years after the theft occurred. The unscrupulous traffickers had cut the manuscripts out of their bindings and were selling them online, page-by-page. The case involved objects that had been smuggled out of Italy and required international cooperation for repatriation. The investigation began when a Columbia University professor alerted Professor Constance Montel Segre, who found the objects for sale on *eBay*, posted by a Bavarian auction house. The TPC were able to intervene to stop the sale, recover the objects and return them to the Archbishop and their home in the ecclesiastical archives. Sadly, many of the pages were still missing (ibid). In 2013 the Carabinieri TPC of Turin recovered *Le Nu au Bouquet*, a fine oil-on-canvas painting by Marc Chagall (estimated value €1.2 million), stolen ten years earlier from the yacht of a US private collector while his yacht was moored in the port of Savona. In 1988 a wealthy US citizen had bought the important painting from an art gallery in New York and exhibited it on his yacht. The yacht was in the port of Savona from February 2002 to January 2003 for maintenance, during which time the painting went missing. The son of the owner (since deceased), his legitimate heir and an art expert, travelled to Italy to collect the yacht and noticed that the original painting had been replaced by a fake. He reported the theft to the maritime authorities who alerted the local Carabinieri TPC nucleus. Images of the missing painting were promptly added to the Banca Dati *Leonardo*.

In 2012, the Carabinieri TPC of Turin identified the painting at the home of an unsuspecting collector while investigators were conducting checks of local art collections in order to intercept stolen works of art sold by an art gallery in Bologna. The Carabinieri of Turin were able to trace the painting's movements: from the US yacht the painting reached Nice in France, where it was exhibited in an art gallery for a short period of time; then it was taken to another art gallery in Monaco, and then came back to Italy – more precisely to Bologna, where it was finally sold to an unsuspecting private citizen.

The Carabinieri TPC, in reconstructing the various 'changes of ownership', discovered that the people who had illicitly removed the painting from the yacht had also managed to convince the Chagall Foundation to issue another certificate of authenticity for it. The newly issued certificate facilitated the sale. With the certificate available, the Turin resident believed he had legally bought a painting from the Bologna art gallery and displayed it in his home until the Carabinieri notified him of its illicit status. A 39-year-old resident of Romania, pretending to be the nephew and heir of the wealthy US citizen, took the painting to the Chagall Foundation and asked for and obtained a new certificate. The Carabinieri was able identify the man's accomplice, another Romanian, who had been a member of the yacht's crew until December 2002 and was aware of the painting's value. The legitimate US owner was able to reclaim the painting and the restitution terms are, at the time of writing, in the process of being regulated by the international agreements between the US and Italy in matters of stolen artworks (Ministero dei Beni Culturali 2013a).

A Turin-based investigation offers another interesting case that brought together the Monza racetrack and the world of counterfeit art in a coincidental way. Flavio Briatore, one-time manager of the Benetton Formula One racing team, is also an art collector. In 2008 he purchased 30 works by Mimmo Rotella from a gallery in Milan called JZ Art Trading, owned by Turin football star Jonathan Zebina. Zebina had hired an individual named Fabrizio Quiriti as artistic director of the gallery and Quiriti asked Briatore if he would like to exchange some of the works that the gallery had in storage for him for other works of art. Briatore evidently agreed and it is possible that at this point originals were replaced with fakes. According to *The Art Newspaper* (Harris 2011), Zebina brought a criminal lawsuit against Quiriti and held him responsible for the failure of the JZ Gallery, which was forced to close in 2010. Briatore, though, expressed confidence in Quiriti, an odd sentiment considering that Quiriti, on behalf of JZ Gallery, had sold him at least four fake paintings. Briatore's opinion adds a fascinating complication to the story, especially considering his very interesting past experiences with Italian law enforcement. Harris' 2011 article even raises the question of the forger's possible identity – an art and carpet dealer named Michelangelo Lanza, hailing from Viguzzolo, a village located just east of Turin. In 2011 the public prosecutor in Turin impounded one of the paintings in question, *Wise* (1962), and Mr Zebina worked with the Mimmo Rotella foundation in an attempt to sort out the fakes from the genuine paintings in the collection. To give a sense of the money involved, it may be helpful to know that a 1962 Rotella collage sold at Sotheby's for over half a million British pounds.

VENEZIA (VENICE)

The Carabinieri TPC nucleus of Venice is responsible not only for the World Heritage Site that is the historic city of Venice but also for the areas of Friuli Venezia Giulia and Trentino-Alto Adige. The nucleus' offices are located in the building of the Nuove Procuratie, in the beautiful St Mark's Square. The building stands on one of the long sides of the square and was built as the replacement for the Vecchie Procuratie, originally designated for the offices of Saint Mark's procurators, the administrators of Saint Mark's Basilica. Construction, by Baldassarre Longhena, began in 1582 and finished around 1640; the intention was to increase the Procurators' office space. In 1806 the viceroy of France and Prince of Venice, Eugene de Beuharnais, required the building to be modified and entrusted the architect Gianantonio Antolini with the transformation of the building into a royal palace.

The building currently houses important offices and museums including the Correr Museum and its library; the Museum of the Risorgimento; the Superintendencies for Historical, Artistic and Ethno-Anthropological Heritage of Venice and the region (known as Veneto); the Superintendency for Architecture and Landscape of the Eastern Veneto; the Archaeological Museum; the UNESCO representative; and the prestigious Marciana National Library (Ministero dei Beni Culturali 2009).

Among the many challenges faced by the Venice TPC is the preservation of cultural heritage for an area that, through the centuries, has been colonised and dominated by many different kings and powers. For over 1000 years, from the 7th through to the 18th centuries, Venice was a very important independent Republic called 'La Serenissima', led by a Doge or Duke elected by a senate-like assembly of nobles. During its independence, Venice dominated the entire Adriatic Sea with its flourishing trade between Italy, Europe and the rest of the world. The empire of La Serenissima extended inland, also ensuring safe trade to the north, reaching as far as the Alps. During those centuries Venice was considered Europe's most beautiful city and its splendour was unrivalled. Venice's richest noble families competed to hire the best artists of their time in order to adorn their residences with beautiful statues and paintings. The rest of the city also glowed in artistic splendour.

After the 15th century, Venice's fortunes began to decline, until Napoleon Bonaparte conquered it in 1797. In that same year Napoleon signed the Treaty of Campoformio, handing Venice and its territory to the Austrian Empire. It was not until 1866, after the Italian Wars of Independence, that finally Venice returned to being part of the land of Italy (Plebani 2010).

The artistic and archaeological abundance of Venice's heritage is spread throughout the Veneto, a region reaching from the Adriatic Sea to the Alps. The geography of such a vast and diverse territory demands extensive coordination between several detachments of regional Carabinieri and the Venice TPC, often using aerial surveillance of the land and maritime surveillance of the sea. Given the maritime nature of the city of Venice, sea surveillance becomes even more important. In his account of rowing and camping throughout the Venetian lagoon, Sean Wilsey (2013) describes what happens when a trespasser attempts to visit one of the uninhabited historic islands. Wilsey approached The Graces, an island measuring 800 × 600 feet and encased in a brick wall topped with marble. The island was originally home to a 15th-century monastery and then became a hospital for people with infectious diseases. When Wilsey landed his small boat he noticed a sign warning of guard dogs, so, for want of any other form of protection, he picked up a shovel he found lying near the dock. As a result, from the point of view of anyone passing on a boat, he looked much more like a potential looter than merely a curious journalist. While exploring the island Wilsey found a Carrara marble table, large enough to seat 12 people, a carved Renaissance well-head, columns with Doric capitals and a 14th-century Madonna statue that someone had honoured with a rosary. Not long after beginning his exploration, Wilsey saw two boatloads of armed Carabinieri TPC speeding towards the island and wisely decided to quietly depart prior to their arrival. This episode certainly added adventure to a Venice rowing and camping experience. It also illustrates the importance of cooperation from the community when the challenge involves attempting to protect a series of uninhabited islands filled with historic material, stretching across miles of seaside lagoon. The episode also demonstrates the Venice TPC's almost instantaneous response time when looting on one of the islands is suspected.

The Venice TPC nucleus is also vigilant across the inland landscape and is responsible for responding to violations that threaten the integrity of the historic landscape. In 2012 the Venice unit, assisted by Nuclei of Carabinieri Helicopters from Bolzano and Treviso, responded to the demolition of a medieval towerhouse in Gorgusello, a remote village near Fumane in the district of Verona. The medieval structure was considered to be an outstanding example of the earliest stone buildings constructed in the Lessini Mountains. The Lessini Mountains are a designated region of Italian Landscape and Architectural Heritage and so are afforded extensive protection under strict laws governing heritage preservation. The Carabinieri's investigation uncovered a series of restoration projects carried out in the absence of authorisation and conservation expertise. The tower belonged to a historic complex of buildings which, owing to a lack of maintenance, had experienced a series of structural failures and the unauthorised and incompetent attempts at restoration had actually contributed to undermine the existing structure. As a result, the instability of all of the structures involved became a question of public safety and portions of the complex had to be demolished. Subsequent poor restoration performed by non-specialist workers led to demolition being extended to areas that were not a safety risk. Carabinieri officers made a case for criminal liability involving three individuals who had directed the unlawful restorations to buildings belonging to public heritage. The local Superintendency pursuant to

Fig 5.4.   Painting on canvas, 17th century, portrait of a Pope. Stolen in 1991 from a house in the province of Viterbo and recovered in 1993 from an antique shop in Vicenza.

the Code of Cultural Heritage and Landscape (Decree No 42/2004) issued an order requiring the town of Fumane to initiate an action plan aimed at proper reconstruction and preservation of the original historical and artistic complex (Ministero dei Beni Culturali 2012).

Art thieves strike in unexpected places. In 2009 the Carabinieri TPC of Venice, cooperating with the Superintendency for Artistic and Historical Heritage of the Autonomous Province of Trento, denounced two women for stealing two oil paintings on canvas forming the 'doors' (portelle) of an ancient chimney of the building called 'Casa Baisi' of Bretonico in Trento. The two panels dated back to the 18th century and depicted a 'bucolic scene with flowers, fruit, and angels'. The paintings were of artistic as well as historic value owing to the fact that they were the work of known and respected artists from Trento.

An even more unexpected theft was from a cardiology department at the Treviso Hospital Ca' Foncello (*Corriere del Veneto* 2013). Each year the department hosts the exhibition *Art is Good for the Heart*, for the benefit of the patients. Imagine the shock of the medical staff when they arrived at work to discover empty spaces on the wall where the paintings should have been. The thieves focused on works by Riccardo Licata and, after news broke of the initial theft of two paintings with details of their commercial value, a third also disappeared. As of summer 2013, the theft remained unsolved.

In 2010 a major operation conducted by the Venice unit made it possible to thwart a criminal group operating in the north-east region of Italy. The group specialised in burglary and handling stolen art and antiques. The Venice Carabinieri TPC unit analysed a series of thefts throughout the region. As they began to identify patterns they were able to trace the evidence to the dwelling located near Brescia. The individuals associated with the dwelling were already known to the authorities for similar thefts from churches and private homes. When agents raided the dwelling they found objects from thefts that had occurred between 2005 and 2009.

The success of the investigation once again illustrates the importance of cooperation between multiple law enforcement organisations. In this case, the Venice TPC worked with Monza, Brescia, Verona, Udine, Pordenone, Treviso and Trento to compare and reconstruct the *modus operandi* of the thefts. A fourth person was also arrested for hiding further stolen items in a storage unit in Brescia. The joint operation led to the recovery of items valued at approximately €60,000 and the return of the stolen items to their original owners (Arma dei Carabinieri 2010). This case also demonstrates that, even across a region as diverse and challenging as the North of Italy, one of the most effective assets in fighting such crimes is the ability of multiple units to coordinate their efforts and succeed together (see Fig 5.4).

6

The Regional Offices: Naples, Bari and the South

The Naples TPC offices are located within a castle – an extraordinary historic structure and symbol of power, visible from throughout the city. The Castel Sant'Elmo dominates Naples from its position on the top of Vomero hill. It is a majestic star-shaped structure with six points and several moats. Originally built by the Angevins, a noble family of Frankish origin, in 1329 and called Belforte, it was restructured into a fortress by Viceroy Pedro Toledo in the 16th century. It has been recently restored and hosts special exhibitions in addition to housing the TPC offices. Visitors can also visit the palace terraces and prisons.

As is the case throughout Italy, the protection of art and archaeology in Naples and the South represents an extraordinary challenge. Along with the ancient cities of Pompeii and Hercula-neum, the multitude of palaces, villas, private collections, archaeological sites, heritage land-scapes, libraries, archives and churches (that are sometimes left open to the public without supervision) require constant vigilance on the part of the Naples CC TPC. Unfortunately there are thousands of stolen artworks and antiquities already recorded in Banca Dati *Leonardo* and art crimes large and small are planned and executed on an almost daily basis.

A recovered statue of Agrippina the Younger, mother of Roman emperor Nero, illustrates one aspect of the range of challenges. Dating from between 100 BC and AD 50 and stolen sometime between 1984 and 1990 from Pompeii, the terracotta statue surfaced in Parma when a dentist who had the statue hidden in his possession for years attempted to sell it through a dealer in Piacenza. The statue was identified and secured by the Carabinieri TPC based in Parma, who also recognised the tremendous historical significance of the object. Both the dentist and the dealer were arrested for possession of stolen archaeological material (*Huffington Post* 2012).

GIROLAMINI LIBRARY DISASTER

The Girolamini Library in Naples (see Fig 6.1) is one of 46 state libraries in Italy. It holds around 160,000 volumes (mostly rare and antique books) including 160 incunabula and 6500 manuscripts of musical compositions dating from the 16th to the 19th centuries. The library is located within the complex of Girolamini Church (Montanari 2012), across Via Duomo from the Cathedral of Naples. The library was opened to the public in 1586 and may be the oldest library in Naples.

This library has an unfortunately long history of being looted; it is believed that, between 1960 and 2007, almost 6000 volumes were illicitly removed from its collection (Montanari 2012) (see Fig 6.2).

One of the most recent and important operations conducted by Carabinieri TPC involved this library. In June 2011 a man named Marino Massimo De Caro was nominated as Director of the Girolamini Library thanks to his political connections, including his long-term friend-ship with Senator Marcello Dell'Utri, a member of Berlusconi's People of Freedom Party and

Fig 6.1.   Interior of the Girolamini Library.

a close aide to the Premier. De Caro misrepresented himself to the Italian public by claiming aristocractic connections and referring to himself as a prince. De Caro was also the owner of an antique book shop in Verona and his passion for antique books was known to go beyond a healthy interest in history and cultural heritage. In March 2005 De Caro had been investigated by the Carabinieri TPC from the Monza office for selling an incunabulum from 1499, *Hypnero-tomachia Poliphili*, stolen from a library in Milan and sold at a book fair sponsored by Senator Dell'Utri. In fact, during a tapped telephone call De Caro was overheard complaining about the Monza nucleus of the TPC, angry that their investigation was interfering with his ambition to be appointed honorary consul to the Congo by the foreign ministry (Stella 2012; Sansa and Gatti 2012). Investigations were subsequently suspended as, after the sale, the book could not be found or physically retrieved (Montanari 2012). De Caro was also said to have been a partner in Imago Mundi, an antiquarian bookshop in Buenos Aires owned by a man named Daniel Guido Pastore, who stands accused of the theft of books from the National Library in Madrid and the Zaragoza University Library.

Meanwhile, De Caro progressed in his political career until he was appointed director at the Girolamini Library. In February 2012 the Carabinieri TPC of Naples conducted their first inspection of the library following De Caro's appointment in response to a report of theft and disorganisation at the library from the art historian Tomaso Montanari, who visited the library with the intention of using the collection for research (Stillman 2013). Following his visit, Montanari wrote an opinion piece expressing his concerns about the Berlusconi government and its systematic failures to protect the cultural heritage of Italy. In addition to his detailed

Fig 6.2.   Rare book of Galileo Galilei, *The Metric and Military Compass*, dating from
the 17th century. Stolen in 1970 from the National Library of Girolamini in Naples and
recovered in 2013 from a safe deposit box at a Swiss bank.

description of books strewn about the library and empty Coke cans on the reading room desks,
Montanari's article also referred to reports by local residents who had observed suspicious activity,
such as vans leaving the library in the middle of the night (Montanari 2012; *Il Fatto Quotidiano*
2012).

The Carabinieri TPC inspection revealed that many volumes had been stolen from the library
and many more were lying in boxes ready to be shipped to England, Japan, Germany and the
United States (see Fig 6.3). The volumes illicitly sold to the United States are now in the process
of being returned, thanks to well-established law enforcement cooperation between Italy and
the US.

Once the investigation began, the number of stolen volumes rose steadily, as did the number
of accomplices. Estimates of the number of stolen volumes are in the thousands, and the library's

Fig 6.3.   Antique and rare books from the Girolamini's collection, as found by the Carabinieri TPC during the investigation.

curator was identified and arrested as an accomplice. In April 2012 the CC TPC arrested five people involved in the crime, including De Caro himself; he later began to cooperate with the TPC. To provide insight into the complexity of the conspiracy, De Caro and his team had even hired a bookbinder in Bologna, over 300 miles away from Naples, to remove from the books the stamps indicating they were the property of the Girolamini library (Stillman 2013). Another member of the conspiracy was a 'runner' who was transporting the books out of Naples.

De Caro was removing antique and rare volumes from the library and selling them for personal profit. Some of the volumes were also shipped to an apartment in Rome owned by Senator Dell'Utri, who himself turned in some of the Girolamini library's books, valued at around €6 million. The senator declared that he did not know of the books' origin and that he simply accepted them as 'gifts' from his old friend. The senator was found guilty of planning the looting of the library with De Caro and was sentenced to seven years in jail for this crime (*Il Fatto Quotidiano* 2013b; *La Repubblica Palermo* 2013).

The Carabinieri was able to analyse details of how the library was systematically looted and uncover the channels used by the looters to place the books in antiquarian bookshops throughout Italy. Several antique dealers also reported the influx of antique books onto the market and alerted the Carabinieri, thereby assisting their investigations. The Carabinieri TPC quickly retrieved 257 of the stolen volumes, found in a storage facility in a small town near Verona, Italy.

The CC TPC promptly coordinated with German INTERPOL in Wiesbaden to halt the expatriation of several Girolamini library books destined for an auction house in Munich. The

Carabinieri suspected that many other books had already been listed in foreign auction houses' catalogues, necessitating international police cooperation for the successful retrieval of the Girolamini volumes.

The investigation was made even more difficult by the criminals' systematic destruction of the sections of the library catalogue that documented the books that De Caro and the library's curator were stealing from the library. De Caro's criminal plan was based on the fact that the Girolamini did not have a complete catalogue, which therefore further facilitated the pillaging of the volumes. One element of the Italian government's response to the tragedy that struck the library was the Italian Ministry of Culture's application for the Girolamini library to be accepted onto the UNESCO World Heritage List (*Corriere del Mezzogiorno* 2012).

As the investigation continued to unfold, the Carabinieri TPC uncovered additional evidence that the same conspirators had also stolen from state libraries in Florence and Rome (Lepri 2013), amongst many others, including one in Montecassino Abbey and the precious collection of the Italian Ministry of Agriculture and Forests. As the tragedy of the Girolamini library enters the pages of history, important points emerge. First, the Carabinieri TPC Monza unit had identified the leader of the conspiracy, De Caro, as a criminal years earlier, before he used his government connections to attack the Girolamini. Second, this case illustrates that criminals in the art sector often do not limit their criminal behaviour solely to the arts. De Caro had also been involved with international corruption in the oil and energy sectors (Stella 2012). The TPC's resulting extensive knowledge of (and experience with) criminality of this type is an asset for dealing with many other kinds of investigations.

The conviction of six individuals in the case of the Girolamini theft will hopefully serve as a warning to others who may be contemplating the theft of rare books and archival material that actions of this nature are not without consequence. De Caro, like Dell'Utri, was sentenced to seven years in jail and is forbidden from ever again holding public office. When handing down the sentence, the judge commented on the magnitude of the loss to the city of Naples, describing the crime as an 'incurable wound' to the city (*ANSA* 2013a).

A slightly more positive outcome of the Girolamini library tragedy is the increased awareness of the importance of protecting library and archival collections. Along with that awareness is recognition that the public may perceive that libraries and archives are assets only of interest to an elite, highly educated proportion of the public as opposed to their true importance and value to the community as a whole. Because ancient books and archival collections require special protection and preservation, it can be difficult to exhibit them and even more difficult to make them available for members of the public to read and appreciate. The Italian Society for the Protection of Cultural Property has declared the need for more public education on this issue (Tabita 2012).

Operation RoViNa

The Naples unit, led by Captain Elefante, is not new to large-scale challenges and has experienced many successes. In fact, in 2011 this unit completed an operation nicknamed RoViNa (Rome–Naples) which culminated in the arrest of 12 people, the reporting of 51 and the investigation of 37. In 2009, the Police of the TPC unit in Rome began to notice an influx of archaeological objects from the Caserta area onto the black market and promptly warned their colleagues in Caserta. At the same time, the local superintendency was denouncing illegal excavations in the same archaeological area. These illegal excavations were always conducted at night, especially in the areas of Riardo (Lagoscelle), Teano (Sette Querce), Casapesenna and Calvi Risorta (Caserta) and Montesarchio Sant'Agata dei Goti (Benevento), all of which were under the jurisdiction of the nucleus TPC of Naples (*Prospero Cecere* 2011). After the initial investigation, the CC was able to identify the same *modus operandi* for all of these illegal excavations.

Surveys conducted using infrared cameras allowed the Carabinieri to identify some local grave robbers (*tombaroli*) who acted at night, armed with car batteries to power portable lights, shovels, picks and sharp, long sticks used to survey the ground in search of burials. These thin, elongated sticks are commonly called 'big pins' or 'big needles'. Grave robbers use these pins to probe agricultural and burial land to identify areas of interest and then dig in search of funerary objects to loot (*Interno18* 2011).

At one such site the CC was lucky enough to find a hat left behind by one of the grave robbers, which led back to its owner. The hat had been used to collect archaeological objects and had been inadvertently left behind. The CC was able to track down the owner and his accomplices, arresting the entire organisation. The criminal outfit that ran these illicit excavations had many members and was well organised. Every morning the grave robbers met at a local bar and planned which sites they were going to 'visit' that night. Later, they would form groups of three or four people and proceed to survey different areas. Once a possible grave was identified, the *tombaroli* quickly performed the excavation and removal of funerary objects, leaving the site and remaining discarded artefacts and features exposed to the elements. An accomplice named Annibale Corvino handled all of the material that had been illegally removed and was responsible for all transactions with potential buyers. Corvino held a prominent position within the organisation and was considered by the thieves to be competent enough in the art and archaeology fields to be nicknamed 'The Professor'.

Corvino was not unknown to the CC. In fact, he had been arrested in 2006 for similar crimes as part of an operation nicknamed AUREA, through which the CC TPC recovered about 750 archaeological items from the Campania region (*Interno18* 2011). Within the structure of his new organisation, 'The Professor' contacted potential buyers, both local and international, and offered them the stolen objects for sale. Corvino was clever enough to mix copies of ancient artefacts into the inventory of looted originals. These copies, commissioned and specifically created for him by artists from the Puglia region, perfectly emulated the period and the manufacturing era of the original pieces. As a result, buyers confidently bought both originals and fakes. Another accomplice was in charge of hiding any objects that the organisation could not immediately sell, waiting for the right market (*Prospero Cecere* 2011).

In 2011 the CC of Naples completed Operation RoViNa, recovering as many as 520 archaeological objects valued at tens of millions of euros. The investigation had also identified an officer of the Mobile Unit of the State Police of Naples as part of the criminal organisation. The damage inflicted on the archaeology of the area was devastating. The grave robbers had acted determinedly for many years and had profited tremendously from the proceeds of their looting and fraudulent activities. The damage was not just limited to the removal of historical artefacts; the objects' *in situ* contexts were also destroyed. Even if they are recovered by the TPC, the stolen items will never regain the associated knowledge that would help people today to understand and interpret their original roles in life and society. The area of Caserta affected by grave robbers now has the appearance of gruyère cheese, not unlike the moonscapes of looted areas of the Middle East. The grave robbers left behind numerous holes, leaving *in situ* only what they could not carry or what they believed had no pecuniary value. All they left behind was their legacy of wanton and unbelievable destruction.

The success of investigations such as RoViNa helps to halt illegal excavations and limit damage to archaeological areas that have not yet been subject to systematic excavation and research. There are sites of potential archaeological and historic interest throughout Italy, which unfortunately makes the CC TPC task of protecting and monitoring the land incredibly difficult. Successful operations once again illustrate the value of both prompt cooperation between the nuclei of different Italian regions and the efficient coordination of their efforts.

CELEBRATIONS OF RECOVERY

It is important to remember that the Naples CC TPC has returned works of art worth millions of euros to the Italian people. Just one example of these recoveries was an exhibition held in December 2012 at the Naples CC TPC headquarters, Castel Sant'Elmo, to celebrate the recovery of 95 paintings previously stolen from churches and private homes in Naples and the region. The Vice Commander of the Carabinieri TPC travelled from the Rome headquarters to accompany Captain Elefante, Commander of the Naples unit, in celebrating the opening of the exhibition (*Il Mattino* 2012).

In March 2013 Captain Carmine Elefante of the Carabinieri Tutela Patrimonio Culturale of Naples recovered the famous painting *Crucifixion* by Mattia Preti, stolen from the church of the Immaculate Conception of Torre Annunziata while restoration work was under way. Artist Mattia Preti was the most famous exponent of the 1600 Neapolitan School of Art, dubbed the 'Calabrese Knight'. This painting was donated to the city of Torre Annunziata by a local wealthy resident and had been on display in the above-mentioned church since its donation. The void created by the theft had been unbearable for the congregation and the painting's recovery was welcomed with solemn celebration and street processions.

The painting was recovered 23 years after it was stolen, in the area of Pescara in the Abruzzo region. Captain Elefante's officers had earlier identified some suspicious antique paintings in a Naples art dealer's shop during one of their routine visits. One of the officers took photographs of the paintings and sent them to the database unit in Rome to check their provenance. The Rome officers immediately identified two of the paintings as having been stolen from two churches in the Italian region of Marche and alerted the Naples unit. The Carabinieri promptly conducted an investigation and found that the shop was owned by a Pescara resident already known to the TPC for crimes against art. The search of the art dealer's home in Pescara led to the discovery of a museum-house of 94 antique paintings, a wooden cross and a small door from a 1700 tabernacle – all sacred items stolen from Italian churches with a value of €2 million. Among the 94 paintings was Preti's *Crucifixion*. The Carabinieri returned the famous painting to the town of Torre Annunziata and its grateful congregation (Salvati 2013).

Another form of celebration occurs when an entire region acknowledges the return of a unique and special object. In 2005 the Getty Museum returned the extraordinary ceramic vessel known as *The Kidnapping of Europa* to Italy and, in 2007, the vessel made its way home to the ancient city of Paestum, located around 85km south-east of Naples. The krater is thought to be the work of Asteas, one of the most celebrated artists of Paestum. Asteas used the vessel to tell the famous story of Europa, a beautiful Phoenician woman. The Greek God Zeus fell in love with her and, disguised as a white bull, came to earth, kidnapped Europa and took her to

Fig 6.4.   *Il Ratto d'Europa*, 4th century BC, Asteas.

Crete. The artist painted the story in breathtaking detail on the 70cm-high krater, a vessel for mixing water and wine, using red figures on a black glaze background (see Fig 6.4). The vessel was uncovered in 1970 near Naples, stolen very shortly afterwards and sold for approximately 1 million lire. In violation of both Italian domestic law and international law, the vessel was sold to the Getty Museum in the United States, where it was identified by the Carabinieri TPC as stolen. It was one of the most valuable objects repatriated by the Getty to Italy during the first decade of the 21st century. After touring Italy, the object returned to its city of origin, Paestum, and was displayed at the museum next to the excavations. In 2010 over 187,000 people had an opportunity to see the krater while visiting Paestum and the object is often mentioned in tourist literature and other discussions of the ancient city.

COSENZA

The neighbouring CC TPC unit south of Naples also has an outstanding record of enforcement and recovery of artworks. The Cosenza CC TPC is based in Palazzo Arnone, built in the 16th century by Bartolo Arnone, the treasurer of the province. It was the first seat of the regional appellate court and for a time served as a prison. The structure was abandoned for a while before being transformed into a museum and arts complex; the palace is also the home of the National Gallery of Calabria. The unit's major activities and accomplishments in the early decades of the 21st century include the discovery and termination of a major contemporary art forgery work-shop, the recovery of thousands of archival documents and the repatriation of significant works of art to the region.

Major Giovinazzo initiated 'Ginestra', an investigation of contemporary art emerging from the region complete with false certificates of authenticity for sale on the internet, with a poten-tial market across the whole of Italy. In collaboration with the deputy regional prosecutor, the Cosenza CC TPC monitored *eBay*, following sales of contemporary art. The nickname of the internet vendor was Ginestra, or 'Broom'. By tracking his behaviour patterns, the CC TPC was able to gather sufficient evidence for a search warrant of Broom's residence. The search yielded all of the necessary tools for a counterfeit operation: a scanner, brushes, paints, enamels – even blank certificates of authenticity. Ultimately, the unit seized 232 fake paintings with a potential market value of over €800,000, with attributions to eminent Italian artists including Renato Guttuso, Eliano Fantuzzi, Mario Schifano, Sergio Scatizzi and Enotrio Pugliese. Approximately 60 angry customers also came forward to give evidence against the accused (Cannataro 2013). In another major investigative accomplishment, the Cosenza CC TPC discovered over 13,000 stolen archival documents hidden in a small community within the province. The CC TPC was able to recover the documents and return them to the Archives of Calabria (*Newz.it* 2013).

One of the more dramatic recoveries of stolen paintings occurred at a house in Mendicino. In January 2010 a businesswoman based in Rome who was originally from Cosenza discovered that five contemporary paintings by the artist Luigi del Bianco had been stolen from her summer home. Luigi del Bianco is a proponent of a style of Italian painting called *Sensivismo*, a philo-sophical celebration and expression of feelings from the deepest melancholy to the greatest joy. During their search of a house belonging to a well-known criminal from Mendicino, the police noticed a series of paintings that did not fit with the decor of the rest of the house. The police were concerned enough about these paintings to call in the Carabinieri TPC for further investiga-tion. It is interesting to note that, in the USA for example, it would be extremely unusual for a question of aesthetics – such as paintings that did not match the decor in a criminal's house – to trigger further criminal investigation. However, the Carabinieri TPC carefully photographed the paintings discovered by their colleagues and, using Banca Dati *Leonardo* at the Central Command in Rome, discovered that the paintings were indeed the Luigi del Biancos stolen two years previously. Two individuals were arrested for the theft of the paintings, which were valued at over €20,000 (*Libero Quotidiano* 2012).

Thorough investigative techniques also led to the recovery of two historic stolen paintings. The investigation began when a collector, who had just purchased a painting titled *Flowers and farmyard animals in a landscape* by the 17th-century Flemish artist De Coninck, double-checked the Carabinieri TPC website and discovered that the painting had been stolen. The collector reported the merchant who had sold him the painting – a dealer in antiquities and art in Reggio Calabria. When TPC officers responded, they also discovered a tiny stolen painting called *Ecce Homo* by Francesco Cairo, also known as the 'Cavalier of Cairo'. This painting had been stolen from a priest in Cremona (*Newz.it* 2012). Two brothers of the shop's owner were arrested for the thefts.

On 17 April 2012 a very special exhibition – *Restitution 2001–2011* – opened in the Palazzo Arnone, Cosenza, at the prestigious National Gallery of Calabria. The Regional Directorate for Cultural Heritage and Landscape of Calabria, in cooperation with the Archaeological Superintendency of Calabria, directed by Simonetta Bonomi, collaborated with the Calabria CC TPC to select and exhibit a series of works of art and antiquities that had been stolen from the people of Calabria and recovered by the CC TPC (Fravolini 2012; Caruso 2012) over the course of the previous ten years. The curator Fabio Di Chirico, with research assistance from Francesca and Valentina Cannataro Cosco, carefully selected the works to tell the stories of theft and loss with the positive endings of recovery. The selected works, including 13 paintings, antiquities and manuscripts of great value, also illustrate the extraordinary wealth of the heritage shared by the people of Calabria. As (then) Captain Raffaele Giovinazzo of the Cosenza TPC pointed out in his opening comments for the exhibition, the works also represent the hard work and dedication of the force required for preservation of cultural property, as well as recovery and return of stolen works of art. By its collaborative nature, the exhibition also stood as a testament to the synergy created by the three agencies continuously working together.

BARI NUCLEUS

East of Cosenza, along the Adriatic Coast, we find Bari in the region of Puglia. Outsiders often fail to appreciate the ties between regional and local communities and the lands they have inhabited for thousands of years. When others think about the people of Italy, they usually think of Italians. It is somewhat unusual to appreciate that the Tuscans of Tuscany are descended from Etruscans, and still have distinct customs relating to food, behaviour and dialect. Tuscans can be distinguished from their neighbours directly to the east, the Umbrians of Umbria. These ethnic distinctions are also important in the south of Italy, where the ancestors of ancient people still proudly welcome visitors to the 'Home of the Messapians'. History indicates that groups such as the Messapians may have managed to maintain their ethnic identity even with the immigration of entire Greek and Albanian communities into their region and the compelling influence of the Roman Empire.

When objects of extraordinary beauty that form part of the ethnic heritage of local communities are removed from the archaeological record, surviving communities become dissociated from their ancestors, heritage and past. An example of a community that actively identifies itself with its heritage and works to preserve its past is Mesagne. Halfway between Mesagne and Latiano, its neighbouring village to the west, Dutch and Italian archaeologists have been working together, bringing to light an ancient Messapian city. As they patiently excavate features such as an olive press, a more sophisticated understanding of daily life in Messapia emerges. The archaeological partnership also works to make the archaeological park part of community life, using it as a centre for concerts and athletic events (Leonardis 2011, *pers comm*). When we think about connections like these between a modern community and its ethnic ancestry, crimes of looting and theft of archaeological material take on an additional layer of significance and loss.

The CC TPC nucleus based in Bari is responsible for the protection of heritage in the regions of Puglia, Molise and Basilicata. The Bari CC TPC headquarters is based at Castello Svevo, a Renaissance-era structure once owned by Isabelle of Aragon. This region is sometimes referred to as the 'heel' of the 'boot' of Italy. The Bari unit faces great challenges in terms of protecting archaeological sites and artefacts, because Puglia is known for the spectacular vases found in the tombs of the region. *Tombaroli* have been stealing these objects for decades, feeding the voracious black market that devours them. Apulian red figure vases are especially prized, particularly those that portray scenes from mythology. To protect the archaeology of the region, the unit works cooperatively with territorial law enforcement as well as with the Bari underwater unit. When officers of the Carabinieri TPC for Bari collated their 2012 accomplishment statistics they noted a series of trends (Ministero per i Beni Culturali 2012, 3) that have been consistent in recent years. As they have been working with institutions and private owners of collections to educate about security and documentation, the number of stolen items from museums in the region has decreased. Illegal archaeological excavations or lootings persist, along with forgery and online sales of illicit material. The Bari CC TPC increased security and surveillance visits in all sectors: museums, libraries and archives; archaeological sites including underwater sites; protected areas of the countryside; and marketplaces where antiquities and works of art are sold (Ministero per i Beni Culturali 2012, 4).

Many people in the region have developed enormous respect for the officers of the Bari TPC and their reputation for professional expertise and excellence. In autumn 2011 a farmer in the district of Cerignola, a community located approximately 100km north-west of Bari, made an extraordinary discovery while ploughing his fields (*Statoquotidiano.it* 2011). As he worked, the soil in one area began to give way. The farmer investigated and found, in the bedrock around 2m below the soil surface, niches that clearly contained ancient artefacts. He reported his discovery to the local police who came to stabilise and protect the site and who also immediately contacted the Carabinieri TPC of Bari. The TPC notified their colleagues from the archaeological Superin-tendency of Bari who came to examine and study the site with them. The discovery turned out to be a tomb complex with an outer chamber that led through a narrow opening to an inner burial chamber. Both chambers were intact and contained all of the objects associated with a funeral, including a pot of aromatic oils. The complex yielded 64 objects composed of numerous ceramic vessels, large and small, including one featuring a scene portraying Dionysus, and bronze sculptures. The discovery was of special value as it was one of very few tombs in the region to be found intact, rather than having been pillaged by *tombaroli*. The farmer's honesty enabled the immediate involvement of the Bari TPC, which in turn brought qualified archaeologists to examine and document the find while recovering the objects that are now available for all members of the community to appreciate.

Just as they respond within local communities, the activities of the Bari CC TPC have also extended around the world. In 2007, Joseph Sisto, a US citizen of Italian ancestry, called the police in Berwyn, Illinois, to his deceased father's home, where he knew they would find thousands of Italian artefacts (FBI 2009) kept by his father John. Joseph had argued with his father over the need to repatriate the items, but John could not bring himself to part with the collection, which included over 3000 parchments, books, manuscripts, paintings, antiquities, religious artefacts and relics and even 100 terracotta heads, known as the Canosa artefacts (Ramirez and Mitchum 2009), once given as offerings to the Roman Catholic Church. The Berwyn police contacted the Chicago office of the FBI Art Crime Team, who in turn contacted the Carabinieri TPC and the Italian Ministry of Culture.

As the Italian experts examined photos of the objects and travelled to Chicago to examine the objects in person, they determined that the collection had originated in the Bari region and that at least 1600 of the objects had been stolen from churches, libraries, archives and private collections. Estimates of the collection's market value ranged from US $5 million to 10 million. It appears that John Sisto's father, Giuseppe, travelled across Italy buying the items and shipped them to his son in the hope that he would be able to sell them in an antique shop he was running in Chicago at the time. However, John became fascinated with the history of the objects, hoarded them and spent much of his time studying them and translating the manuscripts. Members of the public were able to view some of the objects for the first time since their disappearance at a press conference to announce their repatriation, held in Chicago on 8 June 2009. In 2011, the Bari TPC repatriated some of the objects to the Diocese of Trani and, in 2012, 40 parchments from the recovered collections dating from the 14th to the 17th centuries were returned to the Archives of the Diocese of Conversano. Once the lengthy investigation was completed, the Carabinieri TPC nucleus at Bari repatriated all of the objects for which documentation of original ownership was available. The Sisto family was permitted to keep the remainder of the collection (Ramirez and Mitchum 2009).

International repatriation to Bari and Puglia has also taken place closer to Italy. In the autumn of 2012 the Bari Carabinieri TPC reported on the successful repatriation of a collection of objects from Germany. Working with the Operative Unit in Rome and INTERPOL, law enforcement agents had identified a German citizen who was smuggling artefacts from Puglia to Spain, Luxembourg and Germany. Using a letter rogatory in order to gain permission to search the German's cargo, the Carabinieri was able to identify and recover: six red-figured bell-shaped kraters; an *askos* or Greek vessel used for pouring small quantities of liquids; a *pelike* or amphora with open handles, in this case with red-figured decoration; an *olla achroma* or unpainted pot for cooking stews; a *kantheros* or Greek drinking vessel with black glaze; three *antefixes*; and 20 coins and other metal fragments, all dating to the 3rd and 4th centuries BC. One of the objects was an extremely valuable decorated krater or drinking vessel. It had been donated by a German collector to a German museum, but, on finding that the object had been stolen from a private citizen in the province of Foggia, the museum cooperated fully with its repatriation. The value of the repatriated objects was estimated at approximately €300,000 and the items were returned to the people of Puglia for the benefit of the public (*GoCity Puglia* 2012).

The Bari TPC has also participated in discoveries and recoveries in its own community. In one case (*La Gazzetta del Mezzogiorno* 2012) a well-known artist from the community of Francavilla Fontana, located just outside Brindisi, discovered for sale on the internet a papier-mâché sculpture that he had created. The sculpture was an image of Christ on the cross, approximately

105cm tall. It had been stolen in 2009 from a chapel in Squinzano and its image appeared on the internet after a 28-year-old from Bari put the object up for sale. The Carabinieri TPC worked with soldiers from the Triggiano station in Bari and collected sufficient evidence to track down the initial vendor. After arresting and questioning the 28-year-old, the Carabinieri had generated sufficient information to obtain search warrants. Further investigation led them to a house in Bari, where searches yielded an additional 29 stolen papier-mâché sculptures as well as terracotta items depicting religious scenes. Some of the objects dated to the 20th century and the individual could provide no proof of ownership. Enquiries also led the TPC to a trader based in Noicattaro, a town south-east of Bari. With the exception of the sculpture, which had been recognised by its creator, the Bari TPC had difficulty in identifying the objects' rightful owners. Pictures of the objects are featured in the TPC's regular bulletins of recovered objects in the hope that owners will recognise the items and come forward.

The Bari TPC's underwater activities also illustrate the benefits of cooperation between law enforcement agencies, the ministry and academic institutions (*Prima Pagina Molise* 2012). In May 2011 a group of academic institutions in the province of Molise joined with the Bari TPC underwater unit to embark upon a project called 'Atlantis submerged: archaeology, water, and the history of Saepinum-Altilia to Guardialfiera and Buca to Tremiti'. This project was designed to explore a stretch of the Adriatic Coast just off the beach at Termoli and resulted in the recovery of a lead anchor dating to imperial times. Building on the success of this project, the Institute Federico di Svevia in Termoli, a higher education institution that focuses on the hotel and restaurant industry, decided the following year to sponsor a project in the same area: 'From Atlantis to Buca, from Egnazia to Tremiti, from Saepinum-Altilia to Filopoli: archaeology, myths, the sea, history, foods, flavours, spices'. On the morning of 24 June 2012, TPC divers working on this project recovered a lead anchor dating to within 100 years of the birth of Christ. This anchor is also believed to be associated with a shipwreck from the time of the Roman Empire. The archaeological findings will be curated and exhibited at the various academic institutions sponsoring the project.

7

The Challenges of the Island Regions: Sicily, Sardinia and the Palermo, Siracusa and Sassari Nuclei

The Italian region of Sicily has an extraordinary history. Prior to Italian unification, this island, located off the 'toe' of the 'boot', was settled and colonised by many different early civilisations of the Mediterranean area, each leaving behind important urban remains including temples, palaces, castles, mosques and amphitheatres. The Greeks, Carthaginians, Phoenicians, Romans and Arabs all conquered Sicily, leaving traces of their majestic empires. The cultural property of Sicily also offers an historical context for today's society to gain an understanding of how it is possible for people of different cultures to travel from great distances, live together in an island setting and enrich each other's lives.

The then Captain (now Major) of the Palermo and Siracusa units, Giuseppe Marseglia, emphasised the significance of the multicultural dimensions of the cultural property for which he is responsible as he introduced the author (Rush) to the Island of Sicily and its cultural wealth (Marseglia 2011, *pers comm*). He made sure that the tour included the Palatine Chapel – the chapel of the Norman Kings of Sicily – located on the second floor of the Palazzo Reale in Palermo (see Fig 7.1). Beginning with the 12th-century Byzantine apses and mosaics, the architectural elements of the chapel are artistic masterpieces produced by the very best artists and craftsmen the diverse communities of Palermo had to offer. The transept mosaics illustrate the Acts of the Apostles, are narrated with Arabic inscriptions and are framed in a style reminiscent of Eastern icons. Even more remarkable, the Byzantine images are placed within a structure defined by Arabic arches and the Byzantine dome also features Arabic inscriptions.

The ceiling of the chapel is a Muqarnas ceiling composed of detailed geometric inlay, reminiscent of Abbasid designs found in places such as Baghdad, Iraq. The mosaics located outside of the transept, more secular in nature, feature Latin inscriptions and are clearly the work of yet another group of artisans. Perhaps the most powerful symbol of the shared cultural elements and artistry is the Christian cross in the ceiling, formed in part by a pattern of Islamic eight-pointed stars. The juxtaposition of contrasting styles, language and great beauty add spiritual power to this extraordinary sacred place.

The cultural wealth of Sicily extends way beyond its architectural treasures. Like the rest of Italy, the island could also be viewed as an open-air museum and as such it represents an enormous challenge in terms of Carabinieri TPC protection. Segesta is just one of many ancient cities that illustrate the extraordinary archaeology of the island (see Fig 7.2).

The magnificent Valle dei Templi (Valley of the Temples) near Agrigento, to name yet another region filled with antiquity, is a UNESCO World Heritage Site in Sicily. With seven Greek temples still standing, it attracts hundreds of thousands of tourists each year.

FIG 7.1.   A VIEW OF THE PALATINE CHAPEL, PALERMO, ILLUSTRATING THE MULTICULTURAL ELEMENTS.

Fig 7.2. The theatre at Segesta, Sicily, uses the valley as the backdrop with the sea in the distance. Segesta is protected as an archaeological park and filled with intact remains.

To help cover the island more comprehensively, the Carabinieri TPC has two units in Sicily: the headquarters, located in Palermo in the Albergo delle Povere (Hotel of the Poor), and a supplemental detachment, located in Siracusa, with jurisdiction over Eastern Sicily. The Albergo delle Povere was initially built in the mid-18th century and in 1772 was dedicated to the poor and the disabled. In what could now be considered an ironic twist of fate, Phoenician and Carthaginian sepulchers were unearthed on the site during its original construction. In 1898, the Albergo became a place for poor and orphan women. The Palermo TPC officers are extremely proud of the historic location of their offices and a tour of the structure includes the courtyard gardens and a discussion of the benevolent approach to the impoverished inhabitants, who were offered an education and an opportunity to learn marketable skills at the Albergo (Marseglia 2011, *pers comm*).

The Siracusa detachment of the Palermo TPC is housed in the spectacular Castello Maniace, built in 1038 as a fortress to protect the natural harbour of Ortigia. It was transformed into a castle by Federico II in the 13th century and occupied by a series of Bourbon queens. For most of the 15th century it served as a prison and continued to be a military property even after an enormous explosion in 1704 damaged the walls and rained stone over the city. The castle remained in the hands of noble families until the 1980s, when it was sold to the government. In addition to housing government offices such as the Carabinieri TPC, the castle is open to the public and also hosts the annual Ortigia festival.

Although its focus is the eastern region of Sicily, the Siracusa office also responds to and cooperates at regional, state and international levels. For example, in 2012 officers in the Siracusa detachment noticed an embossed silver reliquary urn on the market. The object dated to 1618 and venerated Saint Dominic. After checking the ever-powerful Banca Dati *Leonardo*, they were able to identify the urn as a sacred object, stolen in 1986 from the Church of San Filippo Benizzi, located over 600 miles away in the walled city of Todi, Umbria (*Siracusa News* 2012).

One of the outstanding leaders of the Sicily TPC is the then Captain (now Major) Giuseppe Marseglia, an experienced officer and a veteran of Italy's peacekeeping mission to Iraq. More specifically, the Captain responded to the looting of the National Museum of Iraq in Baghdad, patiently earned the trust of the Iraqi museum staff and also worked with US Civil Affairs Officer Major Corine Wegener to document and recover missing objects. Major Marseglia has been very modest about his contribution to the international effort to assist in recovery at the museum. He courageously visited Iraqi markets throughout the urban area, identifying stolen objects and playing a key role in their recovery. He spent many hours working with the collections catalogue information that remained after the disastrous losses in order to document and provide as much detailed information as possible about the missing objects. The results of his efforts can be seen linked to the Carabinieri TPC website, in the Carabinieri Banca Dati *Leonardo* and also on the INTERPOL website, which also includes a specific link to an inventory of the objects missing from the National Museum.[1] Thanks to the dedication of Major Marseglia, documentation for 2969 objects that have not yet been recovered is available for viewing by interested members of the public and law enforcement agents all over the world. The existence and internet presence of an inventory such as this also means that no collector or dealer can claim ignorance should they choose to buy or sell one of these items, making it a powerful and important asset for law enforcement.

Historically, Sicily has been affected by the worldwide diffusion of a criminal organisation commonly known as the Mafia. From the Middle Ages onward, Sicily was never ruled for any length of time by stable kingdoms, but rather was used as a land of conquest and a source of taxation by various absentee sovereigns. Often the land of Sicily was nominally assigned to different European kings or queens, who never really resided there, but rather acquired dominion over the island by means of marriage. The prolonged lack of central government and its resulting power vacuum, together with a sense of vulnerability on the part of local populations wanting protection and stability, promoted the growth of a criminal organisation that eventually took control.

One theory concerning the development of the Mafia is that it is the outcome of a process whereby feudal lords hired and established their own militias for personal protection and, over time, gained power by establishing alliances with other feudal lords. Soon these lords became powerful enough to rule the entire island, forming an organisation that became criminal. Even after the unification process that saw Sicily become part of the Italian territory, the island has continued to struggle with this form of organised criminal behaviour.

Even though the Mafia's power was diminished following the law enforcement crackdown in response to the assassination of Judge Falcone in 1992 (Facci 2012), the organisation is still active

---

[1]   See: http://www.interpol.int/Crime-areas/Works-of-art/Stolen-Iraqi-items [3 December 2014].

in the region and is responsible for many local crimes, including but not limited to the theft of numerous artworks (Foresi 2006). Palermo TPC officers made a point of showing the author (Rush) the monument to Judge Falcone along the motorway outside Palermo (Marseglia 2011, *pers comm*) and mentioned that this event was the beginning of the end of ubiquitous Mafia power in Sicily.

The Stolen Caravaggio

An example of a masterpiece allegedly stolen by the Mafia is the famous *Nativity* (*Natività*) *with San Lorenzo and San Francesco* by Caravaggio (see Fig 7.3), which disappeared from the church of San Lorenzo (St Lawrence) in October 1969 and, at the time of writing, has not been found. This painting tops the Carabinieri TPC's list of most wanted artworks and they continue to search for it, in spite of the many stories and rumours of it having been damaged or destroyed.

During the night of 17 October 1969 thieves entered the unprotected church of St Lawrence in Palermo and took a Caravaggio painting dated 1609. In Italy, in former times, many churches were open to anybody at any time and this church in particular did not have a rigorous alarm system to protect its treasures. The painting depicted the *Natività con i Santi Lorenzo e Francesco* (Nativity with St Lawrence and St Francis) and was the last masterpiece painted by the artist Caravaggio in Sicily before he passed away in Tuscany one year later.

Stories of damage to, or destruction of, the canvas take many forms. According to one account, in 1996 a Mafia informer explained to Italian police that the thieves had removed the canvas from the frame using a razor blade and rolled it up, making it easy to carry. This rough treatment damaged the canvas and when the individual who commissioned the theft saw the damaged painting, he burst into tears and no longer wanted to buy it. The canvas was then destroyed by burning. Of course, this story could not be verified owing to lack of evidence and at a later stage another repentant mafioso revealed a different version of the story. According to the newer version, members of Mafia leadership still possess the painting and exhibit it during summit meetings as a symbol of power (Grassi 2009). Yet another version claims that the thieves hid the painting in a pigsty and the pigs ate it.

One further version of the story was offered by the English journalist Peter Watson, a columnist for *The Sunday Times* of London. In 1979 Watson met Rodolfo Siviero, the Italian diplomat well known for the recovery of Italian works of art stolen during World War II. At the time, Siviero was continuing his work and leading a small task force. According to Watson's book *The Caravaggio Conspiracy* (1983), Siviero convinced him to look for the canvas instead of just writing about it. Watson assumed the fake identity of John Blake, an avid art collector, and tried to trace the stolen painting. With the cooperation of art dealers and Christie's and Sotheby's auctioneers, John Blake's name became well known among art collectors in a very short time. With his name synonymous with a rich collector, Watson/Blake reached out to anyone who could possibly bring him closer to the stolen Caravaggio. After a few months of investigation, the owner of an antique shop in Naples introduced him to those who supposedly held the missing canvas. A meeting in Laviano, a small town in the Apennine Mountains east of Naples, was organised for Watson to see the canvas and determine its authenticity. That same night, the 1980 Irpinia earthquake struck and decimated the Naples region, preventing the journalist from reaching the meeting place, which was also destroyed by the earthquake. According to Watson, the canvas may have been lost forever during the course of the natural disaster. Interestingly

Fig 7.3.   *Natività con i Santi Lorenzo e Francesco d'Assisi* (1609) by Michelangelo Merisi, called *Caravaggio* (1571–1610). Oil on canvas, circa 268 x 197cm. (Carabinieri file number 00799[1])

enough, none of the Mafia informers who have cooperated with the Carabinieri in order to have their jail sentences reduced have confirmed this version of the story.

No matter how many different version of the story are told, the Caravaggio Nativity is still at the very top of the list of objects most wanted by the Carabinieri, and their investigation will continue until the object is recovered or until the Carabinieri have obtained clear evidence of its fate.

SUCCESS AND THE PALERMO TPC

Even without recovery of the Caravaggio, the Palermo unit's successes are truly impressive. The unit has recovered significant numbers of artworks stolen from a wide range of venues and antiquities removed from archaeological sites both on land and under water. The unit has tracked frauds and forgeries and continues with its education programmes and security inspections. A series of recoveries provide examples of these contributions to Sicilian society.

In December 2012 the nucleus returned 4035 stolen coins made of gold, silver and bronze and 63 bronze objects, including fibulae and rings, to the Paolo D'Orsi Archaeological and Numismatic Museum in Siracusa. This restitution was part of a complicated investigation known as 'Archeoweb', dealing with stolen art objects sold on *eBay*. Among the gold coins there were some dating back to the Byzantine epoch (6th–8th century AD), as well as others dating to the Roman Imperial era. According to the details of the investigation, the thieves claimed that they had come across the treasure when digging at an unknown site in eastern Sicily. However, they made the mistake of putting the coins up for sale on *eBay*, one of the many thousands of websites constantly monitored by the Carabinieri TPC. As soon as the ancient coins appeared, the officers knew there was no possibility of legal origin and information from the website enabled them to track down the criminals and recover the coins (Regione Sicilia 2013).

On 31 October 2012 CC TPC from the Palermo unit retrieved 12 works of art out of 15 stolen from the church of San Nicola (St Nicholas) in Trapani. The theft had occurred at the beginning of that same month and the addition of the information pertinent to the stolen artworks into the databank made it almost impossible for the thieves to sell the masterpieces on the black market. Numerous photographs were promptly made available to the investigators and to all the parties involved in order to identify the pieces. The CC TPC is still looking for three pieces that remain missing, one of which is a wooden statue of Mother Mary (ibid).

Sadly, as demonstrated by the theft of the wooden Madonna from San Nicola, criminals do not limit their ecclesiastical thefts simply to works of art found in churches; they steal sacred objects as well. Another example was the removal of a statue of St Francis from a roadside shrine in the rural village of Modica, located near the south-west coast of Sicily. The image of the empty niche with the words 'S. Francesco d'Assisi, Pregate Per Noi' ('Saint Francis of Assisi, Pray for Us') still printed below illustrates the compelling sense of loss (*Corriere di Ragusa.it* 2014) (see Fig 7.4).

In February 2012 the Palermo TPC recovered the highest number of palaeontological fossils ever found in any Italian region. Over the course of many years, a private collector had amassed a collection of 867 fossils from different areas of Sicily. The fossils dated from the Mesozoic to the Quaternary Eras, covering a temporal span of approximately 200 million years. Among the most interesting pieces were the remains of a dwarf elephant and a dwarf hippopotamus, two extinct species that once lived all across the island. As discussed in Chapter 1, Italian Law

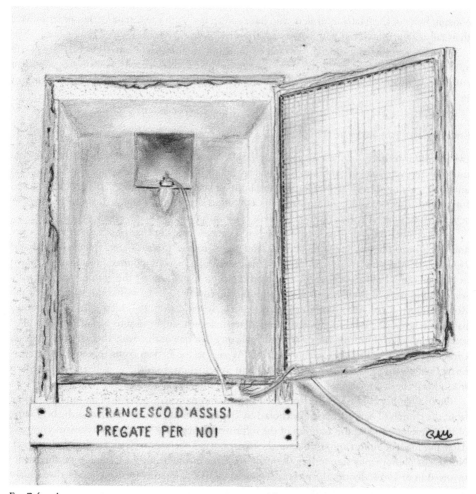

Fig 7.4.   Artistic rendition of an empty shrine from Modica, Sicily.

states that archaeological and palaeontological objects found anywhere within Italian territorial boundaries, regardless of whether the land is public or private, belong to the Italian state and cannot be kept by a private citizen. The fossils were donated to the G Gemmellaro Geological Museum in Palermo (ibid).

In February 2012 the unit led by the then Captain (now Major) Marseglia recovered an important Lekanis Greek vase dating from the 2nd–1st centuries BC. Lekanis vases are a variety of ancient Greek pottery that are low in form and feature a foot, two handles and a cover. Vases of this type were commonly used by wealthy women as containers for cosmetic products. The Lekanis recovered by the Sicilian unit was unusual in that it was much larger than a typical Lekanis and had been used as a burial object in the necropolis of Centuripe, near the city of

Enna. Lekanis vases were largely produced in Sicily during the 1st century BC, and this particular specimen must have been a special order of superior quality. Lekanis vases were usually wedding gifts and often accompanied women into the afterlife as burial goods.

The Sicily TPC found this Lekanis vase while monitoring websites; an Australian collector was selling it on *eBay*. While Carabinieri officers were in the process of contacting all the necessary authorities for the repatriation of the vase, it was bought and shipped to Lisbon, Portugal. The Carabinieri then obtained the vase from the Portuguese collector who had purchased it. In an interview following the repatriation, Major Marseglia discussed how Sicilian artefacts are now sold all over the world through online auctions, incorporating a much larger marketplace than previously and thus requiring extensive cooperation with foreign police forces through INTERPOL (Parisi 2012).

Sicily has also seen objects of great value be returned home, repatriated by some of the world's most significant museums. When the Goddess of Morgantina was returned from the Getty to Aidone, Sicily, the Kepha Foundation[2] sponsored a conference ('Stolen History, From Oblivion to Recovery 1861–2011') celebrating the repatriation. Generale Pasquale Muggeo led the TPC delegation, which also included the then Captains Massimiliano Quagliarella and Giuseppe Marseglia, while other delegates and speakers included Architect Gesualdo Campo, General Director of the Regional Department of Cultural Patrimony and Sicilian Identity, and Patrizio M R Benvenuti, the President of the Foundation. There was also a message from the Italian Under-Secretary of the Ministry for Cultural Patrimony and Activities, Francesco Maria Giro. The event also featured the journalist Fabio Isman, who has written extensively about the Medici investigation, in addition to the Honourable Paolo Ferri and Maurizio Fiorilli, who had become the State Advocate General. With such a distinguished panel of participants, the conference was able to celebrate and learn from key members of the Medici legal and law enforcement teams.

It is interesting to note that, when the Getty returned the statue, the conservation staff packed her extremely carefully in a special, large packing case that could be converted into an earthquake-resistant mount, technically a seismic wave isolator, that would help protect her in her new home. However, no-one thought to measure the doorways of the monastery that is home to the Aidone Museum, so her arrival posed an interesting challenge for the museum staff and her Carabinieri escorts (Marseglia 2011, *pers comm*).

To illustrate a typical year for a Carabinieri regional unit, the following chart gives an overview of the successful activities coordinated by the CC TPC in Sicily in 2011 (see Fig 7.5). This unit recovered a total of 2430 objects with a total value of €1,337,400.

In terms of prevention, the Sicily unit carried out over 740 checks and security inspections, and specifically:

- 118 in museums, libraries and archives;
- 183 at archaeological areas;
- 97 at environmentally protected areas;
- 230 at antique shops;
- 112 in marketplaces and regional fairs.

---

2 The Kepha Foundation is a not-for-profit organisation based in Rome, dedicated in part to respect for culture without regard to ethnicity, to the 'promotion and safeguarding of cultural heritage' and to the preservation of works of art.

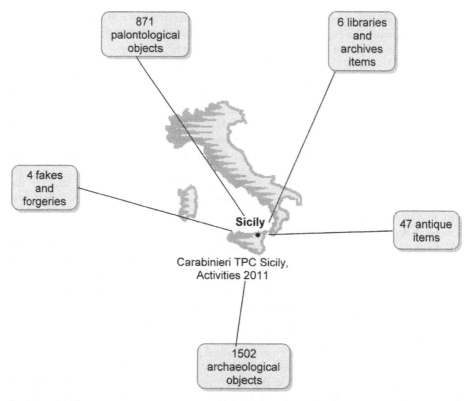

FIG 7.5.   CC TPC SICILY: SUMMARY OF 2011 OPERATIONAL ACTIVITIES.

The statistics for the inspection of museums, libraries and archives are of particular importance. The disastrous thefts from the Girolamini library have attracted increased attention to the question of library and archive protection and the Italian Society for the Protection of Cultural Property has called for public education for greater appreciation of the value of libraries and archives to Italian culture and society. The Society hopes to challenge the mistaken belief that the materials preserved in Italian libraries and archives are simply 'folders on a shelf' (Tabita 2012), the preserve of highly educated scholars and the elite. As the statistics of their annual activities clearly demonstrate, the Palermo unit strives to address all types of cultural property as thoroughly as their resources will allow.

Archaeological inspections are often implemented after locals report signs of looting. Given the extraordinary heritage of the Sicilian region, it is very difficult to predict where and when the *tombaroli* (looters) are going to excavate illegally, damaging and destroying important sites not yet known to science. Once again, the whole territory of Sicily is a place where every inch of soil can hide important archaeological artefacts and many areas have yet to be identified and documented.

The *tombaroli* do not limit their behaviour to undocumented sites. The ancient Greek city of

Fig 7.6.   Major Giuseppe
Marseglia examines a looter
hole at Himera, Sicily.

Himera is located along the north coast of Sicily, just east of Palermo. The ancient city has been designated an historic park area and its museum hosts exhibitions of significant artefacts found in Himera and the region. During the Palermo TPC visit, the officers provided an opportunity to visit the ancient city. The *tombaroli* had struck yet again and the visit to Himera offered an opportunity to watch a looting investigation unfold (see Fig 7.6).

The *tombaroli* had left open holes and backfill across the site. It was clear that they had misinterpreted recent university excavations as indicators of treasure and had made efforts to locate some of their looter holes in the immediate vicinity of the backfilled controlled excavation units. Clearly, the concept of excavation in order to gain insight into the behaviour and culture of past people, as opposed to excavation for the purposes of recovering treasure, was lost on these individuals. Shallow looter holes with discarded modern metal objects indicated that this team of *tombaroli* were also working with metal detectors and were finding the results disappointing. The confidence and carelessness of this group of looters was quite shocking. Not only had they violated the fenced perimeter of a protected archaeological park but they had left behind their breakfast receipts. As a result, the TPC was able to identify the small village they had come from.

When an individual from the United States and its culture of firearms thinks about law enforcement, one of the first thoughts is the potential for violence. In looking across the ancient city of Himera and thinking about the brazen individuals who had just been there, digging holes and stealing objects, it was logical to wonder whether they would return and whether they would be carrying weapons. In discussing this eventuality with the Carabinieri officers, it immediately became clear that violence is not a routine part of the Italian art law enforcement process. Major Marseglia pointed out that the consequences of threatening a law enforcement officer are far more serious than the punishment for looting an archaeological site. The difference is years or decades in prison versus a few days (Marseglia 2011, *pers comm*). It is indeed frustrating for the TPC that crimes and damage to archaeological sites are not treated as seriously as they might be, and one of the very few criticisms of the Italian approach to cultural heritage protection addresses this issue (see Di Fonzo 2012). However, there are advantages to keeping the stakes low, one of which is the reduced threat of bodily harm.

PROTECTION OF THE LANDSCAPE

In the US, zoning laws and restrictions surrounding historic districts help to protect historic landscapes. Additionally, in many states and regions preservation law requires archaeological survey prior to any ground-disturbing undertaking that is supported by public funding. These requirements have resulted in dramatic archaeological discoveries that changed the course of project plans; such examples in the US include The African Burial Ground in Manhattan, New York, and the Miami Circle. The African Burial Ground was discovered during the process of planning the construction of a new federal building in lower Manhattan. It is possible that up to 20,000 African Americans, most of whom were enslaved, were buried in the area during the 17th and 18th centuries. Upon discovery of the site, construction was halted, archaeologists recovered remains and the site was redesigned to allow for a memorial which is now managed by the National Park Service (NPS 2014). Archaeologists discovered the Miami Circle during the course of cultural resources investigation prior to construction of a condominium complex. It appears to represent a circular structure whose posts were cut into limestone and is associated with deposits between 1700 and 2000 years old. Public support for preservation resulted in the site being purchased by the state of Florida and preserved as a park (Florida Department of State 2014).

Italian law also provides legal protection for the landscape in addition to the archaeological deposits under Code of Cultural Heritage and Landscape, in accordance with Article 10 of the Law No. 137 of July 6, 2002 (Legislative Decree No 42 of 22 January 2004, as last amended by Legislative Decree No 63 of 2008). As one might imagine, the tension between preservation and project development can escalate into situations where investors make every effort to move ahead with their project, even in situations where further development may destroy an historic neighbourhood or an archaeological site. In Italy, restrictions affecting landscapes are enforced by the Carabinieri TPC.

Events such as those that unfolded in Siracusa, Sicily, illustrate the enforcement process (*Patrimoniosos.it* 2011). The Balza Akradina is a stunning archaeological area that now lies within Siracusa city limits. The area has been under pressure for housing development since the 1950s when other areas of the city reached capacity. Located on high ground, the Balza Akradina features not only breathtaking views of the city but also burial cavities in the soft stone dating to Greek, Roman and Byzantine occupations. Siracusans traditionally used the area for holiday outings. However, in 2011, developers began foundation excavations for multi-storey apartment buildings located within the protected area. SOS Siracusa, a group dedicated to archaeological preservation in the city, held a sit-in at the site and requested the intervention of the Superintendency and the Carabinieri TPC. On 10 May 2011, at the direction of the public prosecutor, the TPC from the Siracusa section of the Palermo regional office enforced the decree of sequester – the instruction to halt construction. The prosecutor determined that the project had proceeded without the proper planning permissions for construction within a protected landscape. SOS Siracusa estimated that the developer's bulldozers had already caused almost €4 million worth of damage to the archaeological remains present. Even if the site could not be entirely saved, the ability to halt construction enabled salvage archaeology, leading to the discovery of an ancient Greek stone quarry in addition to the tombs already known to be located at the site.

SASSARI

The Sardinian TPC nucleus was founded in 2001 and is located in Sassari at the Polo Museale di Sassari, a major regional museum that includes the Archaeological Museum of Sardinia. It is difficult to know when the first humans might have come to Sardinia, but there is no doubt that the island has been permanently occupied for at least 6000 years. The island features megalithic tombs, standing stone monuments, rock shelters, camps dating to the Roman legions, coastal settlements left behind by Phoenicians and Carthaginians, medieval neighbourhoods and mighty cone-shaped rock fortresses called nuraghi. There are over 7000 nuraghi, some dating as far back as 1800 BC, strategically located as lookouts and defensible positions throughout the island.

Owing to isolation and the island's rugged geography, Sardinians of the past belonged to unique local tribal populations such as the Ilienes, Balares and Corsi, who are known today only by the ancient settlements and structures that they left behind in the form of archaeological sites. However, that same rugged geography and isolation, combined with decreasing populations in some areas, makes protection of those same sites more difficult. In 2001, Francesca Manconi Valsecchi, Archaeological Superintendent for the Provinces of Sassari and Nuoro, described these challenges to an international conference on illicit trafficking sponsored by the Carabinieri TPC and led by General Conforti (Valsecchi 2002). She also pointed out the importance of heritage preservation as an investment in the island's future. The Sardinians, like the Basques, may represent remnants of a population that lived in Europe before the Indo-Europeans, so a greater understanding of the ancient peoples of Sardinia is important for greater understanding of the ancient world, not to mention the origins of all European populations.

The unique and special nature of artefacts found within Sardinian archaeological sites can unfortunately increase their value on the collector's market. Speaking at an event that formed part of the 2012 Culture Week celebrations on the island, the commander of the Carabinieri TPC unit at Sassari, Captain Paolo Montorsi, quoted a black market price of €20,000 per centimetre for Sardinian bronzes (Ambu 2012). These items were stolen from archaeological sites with the greatest incidence of looting in the province of Nuoro, a place described as the Athens of Sardinia. The commander discussed the black market for Sardinian artefacts, with destinations including Germany, the US and Japan, and also described the process of smuggling looted objects to Switzerland, where they can 'lie low' and where criminal dealers fabricate false provenances for them.

Fig 7.7.   These anchors and amphorae, now on display at the Museum at Himera, were recovered from divers who had illegally removed them from the sea floor.

The Challenges of Underwater Protection

In May 2012 the Sicily TPC nucleus discovered 29 marine archaeological artefacts in the house of a scuba diving enthusiast. The pieces date from the Bronze Age up to the 13th century and include several Greek and Roman amphorae. This case highlights, yet again, the challenge of protecting Italy's marine archaeological heritage (ibid).

During a tour of the museum at Himera the then Captain Marseglia (Marseglia 2011, *pers comm*) also pointed out a series of anchors and amphorae on exhibit, originally looted from the Sicilian coast and then recovered by the Palermo nucleus (see Fig 7.7). Objects such as amphorae and anchors offer tremendous amounts of information about ancient seafaring but when they are torn from their original subaqueous contexts the potential knowledge is lost. Clearly, the protection of cultural treasure found underwater all along the Italian coast is a massive challenge and responsibility, and for the TPC nuclei of Sicily and Sardinia it is even more overwhelming given that they are both island landforms with complex coastlines and millennia of seafaring history. A critical element for successful underwater stewardship is cooperation between the TPC, the Carabinieri underwater unit and networks of concerned divers, boaters and archaeologists who all care about this type of heritage.

In 2001 Donatella Salvi (2002, 423–7), the Archaeological Superintendent of Cagliari, began to notice patterns in amphorae that were being seized, recovered and submitted to her office. Analysis of marine encrustations combined with vessel types and styles concluded that some of the amphorae had to have come from the same shipwrecks. As part of the solution to the problem of ongoing underwater thefts, the Superintendency partnered with members of the Sardinia Association of Motor Skiffs. By combining information from law enforcement agencies and the owners of looted objects with the observations of the motor skiff boaters, Dr Salvi was able to determine that the objects came from at least five wrecks of different ages, located within 20–25 miles of the Sardinian coast at depths of 650m or less. The amphorae were from Africa and Spain, and had carried wine, olive oil and fish sauce. One set of amphorae were found in the waters off Villasimius and were the product of a specific 5th-century Punic workshop located near the Straits of Gibraltar.

Ironically, as social values change and underwater looting becomes less socially acceptable, collectors are beginning to discard looted amphorae. Some are handed in anonymously, while others are found abandoned on the sea floor or even floating empty in the ocean, having been discarded by owners who have had second thoughts.

Just as in Palermo and Siracusa, the Sassari TPC also has a proactive approach to protecting archaeological deposits found underwater. An increase in tourism, recreational boating and amateur diving brings increased risk to the natural and cultural resources of the Sardinian coast. The Sassari nucleus has chosen to be proactive in facing this challenge, as illustrated by an archaeological survey initiative along the north-east coast of Sardinia. The Sassari TPC, partnering with archaeologists, worked with the underwater nucleus based in Cagliari on the south coast of the island and the Carabinieri patrol boats of the coastal towns of Alghero and the Maddalena archipelago. Their combined efforts resulted in a series of important archaeological discoveries, including a Roman lead anchor with a design in relief depicting gaming pieces, deposits of amphorae representing different time periods, a Roman shipwreck, building stone for columns, Roman bricks and even a 19th-century anchor from the Admiralty (*Sardegna Reporter* 2011).

8

Investigation Techniques

Having successfully demonstrated to the world that prominent US museums had been purchasing stolen objects from Italy, and following successful repatriation of those objects, the Carabinieri TPC has established a well-deserved global reputation for its investigation methods. For a sense of the scale of the success of the Carabinieri TPC in terms of art recovered, consider the following statistics: between 1970 and 2007, the Carabinieri recovered 202,924 works of art including 8032 found in and repatriated from other countries; 1268 art objects with origins in other countries, discovered in Italy and returned to their country of origin; and over 250,000 fake objects seized by the counterfeiting section (Purarelli 2007) (see Fig 8.1).

As exciting as it is to focus on the aspects of Carabinieri TPC investigative activities that are reminiscent of James Bond films – car chases and agents rappelling out of helicopters in a remote Iraqi desert – the success of the Carabinieri TPC is overwhelmingly due to professional competence, experience, attention to detail, patience, persistence and international legal expertise, plus an ability to partner with subject matter experts and other authorities. These skills apply to solving all types of art crime, whether involving stolen works of art, looted archaeological objects or forgeries. If we think of investigation in terms of essentials, these would include the collection of solid and incontrovertible evidence of guilt on the part of the criminals; identification of locations or hiding places for stolen objects; incrimination of dealers, receivers or buyers; and evidence linking them to the stolen objects.

The Carabinieri TPC's success is even more impressive when one considers the criminal behaviour they encounter. Thieves who focus on works of art represent the type of individual who is willing to steal objects from churches, to cut up sacred paintings and altarpieces and transform baptism fonts into ornamental fountains, confessionals into bars or bookcases, candelabra into table lamps, censers into chandeliers, sacristies into armoires and tabernacles into drinks cabinets. There are *tombaroli* willing to destroy ancient tombs, scattering human remains across the countryside while helping themselves to the jewels of the deceased, and gallery owners who are more than happy to consciously sell forged works of art as authentic to unsuspecting collectors. There are interior and exterior designers who knowingly incorporate stolen art and antiquities into their design plans, sometimes acquiring these objects and installing them in the homes of wealthy clients, perhaps without the clients understanding the objects' origins.

Many art criminals are also extremely skilled and formidable opponents, with talents ranging from artistic expertise (used for forgery) to mastery of neutralising sophisticated alarm systems and overcoming locking devices. The criminals' skills may include expertise in computers and the internet and/or the logistical capabilities required to organise international rings of fences, smugglers and black market dealers. Given the decades of experience of many officers serving on the TPC, some art crimes actually display identifying characteristics that guide the Carabinieri to an individual criminal or group with whom they are already familiar.

Works of art recovered
by Carabinieri CC TPC
from 1970 to 2007

202,924 Italian
works of art
(8032 recovered
abroad)

250,000
fake objects seized

1268 foreign
works of art
traced in Italy
and returned
to country of
origin

Fig 8.1.   Works of art recovered by CC TPC between 1970 and 2007.

Patient Research and Legal Negotiation: The Doria Panel

The recent return of the Doria Panel to Italy is the first of a series of cases that illustrate the investigation capabilities of the Carabinieri TPC. The Doria Panel, named for the Neapolitan family that owned it for over 300 years, had been missing for 79 years. This panel was an antique version of a detail of the lost Da Vinci fresco of 'The Battle of Anghiari 1440', during which troops from Florence and their allies defeated forces from Milan. It was last seen at an exhibition in Milan just prior to World War II. According to a media account of its recovery, it 'passed

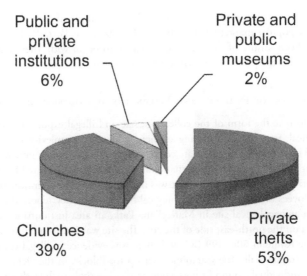

Public and private institutions 6%

Private and public museums 2%

Churches 39%

Private thefts 53%

FIG 8.2. OCCURRENCE OF ARTWORK THEFT. GRAPH BASED ON DATA FROM CC TPC ACTIVITIES SUMMARY 2011.

into the possession of a Swiss art dealer, was sent to Germany for restoration in the 1960s, then turned up briefly at a New York gallery in the 1970s before ending up in the collection of a wealthy Japanese art collector in the 1990s' (Willey 2012). The panel was purchased by the Fuji Art Museum in Tokyo in 1992. Once the Carabinieri TPC knew the location of the stolen panel, it was able to begin negotiations with the Japanese for repatriation. There is no question that the Italians now have the reputation and experience to successfully prove that a 'high profile' object is stolen property and make the case for repatriation in courts of law. This track record gives the TPC and the Italian government an extremely strong bargaining position whenever an object is found, even when, as in this case, on display in a major Japanese museum. Extensive negotiations resulted in an agreement whereby the object was returned to Italy. Upon its return, it was exhibited at the Quirinale (the Presidential Palace), symbolically returning it to the Italian people. The Doria Panel will then go back – on loan – to Japan where it will be featured in temporary exhibitions at the Fuji Museum.

Tracking down stolen works of art is a challenging and complex process. First, there exists a wide range of venues and circumstances through which criminals may help themselves to works of art belonging to others. The Carabinieri TPC has presented these statistics (CC TPC 2011) in an easy-to-understand graph form (see Fig 8.2). Consider for a moment that institutions and museums are the collections most likely to hold inventory information and detailed documentation of their objects. Then consider the chart that illustrates that objects stolen from museums and institutions account for only 8% of all artwork thefts. As a result, the Carabinieri becomes responsible for tracking down objects stolen from private and ecclesiastical collections – the collections least likely to have detailed inventory or documentary evidence that can be easily entered into Banca Dati *Leonardo*. Such losses account for over 90% of all art thefts across Italy.

There are also thefts and losses that go unreported. For example, if someone were to purchase a work of art at a popular market such as the Sunday market at Porta Portese in Rome, where they would have been unsure of the piece's provenance to begin with, they may be unlikely to report the loss should the piece be in turn stolen from them.

DETAILED COLLECTION OF EVIDENCE AND INTERNATIONAL COOPERATION: 'MOZART'

Art theft may also take the form of the collection, sale and illegal exportation of objects looted from archaeological areas. The smuggling element adds the complexity of international law enforcement and criminal organisations are constantly working to design new ways to ensure the safe passage of art and artefacts across international boundaries, as illustrated by a case referred to by the Carabinieri TPC as 'Mozart'. This case was first brought to the attention of the Carabinieri TPC when employees of the Rome Archaeological Superintendency reported evidence of illicit excavations at an archaeological site in Marcigliana Park, an area just outside the greater Rome metropolitan area on the north-east side of the city. The site was Crustumerium, an ancient Latin city conquered by Rome in 500–499 BC, and there was evidence of illegal excavation near the doors of the old Roman wall. The Carabinieri set up roadblocks in the vicinity of the site and began to identify individuals found in possession of digging tools such as shovels and mattocks.

Patterns of evidence that emerged from the observations were strong enough for the Judicial Authority of Rome to authorise further investigation. With more information, the TPC was able to identify how the illegal activity was organised. The large group of perpetrators was divided into two teams. One team was looting throughout the protected archaeological territory surrounding Lake Bracciano. The second group was focusing their efforts on archaeological sites in the northern suburbs of Rome, including La Storta and Settebagni. The suspects were all born and raised in the areas they were looting and thus using their local knowledge to focus on critical archaeological areas. They were also being protected and aided by networks of family, neighbours and friends. As the investigation unfolded, the TPC officers were able to identify the leader of the illegal organisation, an Austrian that the Italians dubbed 'Mozart'.

'Mozart' was an Austrian tour guide who routinely brought tourist groups to Italy with the aim of visiting archaeological sites. During the course of these tours, Mozart would meet with his local Italian contacts, the looters and smugglers, and he would examine their most recent finds. Mozart purchased the materials on-site and hid them on the tour bus, even in the luggage of his unsuspecting tourist customers. Once Mozart's participation was documented, the Italians were able to approach the Austrians for international cooperation on the case. In April and May 2005, searches of Mozart's warehouse yielded almost 4000 artefacts stolen from a range of Italian archaeological sites. The Italians recovered 600 objects upon discovery of the warehouse and the Austrian authorities proceeded to recover a further 3000. Restitution of the objects back to Italy required a complex succession of international judicial administrative procedures.

Through the Mozart case we can see the phases and components of a successful investigation and recovery. First, vigilant stewards report evidence of archaeological looting to the Carabinieri TPC. Second, the Carabinieri TPC takes the concern seriously enough to establish roadblocks in the region. One person found with a digging tool in their car in a relatively rural area would not necessarily indicate a serious crime. However, when the investigators analysed all of the data collected from their traffic stops, a pattern emerged of individuals whose cars contained evidence of illegal activity. This evidence then had to be presented to the Judicial Authority of Rome as a

case strong and compelling enough to warrant authorisation for further investigation. Identification of 'Mozart' would have come as the result of hours of interviews with dozens of individuals,
perhaps supplemented by detailed research into patterns of tourism and international visitation
to the archaeological areas in question. Because Mozart had been successful in transporting
Italian artefacts across international boundaries into Austria, following his identification the
Carabinieri TPC legal team would have had to work cooperatively at international level to prosecute Mozart and recover the objects he had stolen. Mozart was sentenced to four years in prison
as a result of the successful prosecution.

Once the Austrian discoveries had illustrated the magnitude of the theft, the authorities in
Rome permitted additional searches related to the suspects in Italy. These efforts yielded thousands of additional objects hidden in storage areas, outdoors and in the homes of the tomb
raiders and associated collectors. Most of the illegal excavations and damage had occurred in the
province of Lazio, where Rome is situated. As the activities had gone on for so long, the Carabinieri and the Superintendency concluded that it would be impossible to calculate the extent of
the damage to the archaeological sites affected.

EXPERIENCE WITH SMUGGLING ROUTES AND METHODS

As the Mozart case illustrates, the ruse of operating a tour made it very easy for Mozart to
remove antiquities from Italy by crossing international boundaries in a coach filled with tourists.
As the Carabinieri TPC gain experience over the years, they begin to identify patterns within
various forms of criminal behaviour, including smuggling. Common methods for moving objects
included secreting them in lorries with refrigerated compartments for transporting meat and
produce. Compartments of this type are rarely searched thoroughly. Ancient vases and other
ceramic objects of antiquity may be hidden among shipments of similar replicas or modern
products. For a particularly valuable and unique object, smugglers may commission a replica,
ask an archaeologist to examine it, pay for documentation declaring the object to be a fake and
then use the documentation to accompany the authentic object over an international border.
This method can also be used to import an extremely valuable object with paperwork attesting
to far lesser value. A busy border guard who is only superficially scanning cargo that may contain
thousands of objects may not pick up on the characteristics that would distinguish the valuable
antiquity from its ordinary and inexpensive counterpart. Thieves and smugglers are also known
to deliberately break objects into smaller pieces to make them easier to transport in, for example,
personal luggage. Smugglers are well aware that personal luggage, especially in sleeper carriages
of trains crossing Europe, may never be inspected. Ironically, valuable objects can sometimes be
sold for more money if offered piece by piece to culpable purchasers, with the price per piece
increasing as the purchaser comes closer to completing the object, as was seen in the Medici case,
the iconic case against dealer Giacomo Medici, prosecuted by the Carabinieri TPC, that led to
the high-profile repatriations of objects from major US institutions back to Italy (see Watson and
Todeschini 2007; see also Chapter 9 for more discussion of this case).

A major destination for smuggled Italian objects is Switzerland. Swiss law does not require
an art dealer to provide documentation proving that an object has not been looted from an
archaeological site. As a result, for many years looted antiquities traversing the Swiss market
came with paperwork simply stating that the object was from an undisclosed private collection.
In addition, Geneva (Switzerland) has a zone known as a Freeport (Segal 2012). A Freeport is

a district where merchants can rent space to store goods with a great deal of confidentiality or discretion. As long as the goods are in the Freeport, the owners pay no import taxes or duty. If the object is sold within the Freeport, there is no transaction tax either. The purchaser does not pay tax until the object reaches its final destination. As the art market has grown, so have the warehouses, galleries and dealer community in the Freeport of Geneva.

COOPERATION: TPC WITH TPC AND REGIONAL AND LOCAL CARABINIERI, FOGGIA

Numerous successful investigations and prosecutions illustrate situations where regional TPC nuclei have worked successfully with each other, with the operative units at headquarters in Rome and with regional Carabinieri. Just as local Carabinieri officers called upon the Bari TPC when the farmer reported his discovery of the buried funeral chamber, the Bari TPC has cooperated on multiple levels in its battle against *tombaroli* and other forms of art crime. In summer 2013 the Italian press announced that, by working together, the Naples TPC, the Bari TPC and the regional Carabinieri of Foggia had arrested 21 *tombaroli* and recovered 548 looted objects stolen from previously unexplored archaeological sites found throughout the countryside around Foggia. The operation got under way after the archaeological superintendent for Foggia, along with ordinary citizens, began to notice and report evidence of illegal excavations. Working together, the three units identified a well-established illegal organisation composed of looters and fences from Naples who were marketing the objects through a nationwide illicit network. Of the 21 individuals arrested, 17 had committed previous offences. This group of looters was using ground-penetrating radar in addition to traditional metal detectors and tile probes and had caused irreparable damage to the sites they encountered. The area was the territory of the Daunians in antiquity and looting has compromised the research potential for greater under-standing of Daunian culture. The objects recovered were valued at hundreds of thousands of dollars and included coins and intact ceramic vessels including red on black Attic vases (Frisaldi 2013).

COOPERATION WITH THE SUPERINTENDENCY: SATRICUM

Sometimes thefts and associated investigations are as simple a matter as an Italian landowner making a significant archaeological discovery, failing to report the discovery and keeping the excavated objects. In the case of the site of the votive offerings of Satricum (*thaindian.com* 2009), the Superintendency was made aware of a project in which a local farmer was enlarging a small lake and where piles of debris full of artefacts were noticed near the heavy equipment. The Superintendency called in the TPC, who inspected the mounds and determined that significant numbers of artefacts had indeed emerged. Working in partnership with academic archaeologists, the Carabinieri determined that the site was actually a sacred lake and a place of votive offerings. It was probably associated with a water cult and the offerings matched identical artefacts found in the ancient Latin settlement of Satricum, only 4km away. The artefacts dated from the early 6th century BC and included earthen jars and small bucchero – distinctive black-glazed South Etrurian amphorae. It is believed that women may have thrown the objects into the lake as part of ritual offerings. Dr Stefano De Caro, then head of the Ministry of Culture Italian Research Centre, believed that there may have been a sanctuary at the bottom of the lake.

Since the farmer had failed to report any of his finds, the Carabinieri had just cause to search his house. They found over 500 objects meticulously placed in the farmer's bookcase. They also secured both the area where the lake excavations were taking place and the mounds filled with artefacts so that archaeologists could recover the objects and analyse the associated materials.

MATCHING BITS AND PIECES

One method for proving beyond reasonable doubt that an object has been looted is to find pieces of that same object *in situ* or still buried at the archaeological site in the vicinity of the theft. The repatriation of the terracotta head of Hades from the Getty to Aidone, Sicily, announced on 11 January 2013, is an excellent example. According to the Getty's announcement (Ng and Felch 2013), the museum had been working in cooperation with Sicilian officials for over two years. The secret to proving that the head was looted was in matching four terracotta fragments found in the sanctuary of Demeter and Persephone at the archaeological site of Morgantina, Sicily, to the head of Hades that had been purchased by the Getty in 1985. The matching of the fragments unequivocally demonstrated that the head had been looted from the site, smuggled out of Sicily and sold illegally to the Getty. As a result of the determining of the object's true origin, the Getty took the decision to voluntarily return the object to Sicily.

Dr J Papadopoulos, from the Italian Ministry of Culture, provided another example in a presentation offering an archaeologist's perspective on law enforcement. She reminded the audience of the 'Naxos-Heidelberg Arula'. In this case, a portion of a relief had been looted from the archaeological site of Naxos, a Greek colony on the island of Sicily, and found its way to museum collections in Berlin. However, when another portion of the relief was recovered during controlled excavations at the site, photographs illustrating how perfectly the pieces fit together made the return of the fragment to Sicily possible (Papadopoulos 2009).

TRACKING PATTERNS OF BEHAVIOUR

The presence of a law enforcement entity dedicated solely to the arts is a privilege that presents its officers with the opportunity to study the behaviour patterns of art crime and its associated criminals within their jurisdictions. Just as the officers focus on art crime, there are, of course, criminals who also specialise. The opportunity for the officers to focus solely on art crime means that law enforcement agencies can become acquainted, as it were, with their adversaries. A case from Lake Maggiore illustrates this point.

Lake Maggiore is one of the spectacular lakes of the Italian Alps and shares a border with Switzerland. There are a number of expensive villas along its shores and these villas, often holiday homes, are frequently unoccupied. Many of them feature extensive collections of artworks and artefacts, making them an attractive target for art thieves. One such thief was described by the press as 'specialising' in art theft from holiday villas on Lake Maggiore (*Varese News* 2012). The investigation began in May 2009 with the discovery of the theft of a collection of antique stone pestles, a stone basin and an antique ox yoke. A year later, in May 2010, a burglary that was almost an exact replica of the one the previous year resulted in the disappearance of 16 paintings worth €100,000, including works by Carlo Domenici, a well-known landscape painter of the 19th century. The thieves also took two antique vases of Caltagirone, a village on the east coast of Sicily known for its ceramics.

At that point the Monza Carabinieri TPC, recognising the pattern, were able to combine

FIG 8.3.   431 ARCHAEOLOGICAL FINDS OF MAGNA GRAECIA, ETRUSCAN AND ROMAN PRODUCTION, RECOVERED FROM PRIVATE HOUSES IN THE PROVINCE OF ROME DURING 2012/2013.

all of the elements of police investigation – collection of evidence, interviews with suspects and witnesses and the taking of fingerprints and other scientific data – to very quickly identify a suspect. There could be no doubt that the thefts were the planned work of professionals. Because the Monza TPC has so many years' experience in tracking professional art thieves and the illegal market in their region, they were able to identify one of the thieves by name very quickly. Also, being familiar with the illegal networks, by February 2012 they were able to track two of the stolen Domenici paintings to the walls of a private home in Trecate, Italy, over 85km to the south. By October 2012, one of the thieves had been remanded to prison and the search was under way for his accomplices.

Another example of identifying behaviour patterns was the 2013 arrest of a ring of looters and thieves who were working with an interior decorator in Rome. The group clearly catered to extremely wealthy clients with a taste for antiquities and stolen paintings. In an operation coordinated by prosecutors Giancarlo Capaldo and Tiziana Cugini, the Carabinieri TPC recovered over 2000 objects and 6 paintings. The objects included valuable archaeological finds such as vases, kylix, oinochoe, alabaster, kraters, amphorae, cauldron, skyphos, kantharos, lamps, jars, kyathos, friezes, antefixes, bracelets, buckles, scrapers, cameos, gold filigree parure, figurines made of bone and ivory, tools, jewellery and glass ampoules. The seizure even uncovered mosaic floor tiles and marble flooring material dating to imperial Roman structures. The investigation ultimately recovered over €35 million worth of stolen objects (see Fig 8.3) and led to the arrest of

13 individuals (*Tiscali* 2013; DaringToDo 2013) who are likely to serve terms ranging between three and ten years – the usual length of prison terms for robbery in Italy.

STAKING OUT PROPERTIES AT RISK

From time to time, the Carabinieri are tipped off that *tombaroli* are becoming increasingly active in an at-risk archaeological district. One method for catching looters of archaeological material is for TPC officers to stake out the location, sometimes waiting patiently, long into the night. The Bari TPC, in cooperation with the Carabinieri of Foggia, became aware that looters were operating in the area of the ancient city of Arpi, searching for tombs to rob (*Statoquotidiano* 2011). Arpi is located in an area of Puglia once inhabited by an Illyrian people known as the Dauni. According to legend the city may have been founded by Diomedes, a hero of the Trojan War. Arpi was once one of Italy's greatest cities and an ally of Rome against the Samnites. There is no question that tombs associated with such an important city have the potential to yield objects of extraordinary value and beauty. As mentioned above, the area of the Dauni, near the modern city of Foggia, is critically important for understanding this group of ancient immigrants to Italy, so losses due to looting take a significant toll on the potential for scientific knowledge that this region has yet to reveal. The surveillance of the site by the Bari Carabinieri TPC and the Foggia Carabinieri units was so successful that three *tombaroli* suddenly found themselves surrounded by law enforcement officers, despite having posted a lookout. The ability of the two Carabinieri units to move in rapidly in a coordinated effort also prevented the criminals from dropping their digging tools – a critical piece of evidence against them.

BANCA DATI *LEONARDO* AS A STARTING POINT

Effective use of the databank and its comparative information can lead to the recovery of additional objects and the solving of cases. In May 2002 thieves broke into the Church of the Holy Cross of Monterubbiano in the Village of Fermo, south of Ancona, near the Adriatic coast. They stole four oil on canvas altar pieces depicting various episodes from the life of Christ. The following December, thieves struck the Church of St Mary and St James Massignano in Ascoli Piceno, a village situated approximately 70km from Fermo. From the second church, the thieves stole five wooden angels painted in white ivory tones. Representatives of the church had some images and documentation for the objects that they were able to submit to the police. This information was entered into Banca Dati *Leonardo*. In the meantime the Ancona TPC, as part of their routine reconnaissance activities, were completing inspections of restoration laboratories. At one of these locations they photographed a painting of 'The Baptism of Jesus' and two of the ivory painted angels. They were able to use the databank to identify the works as stolen objects. With this evidence, the Carabinieri TPC officers were able to make a sufficient case to the magistrate in Macerata to issue a decree for search and seizure of objects in the restoration laboratory concerned. When officers from Ancona went back they not only recovered the two angels from Ascoli Piceno and the altar piece from the Church of the Holy Cross of Monterubbiano but also found 14 looted archaeological objects and books stolen from a Capuchin Monastery in the Marches (*Quotidiano.net* 2012).

FIG 8.4.   WOODEN SCULPTURE OF SAINT AUGUSTINE COVERED ENTIRELY WITH PURE GOLD, RETRIEVED BY THE CARABINIERI TPC OF PALERMO IN 2011.

THE DATABASE AS SUPPORT FOR LOCAL ENFORCEMENT AGENCIES, VILLAROSA, MONDOVI

The existence of a centrally located comprehensive source of information about stolen works of art strengthens the capabilities of local law enforcement agencies when art and sacred objects go missing. Working from tips and other sources, Carabinieri officers based in Enna, Sicily, were in the midst of an investigation into artworks stolen in their region. The investigation involved searching the countryside and inspecting the ruins of abandoned farmhouses. In the rubble of a collapsed structure on the road to the Sigonella military base the Carabinieri discovered a 19th-century Flemish oil painting stashed amongst debris and completely exposed to the elements. Had the painting been left outdoors for much longer, in those conditions and at risk from the weather, it might have been destroyed, but thanks to the Carabinieri's efforts and thorough searching, it was recovered intact. By using the *Leonardo* database, the officers from Enna were able to determine immediately that the painting had gone missing from the Church of the Mother of St James the Elder in Villarosa, Sicily, and were able to return the painting to a grateful monseigneur and his parish (*vivienna.it* 2012). Similarly, in 2011 the Carabinieri TPC of Palermo retrieved from a private house an important wooden sculpture of 1861, covered entirely with pure gold and depicting Saint Augustine. The Carabinieri was able to use its powerful database to determine the statue's origin – it had been stolen in 1982 from the Church of San

Francesco Saverio of Mondovi in the province of Cuneo. The art object was promptly returned to the church and to the veneration of the faithful (see Fig 8.4).

THOROUGH SEARCHING

Just as the Carabinieri of Enna began to search ruins all over the Sicilian countryside looking for the stolen painting, the Carabinieri TPC of Monza searched innumerable shops and markets looking for a series of wooden panels representing an entire set of Stations of the Cross, stolen from the Church of San Giacomo in the province of Vercelli (Berni 2010). The panels, stolen on the morning of 27 May 2008, were finally recovered in the autumn of 2010. Once the theft had been reported by the parish priest, TPC officers entered documentation of the theft and the objects into Banca Dati *Leonardo*. They then began to search as many antiquarian shops across Lombardy as possible. Finally, in Cormano, they found for sale archival documents that had been stolen along with the Stations of the Cross, which led them to two warehouses filled with stolen goods. This discovery was the breakthrough they needed, leading them to 12 of the 14 stolen panels and two 50-year-old antiquarians handling stolen property in Lodi and Vigevano. Two of the panels, numbers 4 and 14, had been sold for between €1500 and €2000, so were therefore unable to be recovered with the others. The database documentation was critical, as was the database's events category that allowed for connections to be made between multiple objects stolen together at the same time. However, the true secret to solving this case was the comprehensive searching of shops throughout an entire region. Most importantly, the hard work of the officers of the Monza TPC meant that at least 12 of the 14 missing panels could be returned to the parish and community for use in worship.

PATIENCE AND PERSISTENCE: VERGA'S MANUSCRIPTS

Thirty-six manuscripts worth over €4 million that had been stolen and missing since the 1930s were recovered by the TPC in 2013. The archival materials were related to the writer Giovanni Verga, described by some as one of the great Italian novelists. In the 1930s Verga's son lent the manuscripts to an historian in a small town in Sicily and, despite numerous attempts to recover them, the historian refused. He hid the manuscripts extremely well, confounding attempts to find and recover them. It was not until vigilant monitoring of the auction houses revealed manuscripts by Verga for sale at Christie's in Milan that the TPC had the break they needed. The historian's elderly daughter had put the objects up for sale and the auction catalogue provided sufficient evidence for the police to raid her property in Rome, enabling them to recover the collection. The manuscripts included originals of Verga's novels including his first novel, *Love and Homeland*, and *The House by the Medlar Tree*, which was made into the 1948 film *The Earth Trembles*, directed by Luchino Visconti. The TPC returned the manuscripts to their rightful owner, Verga's granddaughter, who has agreed to sell them to the City of Catania where Verga was born (Agence France-Press 2013; *ANSA* 2013b).

THE CHALLENGE OF PALAEONTOLOGICAL MATERIALS, FOSSILS

As mentioned in Chapter 2, the theft of fossils from Italy and the illegal international trade in palaeontological material also falls within the remit of the Carabinieri TPC. One advantage when

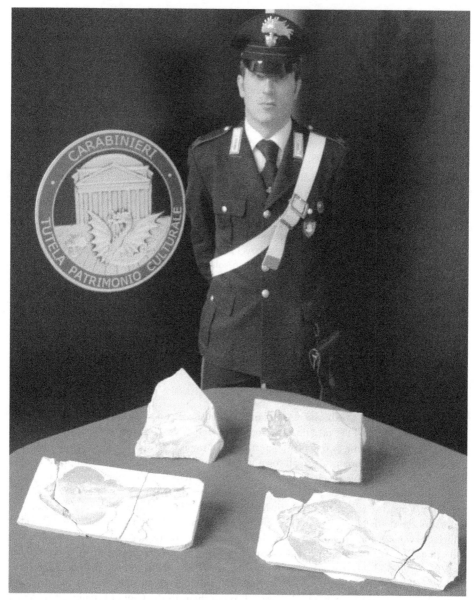

FIG 8.5. FOSSILS FROM LEBANON, RECOVERED IN JANUARY 2008 FROM A PRIVATE RESIDENCE IN ROME AND RETURNED TO LEBANON.

identifying the source of fossils found for sale on the international market is that, quite often, specific species of palaeontological material are found only in very specific geological formations. As a result, the professional expertise of the Carabinieri TPC officers, combined with their willingness to work productively with academic experts, makes them a powerful force for global law enforcement in the protection of palaeontological materials. It was this powerful combination of skill, and a fossil species of panther that is only known to come from Liguria, that enabled the Monza TPC to recover and repatriate the cat skeleton that had made its way to a collector in Dallas, Texas, before ending up at the University of North Carolina. This case also illustrates the power of using customs laws for prosecution. On his customs form the Dallas buyer had listed the object as having no value, which in the US is far more serious a crime than purchasing smuggled fossils. This case also illustrates the value of law enforcement agencies reviewing collections acquisitions. While investigating the Ligurian cat fossil, the Monza TPC also helped the University to discover that they had purchased the skull of a medieval plague victim which had been advertised as an example of a Neanderthal (Ilari 2011, *pers comm*).

While the fossil-bearing grottos of Liguria have been a source of priceless scientific specimens, they have also yielded fossils to smugglers and the international market. In 1999 the Monza TPC, in cooperation with the Genoa TPC, INTERPOL and the Netherlands police, recovered a series of fossils that had been stolen from Liguria. When the objects were recovered, the mayor and community leaders in Toirano allocated funds to set up a museum near the cave entrance and ticket booth so that members of the public and tourists could see restored examples of the remarkable creatures whose fossils had been recovered from the caves. Just as in Liguria, the recovery and repatriation of dinosaur fossils from Mongolia also illustrates the importance of fossils as heritage and sources of pride and economic stimulus for local, regional and national communities.

THE MONGOLIAN DINOSAUR

Another example is the recent recovery from Mongolia of a skeletal *Tarbosaurus bataar*, a form of *Tyrannosaurus rex*. The skeleton appeared at Heritage Auctions, a company based in the US state of Texas, and a Mongolian palaeontologist living in New York learned about the upcoming sale on the news. She contacted an aide to the president of Mongolia, voicing her concerns about the origin of the skeleton. Initially, the auctioneer claimed that the owner/seller was a UK citizen and that there was documentation of legal ownership. However, the only place in the world ever known to have produced a *Tarbosaurus* is Mongolia. In fact, the US smuggler had convinced a British associate to label the objects as being of British origin. It is in combatting this type of deception that it is critical for law enforcement agencies to work with academic specialists; in this example such collaboration meant that the case could easily be made that the *Tarbosaurus bataar* could only have come from geological deposits located in Mongolia. The only source known to science for the fossil in question is the Nemegt geological formation in the Gobi desert. The colours of the deposits within this formation are distinctive and provided further scientific and forensic evidence of the fossil's true source (St Hilaire 2012). The Mongolians enlisted the help of eminent North American palaeontologists and hired an experienced attorney from Texas to represent them (Williams 2013).

Networking also played a supporting role in the recovery of the *Tarbosaurus*. Carabinieri participation in global efforts for law enforcement cooperation and heritage education has helped to establish and maintain international networks for heritage law enforcement. Carabinieri TPC officers participated in a training event held in Mongolia in 2010 that was also attended by agents from US Immigration and Customs Enforcement (ICE) (Rossi 2012, *pers comm*). Given the vigilance of the Carabinieri TPC in monitoring international auctions and markets, it is not surprising that the Italians were also among the first to notice the *Tarbosaurus* up for auction in Texas. As a result, when the *Tarbosaurus* appeared, there was already a network of colleagues in place who had met in person, making it easy to alert the newly acquainted colleagues in Mongolia; the rest is history.

Even though the dinosaur was sold at the contested auction for US $1.05 million, the Mongolian government filed for its return in US federal court. During the course of the subsequent investigation, US agents discovered that the individual who had actually put the dinosaur up for auction – a self-proclaimed 'commercial palaeontologist' named Eric Prokopi from Florida – had allegedly smuggled the fossil into the US in multiple shipments, lying about the value and source of the materials. He had also smuggled additional Mongolian fossils into the US including a *Saurolophus*, a form of duck-billed dinosaur with horns; *Gallimimus*, a dinosaur that looked a bit like an ostrich and that could measure up to 8m in length; and an *Oviraptor mongoliensis*, another bird-like Cretaceous dinosaur. Ironically, UPS delivered the *Oviraptor* as federal agents were searching Prokopi's house and seizing the collections and documents (Williams 2013). He had also imported a *Microraptor*, a small flying dinosaur from China. One of the US prosecutors described Prokopi as a 'one-man black market in prehistoric fossils' (ibid). The efforts of the US agents and prosecutors resulted in the recovery of even more material than the Mongolian government was originally suing to recover, including fossils in the custody of the British associate.

It is important to note what the repatriation of the *Tarbosaurus bataar* and the additional fossils has meant to the people of Mongolia. On the day of the contested auction there were protestors outside the Heritage Auction with signs stating 'National Heritage is Not for Sale' and 'Return our Stolen Treasure'. The Mongolians have recognised their dinosaurs as cultural patrimony since gaining independence in 1924, when they made it illegal to remove and sell fossils from their country. However, this law has proved extremely difficult to enforce, especially after Mongolia opened to the West in the 1990s. Looting and smuggling of fossils out of Mongolia has been widespread but perhaps may diminish now that the *Tarbosaurus bataar* has returned. The day that *Tarbosaurus bataar* arrived home in Mongolia, 18 May 2013, was declared a holiday: National Dinosaur Day (Parry 2013). When the recovered dinosaur went on display at an exhibition hall near the centre of Mongolia's capital, thousands of people came to see it. The Mongolian minister of culture, sports and tourism described the *Tarbosaurus* as a hero in Mongolia due to its potential role as a 'single star who can be a representation of the whole palaeontological heritage that we have' (ibid). The Mongolians have plans for a new dinosaur museum and the establishment of university-level departments of palaeontology that will encourage young Mongolians to study and discover dinosaurs in the future.

INTERNATIONAL COOPERATION AND THE ITALIAN MODEL: A GLOBAL COMPARISON

If we are to consider the Carabinieri TPC as a model worthy of emulation, it is fair to ask about other international approaches to law enforcement with respect to arts, antiquities and cultural property protection. It is also useful to introduce some of the agencies available in international cooperation.

The United States does not have a ministry of culture, so there is no single law enforcement agency in the US dedicated solely to the issue of crimes against art and antiquities. The protection of archaeological sites on US federal land is the responsibility of National Park Service Archaeologists, Federal Agency Cultural Resources Managers and Conservation Police. For crimes involving art, the US has the FBI Art Crime Team, which consists of fewer than 20 agents who partner with experienced prosecutors. From 2000 to 2010 this team recovered approximately 2650 items with a cumulative value of US $150 million. Various major US cities, such as Los Angeles, also have officers who specialise in crimes involving cultural property. At US borders, immigration and customs enforcement (ICE) agents look for smuggled antiquities and stolen works of art. The US State Department, in cooperation with the University of Pennsylvania Museum Cultural Heritage Center, developed a training curriculum for ICE agents regarding investigation techniques, the handling and storage of vulnerable objects and documentation of objects including photographic and analytical methods for the identification and authentication of works of art and antiquities. Experts from ICE, the Department of Justice, the State Department, INTERPOL and the Smithsonian currently offer these courses and over 300 ICE officers have received this cultural property training. ICE takes pride in the fact that the interception of art and antiquity at US borders is their responsibility and its agents take even greater pride when they are successful and able to repatriate objects to their rightful places of origin. From time to time other US law enforcement agents, such as postal inspectors, play a role in recovering stolen objects or investigating the transportation of fraudulent works of art. US accomplishments are important and represent commitment and professionalism on the part of the enforcement personnel. However, when comparing the population sizes of the nations concerned, for the US force to be comparable to the Carabinieri TPC the Americans would require at least 1500 dedicated officers; and, in terms of the geographical area of the two countries, the Americans would require at least 9500 dedicated officers. It is important to note that these estimates do not even begin to factor in an additional 1000 dedicated Italian police officers who assist with art crime issues, not to mention the contributions of the Ministry of Culture and academic partners.

The United Kingdom, Spain, France and the Netherlands also have policing units that specialise in art crime. The UK's Scotland Yard established an Art and Antiques Unit in 1969, disbanded it and then re-established it in 1989. Since 1989, museum theft in London has decreased and the unit has recovered approximately £7 million worth of stolen art each year. The unit's jurisdiction, however, is limited to London and the British officers specialise in preventing forgery and fraud related to art. Even with their outstanding record of recovering property, since 2007 the unit has been subject to serious budget cuts. In late 2010, the UK also identified the need for a police officer with responsibility for focusing on crimes against historic property.

The Spanish art police, la Brigada de Patrimonio Histórico (the Heritage Brigade), specialise in art crime throughout Spain. Like the Carabinieri TPC, they respond to reports of archaeological looting: on average, 300–400 reported cases annually, in addition to investigating art theft and fraud. Antonio Cortes (2002, 317–18), an officer from the Heritage Brigade, emphasises the continuing challenge posed by looters' use of metal detectors on archaeological property. He also characterises three types of looter commonly encountered on Spanish soil: casual pillagers, regular pillagers and 'local experts'. Sometimes the 'local experts' set up local archaeological organisations and it is not unusual for groups of this nature to amass extensive collections and sometimes even start their own museums. Unfortunately, it is rare for such groups to use controlled excavation techniques, meaning that much scientific information and context is lost as a result of their efforts. Cortes (2002, 319) also discusses the smuggling of antiquities across Spanish borders. In fact, he documents a phenomenon whereby Spanish looters smuggle an object out of the country, create a fraudulent transaction and bring the object back as a 'legal' object, purchased abroad.

As Cortes (2002, 321–2) explains, the 'Heritage Brigade' is part of the Spanish Civil Guard, a militarised police force with 70,000 members. The Civil Guard is responsible for security throughout rural Spain and is therefore the primary investigative authority for around 80% of Spanish crime involving art and/or archaeology. There are public security units that protect heritage properties, along with members of the Wildlife and Nature Protection service who are tasked with protecting archaeological sites. There is a maritime service with diving capability that also works with diving activity groups to patrol and protect underwater archaeological sites. The fiscal service is tasked with the prevention of smuggling. The Heritage Brigade is a division of the Criminal Police Investigation Service, based in Madrid, and is ultimately responsible for coordinating information and investigations involving the other units. The Heritage Brigade also manages a database of stolen items. Like the Carabinieri TPC, the Heritage Unit in Madrid also spreads the word concerning stolen goods, publishing a catalogue of stolen art and producing a *YouTube* video of Spain's two most wanted artworks in 2011. Spanish art police are especially interested in collaboration with Italy, Portugal and France, as these countries are the three most likely to receive stolen goods smuggled out of Spain.

Perhaps the world's newest police group dedicated to art crime is based in the Netherlands. Formed in 2006, the Korps Landelijke Politiediensten (KLPD) manages a database of stolen art. According to the FBI website (FBI 2012), combatting art crime emerged as a priority in the Netherlands as recognition of its connection to organised crime increased.

All European and US policing agencies cooperate through INTERPOL, the international policing organisation based in Lyon, France. Given the fact that stolen and forged art and antiquities often cross international borders, it is crucial for all policing agencies interested in fighting art crime to share information and expertise.

International policing related to art crime will, unfortunately, only continue to increase in importance. In 2014 the United States Federal Bureau of Investigation (FBI) estimated that the global value of crimes related to art had risen to US $6 billion per year, ranking its economic impact in third place behind illegal transactions involving drugs and weapons (NRC Research Press 2014). During the course of international investigations into paintings stolen in Ireland, it quickly became clear that stolen artworks that are too well-known or recognisable to be sold publicly still maintain value as collateral among criminals, who may use them to guarantee payment for shipments of drugs or possibly even weapons. Some criminals may even take pride in their 'ownership' of stolen masterpieces. When a work of art disappears into the underworld, it may circulate for years or even decades, lost not only to its rightful owners but also to humanity.

9

Repatriation of Works of Art to Italy: From Siviero to the Medici Conspiracy

Italian works of art are an integral part of western and of world civilisation as a whole. They are signposts along the road to civilisation. To steal them is to deny the foundation of a nation's culture. Their return is an act of justice.

> Susanna Agnelli, Minister of Foreign Affairs, Italy, quoted in her introduction to 'Treasures Untraced, An Inventory of the Italian Art Treasures Lost during the Second World War'.

The Medici Case is not the first time in recent history that Italy has suffered a massive theft of artworks and antiquities, and it is reasonable to question whether mid-20th-century experiences have influenced current Italian approaches to repatriation. Analysis of the case of Rodolfo Siviero and his efforts to find and return cultural property stolen from Italy during World War II offers additional historical context for appreciating the approaches and efforts of the Italian Foreign Ministry and the Carabinieri TPC of today.

RODOLFO SIVIERO AND WORLD WAR II REPATRIATION

From the period beginning on 3 September 1943, when the Italians signed an armistice with the Allies, until May 1945, when German forces in Italy surrendered, German forces – even as an army in retreat – helped themselves to an extraordinary number of artworks belonging to individual Italian citizens, public and private collections and parishes of the Roman Catholic Church. To some extent, the theft of art from the Italian people had begun even before 1943, as Adolf Hitler had pressured Mussolini to sell him Italian masterpieces he coveted, such as the sculpture *Discobolus* Lancellotti, the 1st-century marble copy of the famous Greek bronze Discobolus of Myron. The sale of such objects was in direct violation of Italian cultural property law. In addition, agents working for the German government prior to the declaration of war carefully inventoried art treasures throughout Europe, preparing lists of desired objects for museums and personal ownership in the Third Reich.

As the Allied invasion of Italy began, a controversial individual emerged in the world of heritage in conflict. Born in 1911 in Guardistallo (Pisa), Rodolfo Siviero was the son of the Maresciallo (marshall) commander of the local detachment of the Carabinieri Corps and grew up in Florence. It is possible that Siviero began working as an intelligence agent for the Servizio Informazioni Militari (SIM), the Italian Military Intelligence Service, as early as 1934. In 1937 he went to Germany to study Art History, ostensibly undercover. Like many Italians, Siviero became increasingly disillusioned with the values and behaviour of the fascists and, upon the signing of the Italian armistice, he immediately offered his services to the Allies. As his undercover activities involved association with the fascists, the leading Allied Monuments and Fine Arts and Archives officers serving in Italy, such as Captain Deane Keller, were reluctant to establish a partnership with him.

Nevertheless, Siviero continued to work at preventing further Nazi thefts of Italian artworks. He used the home of his friend, the Jewish art historian Giorgio Castelfranco, as a basis for partisan activity, much of it focused on attempting to trace German truckloads of Italian works of art heading north. The identification of these convoys and the officers in charge of them was not only critical for tracing the movement of the stolen objects but was also used to alert the Allies so that these convoys might be spared during bombing runs (Vicentini and Morozzi 1995, 15). Siviero used his contacts within SIM to gain information about detailed German plans to confiscate and transport collections of artworks from Florence and the region. Siviero and his group were occasionally able to prevent the seizure and removal of specific works of art. Harclerode and Pittaway (1999, 19) describe how two monks working with Siviero's organisation were able to 'spirit away' Fra Angelico's *Annunciation* from a monastery near San Giovanni Valdarno when it became clear that the work appeared on a list of masterpieces to be seized for Goering's personal collection. As a result of his partisan activities, Siviero was captured and held prisoner by the German Gestapo from April to June 1944.

After the war, the Italian government appointed Siviero as lead delegate of the Italian diplomatic mission to the Allied Government in Germany with the goal of recovering stolen Italian works of art that the Allies had seized from the retreating Germans. The Allies were holding the objects at a series of collection points in Germany under the jurisdiction of the Allied Military Government for the Occupied Territories, also known as AMGOT. Siviero wanted all treasures belonging to the Italian people to be returned, including objects the Germans had paid for, such as the *Discobolus*. It was on the subject of these purchased objects that the Allies and Siviero had trouble reaching agreement. Finally, US General Lucius Clay ordered that all of the Italian objects be returned to Italy. His MFA&A (Monuments and Fine Arts and Archives) officer, Colonel Stewart Leonard, Director of the Munich Collecting Point, was so strongly opposed to this decision that he refused to carry out the order and resigned; in response, Clay slowed down the Italian repatriation. However, by 1953, most of the objects identified by Siviero as being in the custody of the Americans and requested by the Italians had been returned. It is interesting to point out that, later in life, Colonel Leonard 'admitted that his own attitude was intransigent' on the issue (Nicholas 1995, 471).

Siviero gained a reputation for being outspoken and for a time he was banned not only from the Munich Collecting Point but also from all of Allied-governed German territory. Nevertheless, his persistence and tactics resulted in the successful recovery of priceless works of art for the people of Italy. Siviero was also a master of the politics required for fruitful repatriation initiatives. After the controversial return of the *Discobolus* to Italy, Siviero arranged for the Italian government to gift a copy of the sculpture to the government of the United States. The Italians used the recovered statue as a mould for a bronze cast, and Florentine artists added detail to the sculpture using Renaissance techniques. The sculpture was then weathered and the Italians completed the gift by offering an Egyptian marble pillar from the theatre of Marcellus in Rome for the plinth. The *Discobolus* offer put President Eisenhower in the difficult position of having to choose between alienating the Italians by refusing the gift or angering the Germans by accepting it. Ultimately, motivated in part by prevailing concerns over Italian sympathy for Communism as a form of government, the president chose the former course of action and accepted the

Discobolus from Italian president Giovanni Gronchi on 29 February 1956 (Kurtz 2006, 194). The replica statue is still on display in Washington DC, near an entrance to the State Department at the corner of 21st Street and Virginia Avenue NW.

POST-WAR RESTITUTION AND RECOVERY

As Italy emerged from the devastation of World War II, politics continued to play a significant role in the progress of finding stolen art and its repatriation. In April 1946 the Italian government transformed Siviero's partisan organisation, referred to as the 'Undercover Protection Service' (Vicentini and Morozzi 1995, 15), into the Office for the Recovery of Works of Art, Library and Archive Material. This office then merged with the wartime Mission for Restitution and the combined organisation became the Delegation for Restitution. Siviero was granted the title of Minister Plenipotentiary for Restitution of Lost Artworks in his role within this delegation (Durney 2009). In 1953 the De Gasperi–Adenauer agreement was signed, which included a provision specifying that the Germans would return all works of art removed from Italy, either purchased by or presented to high-ranking Nazi leaders during their years of alliance with fascist Italy. This agreement essentially ended any further discussion or controversy regarding the return of objects that the Nazis had paid for prior to the war.

It is interesting to consider the terms of the De Gasperi–Adenauer agreement from the perspective of modern Italian approaches to repatriation. The concept of international cooperation towards the shared goals of education and appreciation of cultural patrimony already existed more than 50 years prior to today's negotiation of repatriation agreements. Essentially, in exchange for the repatriation of all Italian masterpieces in question, through the De Gasperi–Adenauer agreement the Italians agreed to restore to the German government all cultural institutes and collections located within Italian borders on the proviso that these cultural assets remain in Italy (Gattini 1996, 76); the Hertziana Library in Rome is an example. Looking back, this solution has ultimately been beneficial, not only to the people of Italy and Germany but also to an international audience of scholars and appreciative citizens.

It is important to recognise that Rodolfo Siviero provided a model for the current Italian standard of repatriation that includes the return of stolen objects to their rightful owners, even if this means a loss for an Italian collection. In January 1947 the Union of Jewish Communities sent Rodolfo Siviero an inventory of property looted from Jewish community members in Italy that had been repatriated by the Allies to an Italian agency called ARAR (Azienda Rilievo Alienazione Residuati) (Agency for the Acquisition of Residual War Materials). The ARAR had begun to auction some of these materials and the Union of Jewish Communities had discovered eight crates of silver objects, clearly of Jewish origin, held in storage on the premises of the Cassa di Risparmio of Milan and of the Milan Tribunal. Siviero intervened and, in less than one month, he had sequestered the crates in question in order to help guarantee restitution to their proper owners. His actions contributed to a change in policy that prevented the further sale of some of the Judaica in the ARAR's custody (Basevi 2001).

In 1963 the Accademia Nazionale dei Lincei (a science academy founded in 1603 and based in Rome) awarded Siviero their gold medal for his efforts. He continued to work on the tracking and repatriation of Italian art until his death in 1983, at which point it was determined that over 700 objects were still missing. One case illustrates the complex challenges of tracking down and recovering art stolen during the war. As the Nazis helped themselves to art all over Europe,

Hermann Goering was amassing his own collection. When the tide began to turn he put his favourite pieces on trains, intending to move them west, where he hoped that at the very least their sale might provide his wife with a comfortable retirement. Instead, German citizens sacked some of the train carriages and, when all of the gourmet food and alcohol had gone, began to take paintings. Almost 20 years later, in 1963, an art restorer in Los Angeles, California, named Arthur LaVigner received two paintings requiring conservation from a German couple who had emigrated to the US. They had been given the paintings by a woman with 'ties to Goering'. LaVigner recognised the masterpieces as having been stolen from the Uffizi Gallery. They were Antonio Pollaiuolo's *Hercules Slaying the Hydra of Lerna* and *Hercules Slaying Antaeus*. LaVigner contacted Siviero, prompting international negotiations which resulted in the paintings being displayed at the Los Angeles Museum of Art prior to their return to the Uffizi (Durney 2009).

By 1969 Italian funding for Siviero's work was in decline. It would be nearly 30 years before *Treasures Untraced, An Inventory of the Italian Art Treasures Lost during the Second World War*, his catalogue of art still missing from Italy, would appear in print in 1995. During the 1970s and 1980s enthusiasm for the aggressive pursuit of property stolen during World War II had waned in some circles. Antonio Paolucci, later to become culture minister, and Professor Luciano Bellosi, an art historian working within the Superintendency in Florence, had prepared a draft manuscript of the 1995 catalogue in 1972 and delivered it to Siviero. However, formal publication of the list at that time would have been problematic owing to political pressure on the Italians and West Germans to maintain positive diplomatic relations. In 1984 an exhibition at the Palazzo Vecchio in Florence titled *Artworks Recovered* presented the issue in the positive light of works that had been recovered, mostly by Siviero himself. He also wrote the introduction to the exhibition catalogue, which featured objects such as a Rubens painting and sketches by Michelangelo. Despite this success, in 1987 foreign minister Giulio Andreotti closed the Delegation for Restitution, the list was placed in the archives of the foreign ministry and the issue was declared 'extinct' (Paolucci 2009, 10; Tagliabue 1995).

However, the Italian people were clearly not ready to give up. In 1988, Law No 400, of 23 August, established an interministerial commission to provide 'assistance and expertise for the co-ordination of activities undertaken to protect the national artistic heritage, with particular reference to the recovery of stolen or illegally exported works of art' (Paolucci 2009). Following the end of the Cold War in 1989 and the opening up of Eastern Europe, the issue of repatriation became an even greater public priority. For the first time since World War II, the governments of Western Europe realised that, by offering to return works of art stolen from the Russians, there might be hope for recovering objects that had disappeared into the East. In 1994, Prime Minister Berlusconi established a Coordinating Committee to support repatriation efforts and, in December 1995, the government of Bremen, Germany, hosted an international conference designed to revive the search for lost works of art (Tagliabue 1995). With the Bremen meeting providing encouragement, keepers of the Siviero archives realised that it was time to press for publication of Siviero's list once and for all, and this was achieved in 1995. The cover of the catalogue featured an image of the marble *Mask of a Faun*, attributed to Michelangelo. This object originally belonged to the collection of the Bargello Museum in Florence, Italy. Italian curators had evacuated it to the Tuscan Castello di Poppi, where it was 'stolen by German soldiers of the 305th Division between August 22nd and 23rd, 1944' (Edsel 2014).

There is no doubt that Siviero's dedication to the repatriation cause still provides inspiration for many Italians, including officers of the Carabinieri TPC. Siviero's ministry archives are currently housed at his office in the Palazzo Venezia, where he continued to serve as head of the Italian Foreign Office Delegation for Recovery of Stolen Art until his death in 1983. A visit to the archives reinforces how inspiring Siviero's example can be to the TPC officers of today who similarly dedicate their lives to returning Italian cultural property to the people of Italy. Siviero bequeathed the Castelfranco house in Florence and all of its contents to the people of Tuscany. It is now an Art Museum called Museo Casa Rodolfo Siviero. As issues of World War II art repatriation began to re-emerge with the publication of *Treasures Untraced*, stolen art belonging to the people of Italy also entered the public realm through the Medici Case.

THE MEDICI CASE: A PARADIGM SHIFT FOR INTERNATIONAL REPATRIATION

The details of the Medici Case – the investigation during which the Italians prevailed over some of the United States' most powerful and wealthy individuals and institutions – have been well documented in such books as *The Medici Conspiracy* (Watson and Todeschini 2007) and *Chasing Aphrodite* (Felch and Frammolino 2011), in addition to extensive media coverage and scholarly analysis. The essence of the case (Quagliarella 2011, *pers comm*) illustrates the strengths of TPC investigation techniques. In September 1995 TPC officers were tracking property stolen from the De Marchi family of San Felice Circeo, Latina, Italy. During a search of a warehouse belonging to Edition Service SA, a Panamanian company, in Geneva, Switzerland, they discovered over 4000 archaeological objects with associated documentation. The owner of the company was Giacomo Medici. Using the seized documents, the TPC was able to reconstruct a network of thieves, dealers, 'middle men' and restorers who were selling illegally acquired objects to museums all over the world. The documentation provided the evidence necessary to support the international letters of rogatory to request judicial support from other countries. These letters led to permission for a series of searches: December 2000, Paris: premises of the dealer Robert Hecht; February 2001, Geneva, Switzerland: premises of the Aboutam brothers, a family known to be trafficking illegal archaeological materials; and March 2001, Zurich, Switzerland: premises of Fritz Burki & Son, restorers who were also involved in sales of illicit property.

When the results of the searches and interviews with the suspects were analysed and compared with the previously acquired documentation, the case tightened. Among the condemning evidence were Polaroid photographs of the objects as they were unearthed from Italian soil, wrapped in sheets of Italian newspaper. In one particularly egregious example, an image of marble griffins encrusted with grime and lying in dirty newspapers in the boot of a car was entered as evidence by the prosecution (Povoledo 2006). The combined evidence provided a chain of custody for many of the objects, beginning with the moment of illegal excavation, their trip via smugglers across the Italian border, sojourns in Switzerland in the dealers' warehouses while their false documentation was established, followed by further travel to auction houses and dealers for sale in the US, UK, Germany, Japan and Australia, and, for many, on to new homes within important exhibitions in prominent museums.

It must be noted that the painstaking and brilliant analysis of the evidence, development of the case and successful implementation of repatriation agreements was also due to the dedication of a series of experienced and talented individuals who demonstrated professionalism and commitment to see the cases through. Prosecutor Paolo Giorgio Ferri worked diligently to bring disparate pieces of the case together and, by analysing every image, transaction and interview detail, even made the discovery that, in addition to all of his other crimes, Giacomo Medici was laundering money and stolen antiquities by selling the objects to himself using major European auction houses (Felch and Frammolino 2011). Maurizio Fiorilli, a senior government lawyer representing the Italian Ministry of Culture, also diligently pursued repatriation options, repeatedly meeting with representatives of the museums who had custody of stolen objects and working in tandem with Prosecutor Ferri, making it absolutely clear to the Americans that the Italian government and law enforcement agencies were committed on all fronts to seeing justice done (Felch and Frammolino 2011, 219). The presence of a leader such as General Roberto Conforti at the helm of the Carabinieri TPC and the gifted, enthusiastic officers he recruited to the force were also clearly crucial to the ultimate success of the Medici investigation.

As the case was brought to court, Giacomo Medici chose to be judged according to summary proceedings on the charges of criminal association, money laundering, illicit export and violation in the matter of archaeological searches under Italian Criminal Codes 416 and 648 and articles 174 and 175 LD 22.1.2004 n 42. The trial ended on 13 December 2004 with convictions and a sentence of ten years in prison plus forfeiture of goods in the sum of €10 million. Other suspects, such as Marion True, curator at the Getty, and dealer Robert Hecht elected to be tried under ordinary proceedings and their trials began on 1 April 2005. Both of their trials eventually ended with expiration of the charges under Italian statutes of limitations.[1]

As the strength of Carabinieri evidence and subsequent case against the dealers and museums became abundantly clear, a series of US museums, including the Getty Museum of Los Angeles, the Metropolitan Museum of Art in New York City, the Princeton University Art Museum, the Museum of Fine Arts Boston and the Cleveland Museum of Art, elected to negotiate with the Italian government. The Italians formed a commission composed of experts from the Ministry of Culture, federal lawyers, the Ministry of Foreign Affairs and the Carabinieri TPC that was intended to collect evidence at each museum to assist in the identification and determination of which objects in the collections were of illegal origin. According to a witness (Settis 2011, *pers comm*), at the end of his first visit to the Getty General Conforti made the gesture of leaving his hat on the desk of the director – in retrospect, a powerful indication that the Carabinieri would prevail. It was also General Conforti who took the decision to expand the search for stolen Italian objects to all US museums that had potentially purchased looted material. The successful investigation methods and high standard of evidence presented by the Carabinieri TPC were such that it quickly became clear to representatives of the US museums that their cases for keeping the objects would never prevail in any court of law. At the conclusion of the meetings with the Italians, some of the museums signed agreements confirming Italian ownership of the objects with commitments for repatriation.

The investigation also revealed that the museums and some collectors were using organisations such as the Art Loss Register and the International Foundation for Art Research to attempt to legitimise acquisition of an illegally excavated object. The Art Loss Register is a business that emerged out of the International Foundation for Art Research and it manages a database of stolen works of art. The concept is that the availability of a comprehensive source of information listing works of art that have been stolen should make it possible to buy and/or sell a work of art legitimately by demonstrating that it does not appear on such a list. However, criminals buying and selling looted archaeological material began to use organisations such as the Art Loss Register

---

[1]   In Italian law, prosecution of felonies must be completed within six years and of misdemeanours within four.

to purchase certificates stating that the objects they wanted to buy or sell did not appear in the stolen objects database. Clearly, though, if an object has been looted from an archaeological site, it will never appear on a list of stolen objects because there is no proof or documentation that the object ever existed. Therefore, attempts by museum representatives to use organisations such as the Art Loss Register to defend the acquisition of looted objects are dubious at best.

The Medici investigation also yielded specific examples of the practice of dealers or 'middle men' deliberately breaking an object so that it could be sold one fragment at a time. As the collector came closer to completing the object, the price of the fragments would increase accordingly. During the course of their acquisitions process, representatives of the Getty purchased fragments and acquired objects in this manner. Also, in 1998, the Getty accepted a donation of fragments from Robin Symes, a dealer in illicit antiquities; in November 2012 the Getty announced that these fragments had been returned to Italy. Getty representatives expressed the belief that the fragments belonged with the ceramic vessels originally looted from Ascoli Satriano, an ancient site in Apulia, southern Italy.

The acquisition of illicit antiquities brings with it a range of associated crimes. One example is perjury, the deliberate misrepresentation of the true market value of objects. In cases involving the donation of illegally acquired objects, significant overestimation of the value of various objects, determined with the complicity of museum experts, encourages donors to claim greater income tax deductions, which is a form of tax fraud. In its early days, a series of Getty donors whose appraisals had been provided by Getty staff were questioned by the US Internal Revenue Service (Felch and Frammolino 2011, 47). A similar type of tax fraud occurs when a donor purchases looted objects and then loans the objects to a museum or university collection, ostensibly giving the curators or scholars an opportunity to study objects to which they would not otherwise have access. If the curator or scholar then publishes the object, confirming its identity and offering dates, the object increases in value. At that point the donor often decides to change the loan to a gift and takes the higher value as his or her tax deduction. This method works especially well for objects requiring translation, such as cuneiform tablets or Aramaic inscription bowls.

When illicitly importing looted objects, sometimes the objects are dramatically undervalued in the customs documentation in order to avoid scrutiny. It was this type of misrepresentation that enabled the Palermo Carabinieri TPC to repatriate the gold phiale, an ancient Greek libation vessel, stolen from the Greek city of Himera. Looters stole the object from its original and sacred location in the Temple of Athena at Himera (see Fig 9.1). Himera was an ancient Greek colony located on the north coast of Sicily, just east of Palermo.

The recent history of the phiale began in 1980, when Vincent Pappalardo of Catania, a known private collector, traded it for approximately US $20,000 worth of material to another collector, Vincenzo Cammarata, who in 1991 traded it to a Swiss dealer named William Veres for approximately US $90,000 worth of objects. Veres contacted a US dealer named Robert Haber, whose client, Michael Steinhardt, was willing to pay US $1.2 million for the phiale. On 13 December 1991 Haber faxed the customs invoice to his broker at JFK airport in New York and brought the object back to the US. Steinhardt kept the object in his apartment for the following three years. On 13 December 1995 the US government filed forfeiture action for the object, based on the fact that Mr Haber had lied about the value of the object on the customs forms. Steinhardt lost on appeal, in part because the bill of sale included a clause specifying that Steinhardt would be reimbursed should the object prove to be illegal. The presence of that clause clearly indicated that Haber and Steinhardt were both aware of the possibility that the object had been looted. When

Fig 9.1.   Original location where the phiale was looted from Himera, now protected.

Fig 9.2.   Ruins of the ancient city of Himera. The location of the phiale is marked by the metal frame seen in the centre of the photo.

Steinhardt argued that confiscation of the object would be a punishment in the form of an excessive fine, the judge ruled that he had no standing as a claimant because the object belonged to the State of Italy. When the Carabinieri officer showed the author (Rush) the phiale at Himera, he proudly reminded her that the infamous violent Chicago criminal Al Capone had also been finally brought down in a similar way, by prosecution and conviction for cheating on his taxes.

ANOTHER CHALLENGE: 'FINDERS KEEPERS' RHETORIC

In the spring of 2011 the author (Rush) encountered an exhibition at the Antalya Museum showing half of a sculpture of Herakles along with interpretive panels explaining that the other half was at the Museum of Fine Arts Boston, and that the Americans were failing to return it. Fortunately, only two short years later, weary Herakles was returned to Turkey and the two halves of the sculpture rejoined. However, it is reasonable to wonder about a worldview that would lead an institution such as the Museum of Fine Arts Boston to hesitate, even for a moment, before returning half of a sculpture that was clearly stolen from an ancient Hellenistic City in Turkey. The 'arguments' and questions often posed by members of the collecting communities of the West follow intellectual pathways composed of interesting twists and turns. The issues discussed in the list below were covered in a presentation given at a regional conference by a representative of an Ivy League University in the US (Johnson-Kelly 2013). According to Gerstenblith (2013), this list is unfortunately all too typical of the 'arguments' used by opponents of the repatriation process and of international laws and agreements designed to protect cultural property.

- *Who rightfully owns the objects?* Perge was first a Greek and then a Roman city in Turkey. Individuals whose goal is to confound the repatriation process would immediately ask, 'Should Herakles go back to Greece, Italy or Perge, Turkey, the location where his upper half was stolen?' This argument is often made with respect to the Euphronios krater, a Greek vessel stolen from an Etruscan tomb in Italy. Opponents of repatriation will often ask the spurious question: 'shouldn't the Euphronios krater have gone back to Greece?' This argument conveniently ignores the probability that the krater was legally acquired and exported to ancient Etruria. It is easy for opponents of repatriation to forget that repatriation agreements offer partial resolutions for modern crimes, not solutions to mysteries of the past.
- *Why should modern people lay claim to objects from the ancient past? What gives the Turks or other peoples of today a right to objects from ancient cities that happen by accidents of history to be found within their borders?* It is not unusual at all for a Western museum or collector to attempt to argue that any museum anywhere in the world should have as much or more right to ancient objects as the people who live on the land where the ancient objects are found. The fact that many of these families still live on the lands of their ancestors and have lived there for thousands of years is again conveniently ignored.

A personal experience offers a compelling rebuttal to the fallacy that modern populations have no ties to their ancient past. On 8 May 2011 it was the author's (Rush) privilege to visit Sardis, Turkey, on the occasion of the spring festival. Every year, on the second Sunday in May, hundreds of Turkish families make the trip up the mountain valley to the ancient city of Sardis. They come in cars and vans, on foot and even in tractors and wagons, carrying all of their extended family members along with all the furniture and food required for an excellent picnic.

FIG 9.3.   AN EXTENDED FAMILY VISITS THE ANCIENT TEMPLE OF ARTEMIS AT SARDIS, TURKEY, DURING THE SPRING FESTIVAL HELD ANNUALLY ON THE FIRST SUNDAY IN MAY. 'WE HAVE COME TO BE IN THE VERY OLD PLACES.'

The valley surrounding the ancient city is filled with vendors and activities, not unlike a county fair in the United States. As we visited the Temple of Artemis, a young Turkish girl approached us and introduced herself. She was very proud and pleased to be practising her English language skills. My colleague also spoke with her in Turkish and asked her why she had come: for the food? For the fair? For the market? The young girl's answer was that she had come 'to be in the very old places' (Luke and Rush 2011, *pers comm*). In retrospect, it became clear that it had been our privilege to meet a young woman who was participating in a spring festival in part celebrating fertility and womanhood – exactly the same values celebrated in association with the goddess Artemis. There is no doubt that the inhabitants of the valley of Sardis and its surroundings have a relationship with this ancient place and its contents that cannot be contested by rational people from any other part of the world.

- *The Museums of the West should be allowed to keep stolen objects because they can take better care of these objects than institutions based in their nations of origin.* Anyone who would seriously attempt to pose this argument has never met the courageous Iraqis, Afghans, Libyans and Malians who have risked their lives to save the cultural property that is part of their heritage. There is no curatorial institution in the world that can guarantee the safety of its contents from all forms of natural and human disaster in perpetuity.
- *Repatriated objects are often stolen again and return to the black market.* There has never been a documented case of a repatriated object returning to the black market for sale to a museum collection and subjected to repeat repatriation. This 'argument' is complete fiction in its purest, most fabricated form.
- *Law enforcement officers should be focusing on far more important crimes than stolen and smuggled archaeological collections.* Clearly, the authors of a book discussing the accomplishments of the Carabinieri TPC would disagree. Tragically, families of murdered archaeological site guards all over the world would disagree even more.

As ridiculous as these 'arguments' may seem to the rational and experienced reader, when stated with confidence by museum professionals and occasionally by judges and scholars they are harmful. The existence of these ideas in Western public discourse can interfere with the progression of good faith repatriation negotiations and the development of sound agreements.

THE ITALIAN APPROACH TO REPATRIATION AGREEMENTS

A repatriation agreement between the Italian government and a foreign cultural institution is technically considered a form of international contract. Such agreements overcome the challenge posed by the fact that quite often there are legal limitations that compel private owners or institutions to return property claimed by another country (Scovazzi 2009, 35). Negotiating agreements also protects both parties from potentially unpredictable court outcomes. A healthy negotiation process also provides an opportunity for the state of origin to establish a proactive, positive relationship with the collecting institution currently holding their property. Most repatriation agreements are confidential, but the agreement negotiated between the Metropolitan Museum of Art and the Italian government has been shared with the public. Scovazzi (2009) eloquently describes the Italian approach to repatriation and its strengths, and cites the agreement between the Italian government and the Metropolitan Museum of Art as an example of what the components of such an agreement can be and what this type of negotiation can accomplish.

The agreement between the Italian government and the Metropolitan Museum of Art defines the philosophical and conceptual positions of both entities and offers a road map for future contributions to society through shared public programming efforts. In the premises of the 40-year agreement the Italians point out that the nation's archaeological heritage 'is the source of the national collective memory and a resource for historical and scientific research'. The premises of the agreement also remind all parties that in Italy it is against the law to excavate archaeological sites without permission from the Ministry of Culture. Such permission requires an application from qualified personnel with a valid research protocol. The museum points out that art museums play an important role in society by preserving and presenting the artistic achievements of civilisations and making it possible for members of museum audiences to experience these objects. The museum also states that it deplores the illicit excavation of antiquities and believes that all collecting should follow the highest criteria of professional practice.

The agreement specifies the objects to be returned and confirms that these objects were illegally excavated. The museum rejects any accusation of knowledge that the objects were of illegal provenance. The agreement also absolves the museum of any liability related to its role in the acquisition of said items. The agreement then goes on to promote cultural cooperation between the Italian government and the Metropolitan Museum of Art in the form of loans. The Italian Ministry of Culture agreed to lend cultural assets of equal beauty and historical and artistic significance in exchange for the objects being returned to Italy. In addition, the Ministry and the Commission for Cultural Assets of the Region of Sicily and the Metropolitan agreed to the possibility of the latter sponsoring authorised excavations that could eventually yield artefacts that could be borrowed by the Metropolitan for research and restoration. A corollary specifies that, after the return of such objects to Italy, these same objects could be considered for loan back to the Metropolitan. A third option offers the Metropolitan the possibility to borrow objects for the purposes of restoration by Metropolitan staff members with subsequent exhibition.

The Italians recognise that repatriation cases are complex and that, in some cases, the destination country may have acquired the objects legally under the morals and rules of the time, and may have cared for the objects in an exemplary manner for decades. Essentially, the suggested principles to follow include: non-exploitation of the weakness of one country over another for cultural gain; cooperation against illegal movement of objects over international boundaries; and preservation of the integrity of cultural contexts for the origins of the objects. The Italian model of negotiation for the repatriation of objects from major cultural institutions at the international level has demonstrated that resolution of these issues through good faith dialogue offers the potential to strengthen sound and productive relationships that can lead to loans, exhibitions and joint excavations.

REPATRIATION AND THE IMPORTANCE OF CONTEXT FOR BOTH LOCAL AND ACADEMIC
COMMUNITIES

From time to time, when stolen antiquities are returned home, the associated scholarship can lead to new insight and a more nuanced understanding of the cultural history of a region. As De Caro (2009, 17) points out, the recontextualisation of works of art from Puglia played a significant role in placing the ancient city of Ausculum in its rightful place within the art and culture of Greater Greece, Magna Graecia. Two of the works were a sculpture of griffins attacking a doe and a painted marble vessel on a base called a podanipter, decorated with Nereids, or sea nymphs, astride sea monsters. Even more importantly, as the Carabinieri reconstructed the origins of these famous works of art and found other looted objects stolen from Puglia, they began to build an entire cultural context which led to a new appreciation of the region's extraordinary heritage.

As world-class works of art, these objects would warrant places of honour in any location in Italy. Through their repatriation to institutions in Puglia, as close to their origins as possible, the sculpture and podanipter now play a critical educational role and give the people of Puglia even more reason to be proud of their important heritage.

MEDICI AND CHALLENGES OF TODAY

Sadly, even though information from the archives of the original Medici Polaroid images of looted objects is accessible to traders around the world, collectors, dealers and even the major auction houses still continue to test the market by putting looted objects up for sale (Sezgin 2014). In addition to the Medici archive, discovered by the Carabinieri in Geneva in 1995, a similar set of images, seized in Basel in 2002, exists for a second unscrupulous Italian antiquities dealer, Gianfranco Becchina. As recently as spring 2014, two items, one documented in the Medici archive and one documented in the Becchina archive, appeared on the London scene for sale – the former at Christie's and the latter at Bonhams. The object at Bonhams was a Greek vessel called a pyxis, a cylindrical box with a separate lid, used by women in the ancient world to hold cosmetics. Women of wealth were often buried with their personal belongings, such as the pyxis, so it is highly likely that the object came from a looted tomb. Becchina sold the pyxis to Ariadne Galleries in New York City in 1987. It appears that the gallery owner had been holding on to the object for over 25 years in the hope that if he waited long enough to sell it, it would not be recognised. The second object, a Greek glass oinochoe for sale at Christie's, was sold by Sotheby's in 1988. Given the fact that Sotheby's had handled hundreds of looted objects for Medici in the 1980s (Watson and Todeschini 2007), the sales history should have served as a warning to Christie's. The oinochoe, an object similar to a small pitcher, was initially sold again in 2013 as part of a collection at Christie's but was then withdrawn from sale owing to being damaged in storage.

The legacy of the Medici crimes continues with the UK liquidation firm BDO, an organisation that has been tasked by Her Majesty's government with selling the holdings of Robin Symes as a way of recovering his unpaid taxes. The Italians warned BDO that many of the objects they were considering for sale were the property of the Italian government, had been illegally removed from Italian territory and were in Symes' custody as a result of criminal behaviour. As of 2014, rumours within the archaeology and law enforcement communities indicated that the firm was planning to sell the Symes collection in the Middle East and especially in Abu Dhabi, where several new museums are being built. If BDO should attempt to proceed with such a sale then an Italian prosecutor may choose to file suit against principals of BDO under the 2003 *Dealing in Cultural Offences Act*. The potential penalties could be up to seven years' imprisonment and unlimited fines (Ruiz and Pes 2014).

Dr Christos Tsirogiannis, a former member of the Greek Antiquities Task Force and now at Cambridge University, has conscientiously compared objects appearing for sale in the London auction houses and potentially by BDO with the images from the Becchina and Medici archive. In addition to calling attention to the two objects up for sale in 2014, he also identified an attempt by Bonhams to sell four looted Roman sculptures in 2010 (Alberge 2010). Sadly, objects looted decades ago continue to be hidden away and will continue to reappear for decades to come. Without vigilance and law enforcement professionals such as Dr Tsirogiannis and the Carabinieri TPC, the crimes committed by individuals such as Medici and Becchina will, sadly, continue to pay.

10

Fakes, Forgeries and Money Laundering

FORGERY IN ITALIAN CULTURE AND SOCIETY

There is no doubt about the importance of art in Italian society or the fact that this cultural value dates back hundreds, if not thousands, of years. Most agree that Italian artists have been among the greatest contributors to Western civilisation. This combination of values has also generated a subculture and tradition of forgery. Some forgers are talented artists in their own right and it is not unusual for Italians to figure among the best. Discussions of the history of forgery in Italy often begin with ancient Roman emulation of Greek sculpture (Fleming 1975, 6). The Romans considered Greek sculpture to be superior, so Roman sculptors worked to copy the style and figures of the Greeks. These activities might not have been considered forgery at the time but appear to be considered by scholars of forgery as one of the first examples of, at the very least, 'imitation' in the Western world. Phaedrus, the fabulist, wrote poetry that included accounts of forgery of silver coinage across the Roman Empire during the reign of Augustus, and there exists archaeological evidence of counterfeiting in Britain under the Romans (Fleming 1975, 6). According to Fleming (1975, 14), the year 1524 marks the first literary documentation of a forgery among paintings. An author named Pietro Summonte described the activities of a Neapolitan artist named Niccolò Antonio Colantonio who, 70 years earlier, was said to have copied a portrait of the Duke of Burgundy so successfully that when the copy was returned in place of the original, the owner did not notice.

It was not until 1735 that a European country, England, issued the very first example of copyright laws – then limited to engraved art (*Engraving Copyright Act*). Up until that point, counterfeiters had not faced any criminal convictions and the worst that could happen to them was to fall from grace and lose the 'protection' of their patrons (Andros 2014).

Following the adoption of these and subsequent laws over the next 200 years, the counterfeiter has come to be seen no longer as an artist with valid talent and skills, but rather as a criminal. In Italy the falsification of artworks was not addressed by specific laws until 1939 and counterfeiters were still condemned under the 'Counterfeiting of Private Writing' article of the criminal code. It was not until 1971 that Italy issued a law regulating the forgery of works of art (ibid).

Currently, the penalty for forging artworks in Italy ranges from three months' to four years' imprisonment and a fine ranging between €103 and €3099, along with publication of the charges in at least three national newspapers. In 2001 the Italian State emphasised that forgers of contemporary art are subject to the same penalties (ibid).

During the second half of the 19th century such dramatic archaeological discoveries as the tombs filled with the treasure of the Egyptians and Etruscans encouraged the collecting of archaeological objects. As the popularity of collecting increased, so did the incidence of forgery, to meet the demands of a burgeoning market. The Vatican may have had the world's first department

FIG 10.1. A WELL-EXECUTED FAKE OF MODIGLIANI'S PAINTING *PORTRAIT OF JANE*, RECOVERED IN 2002 FROM A HOUSE NEAR ROME.

entirely dedicated to authentication, which was also initiated in the late 19th century (Craddock 2009, 1).

The numerous motives for forgery dramatically increase the complexity of the law enforcement challenges. In addition to relatively straightforward creations of fake contemporary art intended for a gullible gallery and collector market, motives for forgery can begin with a famous artist offering his signature to the work of struggling friends. This type of forgery can be difficult to trace as the signature is authentic and the material, methods and possibly style will be contemporary with the genuine artist. There is a suspicion that Modigliani may have signed paintings for friends (see Fig 10.1). A related issue is the existence of contemporary art workshops where teams of artists may create works of art that are ultimately signed by a highly respected individual. In the past there existed 'schools' of artists where apprentices and students learned to master the styles and techniques of recognised geniuses. Sometimes the workshop model also complicates the authentication of indigenous art. For example, in some Australian aboriginal families, a senior family member and artist may 'own' the story and create the essential features of the painting but leave the filling in of tiny dots to relatives (Barkham 2001).

Another motive for forgery is the creation of a duplicate to replace a stolen original in a museum, gallery or private collection, potentially delaying or preventing discovery of the theft. Collectors and institutions sometimes commission replicas for exhibition so that the original object can be secured and stored in climate-controlled conditions. There is consensus in the museum community that replicas of this nature should be created with a feature or marking that easily distinguishes the replica from the original.

To further complicate matters, forgers attempt to stay ahead of the law not just in cases of expressing artistic genius but also by mastering extraordinarily complex techniques and methods. For example, when archaeologists publish new discoveries for understanding ancient technology used to create works of art in antiquity, forgers stand ready to duplicate ancient technology in the creation of a modern object. For example, a Greek vase created using original sources of clay material then fired and glazed using ancient recipes may be more difficult to distinguish from an original than a duplicate made elsewhere and fed into a modern kiln.

There are many techniques for making objects look old, at both the visual and the molecular level. In Afghanistan, for example, talented craftsmen create British Enfield rifle duplicates, bury them in the desert for a while then unearth them looking much older. These objects are very popular for sale to NATO service members. Forgers have even been known to use medical radiation therapy to confound thermo-luminescence dating techniques. In 2012 Italian law enforcement announced the arrest of a ring of thieves that included, among others, an archaeologist who worked for the superintendence of Lazio, a ceramics expert and a nurse. The potter ground up ancient objects and mixed this material with modern clay to create his replicas. In order to jeopardise any attempt to test the authenticity of the object using modern dating techniques, the nurse arranged for the objects to be irradiated using an X-ray machine at a hospital in Tivoli. The extra dose of radiation gives the object a much older thermo-luminescent signature. The archaeologist then authenticated the objects and stored many of them at his home. The operation was uncovered when a wealthy collector who had been cooperating with the thieves became suspicious of the increasing number of objects he was being offered for sale. This individual was finally confronted with the truly criminal nature of his accomplices first-hand when assailants broke into his home to steal an object that the group had indicated they wanted (Di Chio 2011).

THREE TYPES OF FORGERY IN MODERN ITALY UNDER THE LAW

A major component of the Carabinieri TPC law enforcement efforts targets crime associated with fraudulent artwork and the network of illegal activity surrounding it, such as smuggling, black marketeering and money laundering. Cases of forgery are handled by the forgery division of the operative unit in Rome in cooperation with regional units that encounter fraudulent works of art on a regular basis. Italian law, Article 178, Legislative Decree 42/2004, Code of Cultural Heritage and Landscape defines three different types of forgery. The first is counterfeiting, where a work of art is meticulously copied so that the reproduction can be mistaken for and sold as the original. Colonel Cortellessa used a seized example of Morandi's 'Flowers', oil on canvas, as an example of counterfeiting in his presentation at Basel (Cortellessa 2012).

Second is alteration: changing the essence of an original work by adding or removing details or making other kinds of modifications. Alteration can also include changing a work of art to facilitate its illegal export, for example by painting over a stolen canvas with removable pigments. One example of alteration presented by the Carabinieri was the attempt to smuggle a Guercino out of Italy by painting a contemporary work over it. The border officer noticed that the canvas seemed too old when compared with the image on its surface. He seized the painting and the stolen Guercino was discovered underneath (Manola and Ragusa 2012). In cases of alteration, the changes could make the work attributable to a different artist. Alterations also include sectioning, where a stolen painting is cut into sections, so that the portions are more difficult to trace and can be sold separately.

The third type of criminal forgery under Italian Law is reproduction, where original works of art are copied and sold as originals. Reproductions may be unauthorised lithographs, etchings, silk screens and multiple castings of sculpture. Criminal reproduction also includes making more copies than the artist has authorised. A significant related crime is authenticating a work of art that is known to be false.

A very important aspect of Italian law governing forgery is that it is designed to hold every contributor responsible for every phase of the crime. If we consider forgery as a process, the potentially guilty individuals could include (Croce 2007):

- the artist who created or altered the false object;
- the gallery owner or merchant who facilitated the sale of the false object;
- the scholar who provided a false statement of authentication in return for money;
- the forger who prepared false documentation concerning the history of the object;
- the smuggler who transported the object across international boundaries;
- the actor who pretended to be the artist, greeting and reassuring the collectors who purchased the false object.

THE ITALIAN MARKET

There are many gifted Italian artists who are capable of creating convincing forgeries and reproductions, especially of objects of contemporary art. They either sell these objects or work directly with criminal networks that traffic the objects via sophisticated international markets. One common approach is to illegally export the objects to countries that have not signed international treaties governing trade in cultural property and then move them back into the mainstream international networks. International law enforcement agencies are faced with complex and well-established criminal organisations; successful investigation requires international cooperation.

It is critical to remember the economic impact of these illegal activities. In the first half of 2012 alone, the economic value of forged artwork seized by the Carabinieri TPC was approximately €40.4 million. In the first six months of 2012, the Carabinieri TPC recovered 3426 forged works of contemporary art, 577 false archaeological and palaeontological objects and 239 fake antiques, books and archival items; in total, 4242 forgeries. Some forgeries were attributed to the Chinese, but the Italians take credit for the perfect copies as 'made in Italy' (*Inside Art* 2012). Internet sales, unscrupulous dealers and fake catalogues all help to move the fake objects through the art market. This highly significant multi-million-dollar black market affects the potential not only for legitimate jobs but also for the contribution of taxation of legal transactions to the Italian economy (*paperblog* 2012).

OPERATION 'PLOTTER'

Operation 'Plotter', the first case to be prosecuted at the international level under Italian legal code 146/2006, is an example of the international market in fraudulent contemporary art. The Italians received information that galleries in Florida and California were selling fakes. It is interesting to note that of the fakes and forgeries seized by the Carabinieri TPC from 2010 to 2011, 84% were fraudulent works of contemporary art (Cortellessa 2012). As they continued the investigation, the TPC staked out the premises of the suspected forgers who were working in Italy, took photographs of the counterfeiters carrying the paintings wrapped in brown paper and, in one case, even got a picture of one of the forgers signing his fake painting outdoors, using the boot of a car for support (Ilari 2011, *pers comm*). In late 2010, officers from the regional office in Monza testified in San Francisco, one of the locations where an art gallery was selling the forged works of art created in Italy. In order to successfully investigate and prosecute this case, the Carabinieri cooperated with the US legal attaché in Rome, the US Federal Bureau of Investigation (FBI) and even US Postal inspectors, as one aspect of the case was the use of the US Postal Service to transport fraudulent material.

THE MODIGLIANI AFFAIR

Forgers can be unbelievably bold. In the autumn of 2010 the city of Palestrina hosted an exhibition of the works of Amedeo Modigliani at the National Museum of Archaeology of Palestrina (see Fig 10.2). This exhibition was a major event for Palestrina and the community organised other activities and festivals to celebrate the arrival of the masterpieces. There was evidently some suspicion surrounding the exhibition titled *Modigliani from Classicism to Cubism*, so Carabinieri TPC officers filmed the content. Examining the film, they realised that not all of the works could be authentic, and found that 22 of the approximately 50 works on display were forgeries (*La Stampa* 2012a). As they began to investigate further, it became clear that the exhibition in Palestrina was not the only event at which fake Modigliani masterpieces were appearing; the criminals had in fact organised an entire exhibit tour with venues in Italy (such as the Ursino Castle in Catania) and abroad (as far away as Bangkok, Thailand). One of the main purposes of these exhibitions was to give credibility to the fraudulent works of art in order to increase their value for sale to unsuspecting art collectors.

Fig 10.2.   The National Archaeological Museum of Palestrina is located in the Renaissance Palazzo Barberini. It would require considerable bravado to organise an exhibition filled with fakes intended to travel the world and even more bravado to include high-profile national museums as venues.

As the investigation unfolded, it became clear that the fraudulent activity dated back to at least 1984 – the 100th anniversary of the artist's birth. At that point, there was a legend in Livorno that Modigliani had attempted sculpture, become discouraged and thrown his efforts into a canal called the Fosso Mediceo. In order to attract publicity for a local exhibition honouring the centenary, the organiser, a woman named Vera Durbè, along with the Livorno City Council, decided to dredge the canal, looking for the sculptures. After eight days and many jokes about the objects that were dredged up, a granite 'head' emerged, followed by two more. Vera and her brother Dario, curator of the Modern Art Gallery of Rome, declared the objects authentic Modiglianis and the exhibition attracted the audience that had been hoped for. Only the art historian Federico Zeri was sceptical and declared the objects to be 'immature' if authentic (*Livorno Now* 2009). In reality, four teenagers had created one of the heads using a Black & Decker drill, and they happily reproduced their effort on Italian television. The producer of the others was a dock worker and art lover named Angelo Froglia (Norese 2007). Imagine the surprise of the teenagers and the dock worker when fake sculptures appeared that were not their own.

Although the episode appeared to be a joke, Jeanne Modigliani, the daughter of the artist, had been outspoken in stating that these sculptures could not have been her father's work. Around this time, she was found injured at the foot of a staircase in mysterious circumstances and died very shortly afterwards of a cerebral haemorrhage. There were suspicions that her death was murder, but the case was dismissed (*La Stampa* 2012b; *La Repubblica* 1984). Now, however, her death takes on even greater significance as it appears that her colleague and confidant, Christian Parisot, the president of the Modigliani Archives, has been organising the forgery and sale of fake Modiglianis ever since. Parisot even sought to enhance his reputation by offering his expertise as a consultant to the Carabinieri TPC. Jeanne's daughter Laura has been unsuccessful in the Italian courts in her attempts to regain control of her grandfather's archives from Mr Parisot (Cohen 2014).

Careful examination of the fraudulent works revealed some of the forgers' methods. For the two-dimensional paintings, the authentic works were scanned, reproduced and affixed to vintage or aged paper with hand finishing (*La Stampa* 2012a). The bronzes were complete fabrications and have since been traced to a foundry in New York, USA (ibid). The method for selling the forgeries was simple: after the objects appeared in high profile exhibitions the dealer offered them for sale, while Mr Parisot provided authentication and reassured the buyers. Mr Parisot's former affiliation as a consultant to the Carabinieri was even used to the criminals' advantage. The financial rewards were significant. The fake Modigliani drawings sold for €60,000–70,000 each, while the bronzes started at €75,000. In late 2012 Mr Parisot was put under house arrest, facing criminal trial. It is also interesting to note that a respected art historian named Marc Restellini ceased work on an authoritative survey of Modigliani's work when he began to receive death threats from angry collectors who feared that works in their collections would be declared fakes (Cohen 2014).

PREVENTING FORGED WORKS OF ART FROM ENTERING THE MARKETPLACE

From the perspective of the police, preventive measures include very careful observation of the art markets and paying attention to works of art moving through galleries and on the internet. Unscrupulous gallery owners and art dealers begin to gain a reputation for fraud and the Carabinieri follows their activities very closely (Cortellessa 2012). Once these individuals and businesses are identified it becomes easier for law enforcement to discourage them from selling forged material with the threat of investigation and documentation leading to criminal prosecution. Some of the most helpful sources of information are fraud victims. Once a customer realises that the artwork they have purchased is a forgery, they can provide extremely helpful information regarding the source of the sale. Another powerful tool in curbing the market in forged contemporary art is the education of prospective buyers, encouraging them to conduct careful research and purchase cautiously. The existence of more than one known 'original' and the presence of more 'originals' than a famous artist is known to have created are both huge warning signs of forgery.

IL MUSEO DEL FALSO

Policing methods for detecting fraudulent art can be as simple as inspecting print shops, galleries and warehouses across Italy. The Carabinieri TPC also pursues scientific investigation of fakes and forgeries. This interest, combined with the fact that many of the fake artworks are extraordinary works of art in their own right, resulted in a 2003 agreement between the Carabinieri TPC

Fig 10.3.   During house searches in Naples in September 2011, the CC TPC seized 62 paintings, skillfully forged and fraudulently attributed to famous Neapolitan artists of the 1800s and 1900s such as Pratella, Asturi, Iroli, Lautrec and Guttuso. The Carabinieri's monitoring of online auction websites led to the discovery of the fake paintings.

Corps and the Museo del Falso (Museum of Fakes) at the University of Salerno. In the past, the Carabinieri destroyed all of the fraudulent works of art it seized, but, following the creation of the Museum of Fakes in 1991, the Carabinieri TPC donated thousands of confiscated objects, providing tangible evidence of fraud to art experts and collectors (see Fig 10.3).

Unfortunately, owing to a lack of proper funding and a decline in interest from the field, the Museum of Fakes closed 20 years later, in 2011, having widely served its purpose of fighting counterfeiting. Among the counterfeited artworks the Carabinieri Corps donated to the Museum were fake Warhols and paintings attributed to a famous Italian contemporary artist, Mario Schifano. To provide perspective on the sums of money involved, a legitimate Schifano would sell for US $500,000. The forgers were so convincing that fake Schifanos showed up in an exhibition at the Royal Palace in Caserta. In some cases, forgers or criminal dealers have been known to hire actors to pose as contemporary artists in order to convince collectors that the object is real; one such duped collector was sure that he had met Schifano (Modianot-Fox 2008).

The mission of the Museum of Fakes was to 'analyze the evolution of forgery, from technique to organization, and to give visitors the opportunity to see firsthand how the counterfeiters carry out their deception' (ibid). In addition to the sample works of art, the museum also had an extensive and representative collection of the tools and materials 'of the trade', offering an

opportunity to research methods for forgery, leading to the development of increasingly sophisticated techniques for authentication.

When the museum closed in 2011, its Director, Professor Casillo, declared that 'the Museum
had served its purpose by generating broad awareness of the spreading of fakes and forgeries,
providing tangible examples to the most sceptical art experts' (Bojano 2011).

In general, the authentication of artwork begins with visual inspection of the object.
Depending on the skill of the forger, sometimes detecting a fake can be as simple as noticing
that the forger misspelled the signature of the alleged famous artist or recognising that the
clothing on characters in a painting would be impossible to take off or put on. Thorough and
detailed scholarly knowledge of objects, especially objects of antiquity, also contributes to the
analysis. For example, Attic painters, named after their Greek province of origin, were known to
begin decorating their vases with sketches and engravings beneath the finished images and they
sometimes divided the objects into horizontal sections (Fleming 1975, 18). Visual analysis can be
augmented by using microscopes to examine the surface of the object for ageing and X-rays to
determine the presence or absence of other images beneath the surface. Another example would
be an understanding of ancient Egyptian sculpture. The ancient Egyptians viewed inanimate
versions of living creatures as having living spirits of their own. It would therefore be unlikely
that an ancient Egyptian would create a statue of a creature such as a cat where the animal and
its base were one single sculpted object; one would expect the cat to be sculpted as an individual
entity and then attached to a base if necessary. Recently, while working on an Egyptian sculpture
that had been in the collection for a very long time, a conservator at a prominent US museum
discovered that the subject and base had been sculpted as one object and as a result suspects the
object of being an historic forgery.

The examination of scientific variables also provides insight into whether an object is an
authentic work of art or antiquity, beginning with determination of the object's true age. Ageing
techniques are based on the materials involved, so dendrochronology – tree-ring dating – is
appropriate for objects made of wood or paintings on wood panels; radiocarbon dating for any
object with organic components; and thermo-luminescence dating for ceramics. Art historians
have aggregated vast amounts of detailed data concerning components of pigments over time,
enabling the authentication of pigment within the paintings in question. For example, if a
pigment contains a form of titanium dioxide white that was unavailable prior to the 20th century
then the painting has either been subject to restoration or cannot be original.

The above-mentioned Professor Salvatore Casillo, a sociologist and former director of the
Museum of Fakes in Salerno, has over 20 years' experience of studying fakes and forgeries. Statistics relating to the sheer numbers of forgeries in circulation, in collections and on the market, are
staggering; furthermore, there are multiple motives behind the creation of forgeries. According
to Professor Casillo, as of 1961 in the US alone there were over 100,000 paintings attributed
to Jean-Baptiste-Camille Corot (1796–1875), even though he was known to have actually only
painted 3000 canvases during his lifetime. Forgery of fine art is a trade that dates back hundreds
of years and is steeped in a fascinating history of colourful characters.

WIDER GLOBAL MARKETS AND MONEY LAUNDERING

As devastating as it may be for a buyer who bought in good faith to discover that they are in
possession of a forgery, stolen art, fakes, forgeries and art smuggling all provide criminals the

opportunity to conceal even more significant crimes. As illustrated by the Ferreira case (Cohen 2013), the purchase of works of art and their subsequent transportation to foreign countries using false paperwork is one way to protect illegally gained assets that may be subject to seizure in the country of origin. False documents can range from simple statements of (far lower) value to completely false identities and origins for the objects. As an example, as part of Ferreira's efforts to move his ill-gotten gains from Brazil to the US, the painting 'Hannibal' by Jean-Michel Basquiat arrived in New York with a customs valuation of US $100, causing it initially to clear automatically when in fact it may be worth as much as US $8 million.

Money laundering is not only a feature of attempts to hide assets that may be subject to taxation or seizure; it also is a crucial component in realising profits from a wide range of illegal activities such as drug running and arms dealing. When someone is making large sums of money that cannot be explained through legal enterprises, that individual needs to devise a way to hide the illegally gained sums and make them appear as legitimately earned income. As Cohen (2013) points out, the discretionary nature of the art market offers many opportunities and advantages for criminals and criminal organisations. The advantages of using trade in contemporary and forged works of art include the fact that the valuation of contemporary art can be arbitrary. The art market is easily manipulated and valuations of works of art can vary by millions of dollars (Shubert 2013). To compound the issue, the identities of collectors, buyers and sellers are kept secret by galleries and auction houses, a huge advantage for criminals in contrast to, for example, real estate transactions, where identities have to be included in deeds and titles.

In 2006 and 2007 presentations to the European Police College (CEPOL), Officers of the Carabinieri TPC warned European police forces of this issue. The Italians pointed out the diverse set of roles that criminal organisations can play within art markets:

- they can put stolen works of art and looted archaeological materials up for sale;
- they can act as intermediaries between private collectors and professional thieves;
- they can use dealers to artificially raise the value of works of unknown artists, and buy the paintings or other art objects from themselves at astronomical prices. They can also use this process to sell the paintings to innocent collectors at artificially high prices;
- they can use illicit funds to buy works of art that they sell at public auction, receiving valid cheques signed and certified by the auction houses.

The presentations also identified weaknesses in law enforcement that make these activities easier for potential offenders:

- lack of forces that specialise in art crime in some countries;
- lack of coordination between different police forces both within countries and at the international level and various official administrative offices;
- lack of enforcement agency familiarity with all of the diverse methods for selling cultural objects of illegal origin;
- slow exchange of information between countries affected by illicit trafficking;
- the failure by many nations to establish specialised archives or data systems dedicated solely to works of art and antiquities;
- inconsistencies in and, within some countries, the complete absence of legislation concerning money laundering;
- many countries' failure to sign and ratify international accords.

One of the purposes of the CEPOL course was to emphasise the importance of combatting art crime by reminding representatives of policing agencies of the magnitude of the problem across Europe. The course was also designed to improve networking between officers and policing agencies in order to improve international cooperation in combatting the trafficking of illicit cultural property.

BASEL

It is interesting to note that the not-for-profit Basel Institute for Governance has raised the issue of the art market's role in current underworld crimes and transactions. The Basel Institute is an independent organisation that specialises in corruption prevention and public governance, corporate governance and compliance, fighting money laundering, criminal law enforcement and the recovery of stolen assets. In 2009 the Institute hosted an international conference titled 'Governance of Cultural Property: Preservation and Recovery', a gathering intended to draw attention to increasing international concern surrounding crime and the art market. The Basel conference offered a series of workshops including 'The Role of Museums and Collections', 'Art Business: Where to Draw the Line', 'International Conventions and National Laws' and 'Self-Regulation and Voluntary Codes', all featuring internationally recognised speakers. On the second day there were two additional workshops covering 'Technical Aspects of Recovery/Money Laundering' and 'Protection of Cultural Property in Conflict Situations'. The plenary session featured one of the academic community's leading advocates for cessation of an institutional market for looted antiquities, Dr Neil Brodie.

It is especially appropriate for the Basel Institute for Governance to take a proactive interest in the issue of art crime as Basel is also the home of Art Basel, sometimes referred to as 'the Olympics of the Art World'. Through its focus on contemporary and modern art, Art Basel is one of the premier international venues for presenting authentic masterpieces to the world.

From an historical perspective, art forgery may have begun shortly after the very first work of art was exchanged for money. Motives for faking art can range from creating objects that can be used to launder money to a talented but unappreciated artist wishing to embarrass an artworld that has offered only rejection. As long as the potential for illegal profit exists, forgery will continue, but the Carabinieri TPC offers formidable opposition.

11

Who Are the Officers of the Carabinieri TPC?

Members of the Carabinieri TPC are, first and foremost, police officers. In order to become a member of the TPC Corps, regardless of academic background you must first serve in the general law enforcement units and gain as much experience as possible in developing police investigation skills. One of the TPC captains interviewed by the author (Rush), whose credentials included a doctoral degree in archaeology, spent ten years focusing on mafia investigations before qualifying for TPC training. If a serving Carabinieri TPC officer is asked whether he is an archaeologist, a lawyer or a data analyst, he will respond patiently to such a strange question: 'I am a police officer'.

Lieutenant Colonel Roberto Colasanti graciously explained to the authors some of the selection criteria and summarised the four phases of training for a serving officer in the Carabinieri TPC (Colasanti 2013, *pers comm*). These begin with an introductory course in law enforcement roles and responsibilities before moving on to a practical phase during which the new officer can learn on the job and where their attributes as a TPC candidate are evaluated. The process continues with a third phase during which the selected TPC candidates receive specialised TPC academic training. A field assignment represents the fourth and final phase, during which the candidate is deployed alongside an experienced colleague in order to gain experience under close supervision while continuing to be rigorously evaluated. Ultimately, in order to be permanently assigned to the TPC Corps, the new candidate must complete all phases of training, achieving a level of 'excellent' or 'above average'.

All Carabinieri officers, regardless of their ultimate specialty or assignment, begin service at Phase One with an educational introduction to law enforcement principles and general policing appropriate to their professional and academic background. As stated above, this training focuses on Carabinieri law enforcement roles and responsibilities. Introductory training is also custom-ised to fit the officers' future roles within the force, either as a Commanding Officer, Captain, Major, Colonel or General; a non-Commanding Officer, Marshal or Brigadier; or a serving law enforcement officer or policeman. The Commanding Officers will serve in positions of respon-sibility at the executive or director levels; the non-Commanding Officers will be responsible for command of smaller units. The serving police officers in 'the ranks' will be destined for operational tasks. The relationship between Commanding and non-Commanding officers in the Carabinieri is similar to US military service, where there are Commissioned Officers who train at the Academies or with the Reserve Officer Training Corps and non-Commissioned Officers who emerge out of the enlisted ranks (Ministero per i Beni Culturali 2008).

All potential candidates must also complete Phase Two. In contrast to academic Phase One, Phase Two offers practical experience. New officers are assigned to regional units of Carabinieri and work in routine law enforcement, learning methods associated with the regular duties of maintaining order and public safety at the community level. For an officer potentially interested in joining the TPC, this phase is especially important as the trainees' direct superiors assess their performances for skills and attitude. The trainees are ranked on a scale: excellent, above average, average, below average or not meeting the standards. If a candidate shows aptitude for the TPC during the course of Phase Two, they are given the opportunity to transition to a specialised academic cultural property policing course, or Phase Three.

AFTER PHASES ONE AND TWO: CRITERIA FOR SELECTION OF POTENTIAL TPC CANDIDATES

Carabinieri officers are selected for the TPC section using a wide range of criteria, but are always chosen from active officers of the Carabinieri Corps (CC) who have successfully completed Phases One and Two. The non-Commanding officers may be selected from those who graduated from a high school specialising in the humanities (where Latin and Greek are compulsory), an Art Institute, or a Technical Institute. These are three of the many high school options available to middle school students in Italy. Applicants to the position of non-Commanding officer who possess only a high school diploma should also demonstrate an interest in fields related to sculpture, painting and/or precious or semi-precious metal artwork.

TPC Corps candidates can also be individuals who have completed a university or college degree from a private or public university in the fields of Architecture, Archaeological and Environmental Sciences, Archival and Library Sciences, Restoration and Conservation of Historical, Artistic and Cultural Heritage, Archaeology or Law prior to becoming active Carabinieri. These candidates may continue their education within the Carabinieri Police Academy as they work towards becoming Commanding Officers.

Candidates that are already Commanding Officers within the Carabinieri and have completed two years of Military Academy coursework in Modena and three years at the School for Officers in Rome may also apply to become CC TPC officers. Upon completing Military Academy, a Commanding Officer for the TPC usually obtains a Doctoral Degree in Strategic Sciences, Archaeology, Art History or Jurisprudence.

Candidates for the TPC Corps may thus stem from a variety of backgrounds but it is their personal interests, attributes and education that ultimately determine whether they are chosen to become part of this specialised section of the Carabinieri Corps. In addition to the above-mentioned credentials, additional factors may be candidates' specific interests in any of the following areas: sacred art, numismatics, the history of past civilisations, world history, photography or advanced fine arts education in areas such as painting and drawing or printmaking (Tiberi 2008). In general, TPC Corps candidates with postgraduate training in any of these arts-related areas are usually very well received.

Another skill sought in potential candidates is written and spoken fluency in several languages. Knowledge of foreign languages is considered a necessity for an effective TPC officer and especially for the new candidates, who are required to travel and stay abroad for long periods of time. The Carabinieri TPC is in constant collaboration with foreign police forces; thus, the ability to speak many different languages ensures the timely and efficient exchange of information crucial for productive investigations.

PHASE THREE – ACADEMIC INTRODUCTION TO CULTURAL PROPERTY AND RELATED ISSUES: COURSE FOR POTENTIAL TPC OFFICERS

The preferred candidate for the TPC section is an officer who has already undergone a considerable amount of training, in addition to having excelled during the practical assignments and investigation techniques experienced during Phase Two. Following initial selection, the TPC candidate undergoes intense preliminary training for four and a half weeks to acquire basic knowledge in cultural heritage and issues related to its protection, as well as investigative techniques specifically aimed at fighting crimes against art. The training begins with an historical and organisational introduction to the TPC very similar to the chronology and information offered in the introductory chapter of this book (Chapter 1).

INTRODUCTORY COURSE PART ONE

The new officer is introduced to the specific law enforcement responsibilities of the Command:

- controlling archaeological areas and commercial activities related to archaeology;
- specialised investigations with the goal of recovering cultural property and art objects and monitoring dedicated websites;
- the establishment and management of Banca Dati *Leonardo*;
- specialised consultation on behalf of the Ministry of Culture and its regional organisations.

More specifically, the officers are reminded that they will be responsible for:

- investigating crimes resulting in damage to art, whether those crimes are related to theft, fencing stolen objects, illegal archaeological excavations or counterfeiting, and then preparing the cases for referral to judicial authorities;
- recovering cultural property that has been stolen and/or smuggled outside of Italian borders, working together with INTERPOL in addition to the police forces and judicial authorities of other nations;
- aiding the identification of violations of the standards of protection for the landscape;
- providing security for exhibitions and antiquities markets and tracking the catalogues of the important auction houses, in addition to monitoring sales online, in antique shops and objects appearing in restoration laboratories (and other activities within the heritage sector);
- effectively preventing damage in sensitive archaeological areas in cooperation with regional police, airborne enforcement, mounted police and maritime security.

New officers are also reminded that, using the databank, they will be responsible for tracking the activities of known criminals in the arts sector and documenting events resulting in theft or damage to art or antiquities. The purpose of collecting and managing these vast amounts of data is to assist the force in elucidating patterns of behaviour and crime – knowledge that can be applied to future investigations.

Once an understanding of the TPC's basic organisation and its essential responsibilities has been established, training shifts to current or new initiatives and partnerships. For example, in 2008, examples of cooperative effort included the TPC's partnership with the Museum of Fakes at the University of Salerno, an archaeological site documentation and mapping programme at the University of Lecce, the EU COINS (Combat Online Illegal Numismatic Sales) project, the 'Discovering Magna Graecia' project (a joint effort with the Region of Calabria that included monitoring sites using satellite photography) and, through the Agency for European Integration and Economic Development based in Austria, a twinning project with the Romanian Ministry of Culture and Religious Affairs, designed to help the Romanians to protect their cultural heritage. There is no question that the collaborative nature of Carabinieri operations is emphasised throughout the introductory course, as is the importance of the ability to work effectively with police forces from around the world and with INTERPOL.

INTRODUCTORY COURSE PART TWO

The course's second set of topics introduce crimes specific to the arts. Discussion begins with an introduction to the nature of criminals that Carabinieri officers are likely to encounter during their careers. The course points out that, in recent times, criminals have begun to specialise and to form organisations that specialise, in specific types of crime. Art criminals often specialise in types of targets. Some may focus on stealing paintings while others may be more interested in manuscripts or antiquities. Criminals also pride themselves on having special skills. Some may be talented forgers while others are experts at picking locks, discovering tombs or crossing international borders while carrying stolen objects. The course goes on to introduce all of these skills and methods in the greatest possible detail, concentrating on:

- methods for altering an object to make it more difficult for law enforcement to identify, whether intercepted during smuggling or when it reappears on the market;
- methods for altering an object to change the original function, such as changing a stolen historic confessional into a bar or piece of furniture;
- smuggling with an emphasis on the networks that collaborate to move objects across international borders, methods for hiding objects in vehicles and luggage and methods for disguising valuable works of art;
- falsification of documentation in order to provide provenance and authenticity for stolen and looted objects;
- methods for bringing stolen and illicit objects to the market, from individual internet sales to lots at the world's most elite auction houses;
- illegal excavations with discussion of the variation amongst individuals who loot archaeological sites, the devastating damage caused and the loss of knowledge that results from these crimes;
- forgery or falsification, an extremely complex subject that can apply to alterations of artworks as mentioned above, but can also result in the creation of objects designed to duplicate famous and valuable works of art to be sold as authentic originals. Antiquities can also be falsified.

The course also emphasises that the law is designed to hold everyone in the chain of forgery responsible for their crimes. As a result, everyone from the 'artist' who creates the forged, falsified or altered object through the person who advertises the object for sale to the person who delivers the object to the unwitting purchaser can be arrested, charged and convicted of the acts committed through their part in the illegal process. In order to ensure law enforcement is as effective as possible all along this chain, the officers in training need to become familiar with all aspects associated with the forgery and sale of fraudulent objects.

Introductory Course Part Three

The third major section of the course is a comprehensive introduction to Italian legislation as it relates to the protection of cultural property. In contrast to the US, which first began to enact heritage law more than 100 years after the creation of the federation, the protection of cultural property is clearly articulated in Article 117 of the Constitution of the State of Italy. As the course progresses systematically, it begins with the constitutional reference and immediately introduces the essential principles of conservation and preservation. The course then moves on to definitions of cultural patrimony and types of cultural property, with characterisation of what is meant by protection. The role of the State is introduced with discussion of the responsibilities delegated to the Ministries along with explanation of the structure for regional cooperation. The significance of cultural property in community identity is also acknowledged, in addition to recognition of the critical value of sacred objects. In essence, the legal basis, definitions and guidelines for all aspects of Carabinieri TPC law enforcement actions are laid out for the new officers in exquisite detail.

Following their preliminary training, the candidates undergo even more specific preparation to hone their knowledge and skills as applied to art crimes. The new candidates attend courses offered by the Cultural Heritage Ministry, usually delivered by university professors who specialise in the subject areas being covered. Some of the courses cover legal and historical problems for selected geographical areas, in addition to training in the use of specific software, internet search engines and applications for web-related investigation.

Phase Four: After the Formal Course...

After completing Phase Three of the training, the new CC TPC candidate is ready for Phase Four. At this point, he or she is transferred to the detachment or regional office where there exists the opportunity to learn in the field from veteran officers who serve as mentors while observing the candidate's performance. At the end of the year, two Superior Officers evaluate the new candidate using the 'excellent' to 'below average' ranking system. In order to achieve a permanent assignment to the TPC, the candidate must rank at the excellent or above average level.

Once within a regional assignment, there are also opportunities to attend more specific courses, usually coordinated with local universities or other higher art institutions, as needed. Continuous, diverse opportunities for education and training ensure that each individual officer becomes a unique and specific asset of the CC TPC organisation with his or her own specialty and knowledge. As needs arise, officers of the TPC receive additional training in new fields and techniques of art crime investigation. Maintaining an efficient exchange of information between each of the TPC operative departments and regional offices is crucial for success because every department and officer brings a unique set of skills and experience that mature over many years of fighting crimes against art. Many private museums, art galleries, private collectors, businesses and enterprises also cooperate with Carabinieri TPC in order to benefit from this special expertise.

After many years' experience in fighting and preventing art crime, a TPC officer becomes an increasingly effective adversary to criminals while at the same time emerging as a unique and valuable source of information for his or her colleagues, both inside and outside law enforcement.

Training Offered by International Organisations

Courses available to the Carabinieri TPC are also offered by several international organisations, including ICCROM (International Centre for the Study of the Preservation and Restoration of Cultural Property, founded by UNESCO) at several sites, one of which is located in Rome; ICOMOS (International Council on Monuments and Sites); and ICOM (International Council of Museums). These international organisations are not the only institutions that offer training for Carabinieri or other professionals in the cultural heritage protection field, but they are certainly among the most important.

ICCROM and ICOMOS were named in the 1972 UNESCO World Heritage Convention as two of the three Advisory Bodies to the World Heritage Committee (WHC); they offer advice and training on conservation issues to Member States and in general to professionals in the field. ICCROM training programmes are taught by cultural heritage experts and are often offered in response to specific or high-demand needs of the Member States (ICCROM 2013).

ICOMOS focuses on the conservation and protection of cultural heritage places and is dedicated to the diffusion of theories, methodologies and scientific techniques necessary for country-specific preservation of architectural and archaeological heritage (ICOMOS 2013). This organisation hosts workshops, seminars and symposia throughout the world and its website, which includes an online archive of publications, is an excellent source of information. Another international organisation, ICOM, dedicated to the conservation and protection of cultural assets, also organises training modules and exhibits (ICOM 2013).

The International Institute of Humanitarian Law (IIHL) in San Remo, Italy, organises courses and specific training for military personnel and civilians. The Carabinieri TPC participates not only as students but also as invited specialists, to train other military forces. As the right to one's heritage emerges as a component of international human rights law, the IIHL is beginning to add the protection of heritage, especially during times of crisis and conflict, to its curriculum. In December 2010 the IIHL delivered its first week-long course dedicated to the topic. Colonel Alberto De Regibus of the TPC participated as a faculty member and two Italian police officers also took the course. In the spring of 2011 the IIHL also offered a session on heritage protection to an international group of military officers studying at Italian Defense College in Rome.

Located in the renovated monastery of San Francesco a Ripa in Trastevere, the operative departments in Rome are next door to the ICCROM headquarters. This fortuitous juxtaposition makes it even easier for the two agencies to train and work together. The relationship provides opportunities for ICCROM faculty and TPC officers to both teach and study on each other's programmes. The following list outlines some of the courses offered by ICCROM that are available to Carabinieri officers. On occasion Carabinieri TPC officers host field trips and teach components of the following courses:

- Architectural-Archaeological Tangible Heritage in the Arab Region (ATHAR) Programme – Course on Documentation and Management of Heritage Sites in the Arab Region
- Preservation and Restoration of Cultural Heritage in the Asia-Pacific Region: Research, Analysis and Preservation of Archaeological Sites and Remains

- Archaeological Conservation in Southeast Europe 2006: Documentation, diagnosis and planning for conservation of archaeological heritage
- ATHAR: Conservation of Archaeological Heritage
- Regional course on archaeological conservation in Southeast Europe
- Reducing Risks to Collections
- Field School of the UNESCO-ICCROM Asian Academy for Heritage Management (AAHM) on Cultural Impact Assessment and Maritime Archaeology
- Management Planning for Cultural Heritage
- First Aid to Cultural Heritage in Times of Conflict

Understandably, the training of a Carabinieri TPC officer really never ends. It is a continuous process, reinforced by learning about new issues and new methods for counteracting and, even more importantly, preventing crimes. The more a CC TPC unit is exposed to these workshops, the greater their advantage in terms of staying up to date on worldwide issues related to protecting cultural heritage. Owing in part to its proactive approach to continuing education, the CC TPC is now the leading force in cultural property protection and a model for other police forces worldwide. The training it permanently offers to foreign police officers also creates an international network of cooperation and helps to halt the smuggling, looting and destruction of cultural assets, as seen in Iraq during and after Operation Antica Babylonia or Operation Ancient Babylon (see Chapter 12).

TRAINING OF FOREIGN POLICE OFFICERS

Most of the courses offered to foreign police force trainees are delivered at the Carabinieri Officers School in Rome, while courses on international stability are usually held at the Centre of Excellence for Stability Police Units (CoESPU) in Vicenza. Specialised training of foreign police in Italy takes place within the context of Italian police academy programmes that offer comprehensive secondary education in law enforcement. The initial courses are offered to reserve, non-commissioned and warrant officers who are due to be promoted to the rank of Lieutenant in permanent service, especially those officers destined to serve in special branches comparable to the TPC. Courses offered to foreign forces cover: Professional Techniques, Criminal Law, Criminal Procedure, Public Law, Investigation Techniques, Military Law, Military Police and National Security, Legal and Insurance Medicine and Information Science. Successful graduates of this year-long course may attend the two-year programme at the Military Academy in Modena. Upon graduation from the Military Academy, candidates can qualify for a further three-year programme that will lead to a Masters Degree in Law.

Examples of courses attended by foreign police officers trained by Carabinieri Corps are:

- Protection of Human Rights in Police Activities, where candidates learn about 'professionalising foreign Law Enforcement personnel in accordance with the international standards on human rights protection in policing activities' (Ministero della Difesa Italiana 2011);
- Criminalistics;
- Specialised Police Units and Multinational Specialised Units or MSU Deployment in International Crises Management Operations;
- International Military Police (ibid).

APPLICATION OF THE TPC OFFICER MODEL AT THE INTERNATIONAL LEVEL

The self-identification of TPC primarily as police officers, regardless of training, specialisation or background, offers a robust model for military and policing forces who wish to develop or improve enforcement and/or deployment capabilities related to implementation of the 1954 Hague *Convention for the Protection of Cultural Property in the Event of Armed Conflict*. When a uniformed individual also has experience and expertise in the arts and/or archaeology they emerge as a valuable asset, whether they are applying their knowledge in a conflict setting or are part of an operation responding to crime or disaster. The venerable Monuments Fine Arts and Archives Officers, more commonly referred to as 'Monuments Men' of World War II, offer a similar successful model. However, following the end of World War II, this capability was nearly lost in the US and in many allied military organisations. As the US, UK and other NATO member nations and partner countries struggle with the challenges of protecting cultural property in the conflict zones of the 21st century, the Carabinieri TPC offers a model of officer selection and training worthy of serious consideration as others work to develop similar capabilities.

12

The Carabinieri, Peacekeeping and Foreign Relations: The Carabinieri Mission to Iraq

In retrospect, it makes sense that many of the most robust and meaningful responses to the destruction of cultural property in Iraq came from the Italians and more specifically the Carabinieri TPC and the Centre for Archaeological Research and Excavations of Turin (CRAST). CRAST had been working in Iraq since 1964 and had established the Iraqi–Italian Institute of Archaeological Sciences and the Italian–Iraqi Centre for the Restoration of Monuments. In the aftermath of the first Gulf War, many of Iraq's regional museums were looted, with losses in Basra, Kufa, Assur, Sulaimaniya, Babylon, Maysan, Qadissiya, Kirkuk and Duhok. CRAST and the Carabinieri TPC worked together to identify, catalogue and publish information concerning the missing objects (Parapetti 2008, 229).

After the 2003 invasion of Iraq and the associated destruction of cultural heritage, there were, in essence, three additional Italian missions. The first was the Iraq Museum project, in which the Italians sent Carabinieri officers to work in partnership with Italian academics in order to help rebuild the museum in the areas of documentation, recovery of looted objects and virtual interpretation. The second mission was a community-based policing initiative that sent a multidisciplinary force to the south of Iraq as peacekeepers and the third was an archaeological site protection and enforcement mission established following the tragic bombing at Nasiriyah.

The Iraq Museum Project

Italian peacekeeping and missions to Iraq began with an expert response to the situation at the National Museum of Iraq in Baghdad. In response to a UNESCO conference held in Lyon, France, on 5–6 May 2003, the Carabinieri sent experienced personnel to the National Museum of Iraq to aid its recovery from the extensive looting and damage suffered by this extraordinarily significant institution. At the Lyon conference an international group of museum directors, representatives of ministries of culture and distinguished officers from policing organisations decided to create a database for archaeological objects stolen in Iraq, create an INTERPOL experts group for stolen heritage and create a special INTERPOL unit for the recovery of stolen heritage, known as the INTERPOL Tracking Task Force (ITTF). Given its domestic accomplishments and experience using database information in the recovery of stolen property, the Carabinieri TPC was the ideal choice to respond to events at the National Museum in Baghdad. Co-sponsored by the Italian Ministries for Foreign Affairs and Culture, two Carabinieri officers reporting to the Senior Adviser for the Minister of Culture were sent to Baghdad for six months from June 2003 until January 2004. Their goal was to compile description cards of stolen objects in order to create a catalogue that could be sent to the Carabinieri database of stolen objects in Rome which would in turn link to the international INTERPOL database. The Italian officers were also hoping to create an Iraqi INTERPOL liaison office and were anxious to trace the illicit exportation routes out of Iraq through associated investigations into the destinations and markets for stolen materials (Azzaman 2011).

As a Carabinieri officer in Baghdad, then Capitano (now Major) Giuseppe Marseglia played a key role in the recovery of the museum. Major Marseglia's patience encouraged members of the museum staff's trust and they slowly began to share artefact documentation that had survived the looting and vandalism. He compiled this evidence into the Carabinieri database format and uploaded it to the Italian system. This information is still available today on the Carabinieri website, where it can be accessed immediately should any of its objects reappear in the market-place or on public display. The captain also spent hours, days and weeks perusing the markets of Baghdad and talking with vendors, looking for objects with tell-tale Iraq Museum numbers recorded in ink. Again, his patience prevailed as he convinced Iraqis to return objects that did not belong to them. In cooperation with the University of Torino, the Italians also created The Virtual Museum of Iraq, a compelling tour of the collections and interpretation of the history of Mesopotamia for people who may never have the privilege of visiting the Iraq Museum galleries in person.[1] Major Marseglia also collaborated with officers from the TPC who were serving on the Nasiriyah peacekeeping mission and played a key role in the development and implementation of training for Iraqi archaeological site guards.

Operation Antica Babilonia, Ancient Babylon

When the Carabinieri TPC deployed to Iraq's Nasiriyah Province in 2003 as part of a UNESCO peacekeeping mission,[2] their operations and success in the area of heritage preservation demon-strated to the entire world the unique capabilities of the Carabinieri TPC. As advisers and subject matter experts study the Carabinieri mission (Stone and Farchakh Bajjaly 2008), it quickly becomes clear that this mission may be used as an example and model for developing similar capabilities in departments and ministries of defence in other nations. However, in order for future international military operations to benefit from the full learning potential offered by the Operation Ancient Babylon mission, it is crucial to begin by understanding the context and structure of the Italian deployment in 2003.

The Italians had been offering support to Iraq through bilateral and multilateral partnership agreements since the 1990s. In 2003 the Italians sponsored over 100 projects in Iraq. Culture, education, archaeology and heritage were initiatives among others including health, environment, public administration, irrigation, rule of law and agriculture. As a multidisciplinary law enforce-ment organisation, the Carabinieri is ideal for implementing these types of projects and missions. The structure of its force in nucleated subdivisions enables it to offer specialised policing in a wide variety of areas. The Carabinieri mission to Nasiriyah included not only two officers from the TPC – one from Monza and the other from Sassari, Sardinia – but also officers specialising in food safety, depleted uranium, DNA analysis and ballistics. Carabinieri officers also make excellent peacekeepers because of their approach to and experience in domestic and community-based policing. Quite often in small Italian villages key community leaders include the priest, the

---

[1] See: http://www.virtualmuseumiraq.cnr.it/prehome.htm [8 December 2014].
[2] It is important to note that UNESCO missions are distinct from NATO missions.

mayor, the physician and the marshal of the Carabinieri. As a result, these officers gain experience in keeping track of community activities and dynamics of all types. At the local level there is also latitude and responsibility for managing the resolution of disputes so Carabinieri officers have the opportunity to gain experience with proactive approaches for keeping the peace in very local contexts. Much of the initiative for the Iraq mission came directly from the Carabinieri and the force selected its very best officers for duty in Iraq. Prior to deployment, the nominated officers spent 40 days training in Vicenza on a course taught by the Carabinieri about what the situation would be like for Italians in Iraq. There was no specialised discussion of their respective areas of specific expertise, but rather a general introduction to Iraq and the Middle East.

The deployed Carabinieri officers worked together as a team, assisting each other in their respective missions. For example, if the goal was to inspect food supplies, the food safety officer would provide the necessary information and training to the entire team and they would all work together towards a successful inspection mission. Similarly, the TPC officers helped to prepare the entire team for the anti-looting and archaeology protection missions. The goals of these missions were to document and map sites in Nasiriyah and Di Qar Provinces in the south of Iraq, in addition to the mapping and documentation of sites in and around Baghdad.

When the Italians arrived in Nasiriyah in July 2003, they assumed responsibility directly from the reserve unit of the 2nd Battalion of the 25th US Marines, some of whom had used the local museum as quarters. When the TPC officers approached Abdulamir Hamdani, the antiquities inspector for the province of Nasiriyah, the tensions inherent to the situation led him to be initially wary of interacting with individuals in uniform. It is important to note that the Iraqis did not report to the Italians any thefts from, or damage to, the provincial museum by US forces and in fact the Carabinieri officers felt that the behaviour of the marines in Nasiriyah had been careful and appropriate. Photographs taken during this occupation support the accounts that the marines treated the structure, exhibitions and collections with care (see, for example, McCurry 2003). From a military perspective, the provincial museum building was strategically located near the Euphrates River, which had at one point been the front line between US and Iraqi forces, so it is understandable that this relatively secure structure would have been selected for bedding down US forces as a point of military necessity.

After establishing an initial introductory relationship with Mr Hamdani, the two Carabinieri TPC officers, LT Schivo and his colleague from Sardinia, began by asking for a map of archaeo-logical sites in the area so that they could begin logistical planning for site protection. The Italians knew that there was a substantial amount of looting going on all around them. The challenge they faced was exacerbated by the fact that critical sites being subjected to looting were located at great distances across the desert from the Italian headquarters in Nasiriyah and from each other. The great city of Umma, for example, where University of Chicago excavations had previously been located, was a four-hour drive across the desert from Nasiriyah. As it turned out, there were no real maps by modern standards and the Italians described the management document that Mr Hamdani was using as an 'old book'. Nevertheless, during the first phase of the Italian deployment for archaeological site protection in Iraq, the Italians completed 39 cultural prop-erty missions, visiting 23 archaeological sites, completing 6 flyovers, recovering 92 objects and identifying 54 looters, 19 of whom were arrested. The TPC officer from Sassari completed the aerial photography and documentation for many sites during the helicopter missions. In at least one case the Carabinieri used Italian Navy and Air Force helicopters to 'herd' the looters to one side of the site, where ground forces were waiting to arrest them. During the course of interdic-

FIG 12.1.   IRAQ, 2009. PROFESSOR BRIAN ROSE EXAMINES THE LOOTED NECROPOLIS LOCATED NORTH OF
THE ANCIENT MESOPOTAMIAN CITY OF ERIDU, IN THE NASIRIYAH PROVINCE. IN THE BACKGROUND TWO
MEMBERS OF THE COMBINED IRAQI AND US INSPECTION TEAM ARE STANDING IN ONE OF THE LOOTERS'
HOLES AND ON THE SPOIL MOUND. THE DEGREE OF DAMAGE EVIDENT IN THIS IMAGE ILLUSTRATES THE
SERIOUSNESS OF THE SITUATION ENCOUNTERED BY THE TPC OFFICERS IN SOUTHERN IRAQ.

FIG 12.2.   IRAQ OPERATION 'ANCIENT BABYLON', 2003–2006. CARABINIERI OFFICERS INSPECT LOOTED ARCHAEOLOGICAL SITES.

tion, the Italians also confiscated looting tools such as shovels and probes in addition to rigs for electrical lighting designed to run off car batteries. By the time Operation Antica Babilonia was completed, its accomplishments included 90 missions performed, 60 sites inventoried, 24 helicopter missions completed, 302 objects recovered, 94 looters identified and 46 looters arrested.

In recounting these events, the Carabinieri officers involved articulated a sophisticated understanding of the complexity of world events that drove desperate Iraqis to loot; they also expressed compassion for these individuals (Celentano 2011, *pers comm*). For over 100 years an economy had developed in the Middle East that was supported by archaeological excavation activities. Archaeologists and their students came from throughout the Western world to dig, not just in Egypt but also throughout ancient Mesopotamia, the Mediterranean, Persia and South Asia. In local regions where ancient cities, temples or tombs were located, many Western higher education institutions established archaeological missions where they built dig houses and returned year after year. The presence of foreigners helped to support local economies, as the archaeologists purchased goods and services. Even more importantly, it was customary to hire local labourers to assist in the excavations. As the years passed, relationships between local on-site labourers and the archaeological missions became generational and members of local communities developed detailed knowledge of the sites, in some cases perhaps rivalling the archaeologists'. Sheik Altubi, whose family lives on the ancient site of Uruk, is an excellent example. His knowledge of the ancient city is extensive and he can describe its features using the German archaeological terminology of the Institute colleagues who used to excavate there (Altubi 2009, *pers comm*). At Uruk

Fig 12.3.   Monument to the Carabinieri officers lost at Nasiriyah, Giove, Umbria.

the German Institute provided the funds to pay the Altubi family to protect the site and delivered these funds via a cultural property officer from the Netherlands with a US escort (Kila 2012) so that the site remained almost intact throughout the years of conflict.

However, Uruk was, unfortunately, an exception. Labourers living on and around archaeological sites throughout Mesopotamia found themselves, following years of sanctions and then the imposition of violent conflict, without the means to support their families when the missions no longer came. Some began to use their detailed knowledge of the sites to target the most 'productive' (marketable) objects by, for example, deliberately excavating into royal tombs and cuneiform tablet libraries. The long-term effects of sanctions, exacerbated by conflict, meant that not just archaeological labourers but all sections of society were affected by the destruction of the economy. One of the looters arrested by the Carabinieri was a schoolteacher who was deeply ashamed to have participated in the looting but whose children were starving. In some cases, the children themselves were also looting. As LT Schivo eloquently pointed out, in order to save archaeological sites in a crisis area it is essential to support members of the local population in the protection of their own cultural property.

A suicide bombing at Nasiriyah was a tragic turning point for the Italian mission. It is possible that the success of the Italian mission and its resultant emerging partnership between the Italians and the Iraqi citizens increased its priority as a target for terrorism. Rumours of an impending attack had been sent up the chain of command but unfortunately there had been insufficient information available to establish a proactive and viable defensive plan for the Nasiriyah headquarters. On 12 November 2003 a decoy car ran a roadblock in front of the three-storey Nasiriyah Chamber of Commerce building where over 300 Carabinieri officers and 100 Romanians were based. As the guards fired at the car, a fuel lorry appeared from the opposite direction, ramming the gate at very high speed before exploding. A total of 21 Italians were killed, including 12 Carabinieri officers, 6 soldiers and 3 civilians. At least 8 Iraqis were also killed. According to the Italian survivors, most of the Iraqis who were killed and injured were children who often lingered near the gates to the compound. Over 100 people were injured, including more than 70 Italians.

The bombing came just two days prior to a major rotation of personnel, so many of the dead and injured had been just about to return home to Italy. On that day, the two Carabinieri TPC officers in Nasiriyah had decided to complete one final patrol at Babylon. They invited the other four members from LT Schivo's multidisciplinary team to join them, but they declined and were lost in the attack; LT Schivo still has their group photo on his desk. As the TPC officers returned to Nasiriyah from Babylon, they saw the fire and the aftermath of the bombing. Their first-hand accounts of encountering the destruction and the loss of their friends and colleagues is heartbreaking. After the bombing, LT Schivo and other officers stayed a few extra days in order to assist the transition for the incoming personnel.

The Carabinieri officers view the experience in Iraq as two distinct missions: before and after the bombing. After the bombing, community relations were badly damaged and the spirit of the mission necessarily had to shift away from truly community-based peacekeeping. It was very difficult to continue day-to-day interaction with local people due to increased security. It transpired that the bombing was most likely the action of a terrorist organisation and the driver of the truck was probably not even Iraqi. The bombing was also a great tragedy and betrayal for the Italian people. The Italians had sent their very best people forward in a genuine attempt to help the Iraqi community of Nasiriyah and the resulting casualties represented the greatest Italian military loss since World War II. It is not unusual to see monuments to the lost members of the Nasiriyah mission in piazzas within communities large and small, all across Italy (see, for example, Fig 12.3).

TRAINING AND IMPLEMENTATION FOR A SUSTAINABLE IRAQI SITE PROTECTION PROGRAMME

During the course of the overall Carabinieri mission, with all associated site documentation and interdiction activities, the Carabinieri TPC officers recognised that long-term success would require a sustainable site protection and archaeological programme that could be implemented and run by Iraqis following the Italians' departure. So as the Carabinieri team monitored and patrolled sites and followed looting activities on a day-to-day basis, it also initiated an Iraqi site guard implementation and training plan. It soon became clear that criminal elements were exploiting the situation in Iraq, in some cases paying wages to looters and collecting looted objects for international sale. Involvement at this level shifted the dynamics of looting from the desperate activity of local community members to deliberate, organised theft committed by armed personnel. The Carabinieri began to uncover the international network involved and as officers worked on the issue and began to cooperate directly with Iraqi site guards, it became increasingly clear how truly dangerous this work could be for the Iraqis. In some cases a single unarmed Iraqi site guard might be faced with 30 armed looters and occasionally, fearing for their lives, Iraqi site guards failed to report for work, despite being paid to guard the site. More comprehensive solutions were clearly needed.

The Carabinieri recognised that a sustainable programme required the following key elements: mapping and documentation of the known sites; professionalisation of the force; and archaeological education and reform. Officer Celentano from the Rome Archaeology Unit of the TPC arrived in Nasiriyah the day after the bombing. Fire had destroyed the archives of the mission, so much of the documentation work had to begin again. The Italians worked extremely hard to map and remap all of the key sites in Nasiriyah and Di Qar provinces so that they could use the geographic documents to organise the new site protection system. With aerial reconnaissance and interdiction missions continuing, the new maps used aerial reconnaissance and photos to provide detailed map information for over 60 sites in the region.

In order to professionalise the Iraqi FPS (Facilities Protection Service), the Carabinieri had to transform it into a professionally recognised force that would be paid for its services. The first step was to select trustworthy site guards and obtain ID cards from the Iraqi police that governed the site guards' capability to legally carry a weapon. The Italians also advocated for and established uniforms for the FPS. The site guards' training also introduced additional and essential policing skills, including how to collect evidence and organise and write reports. The archaeological component also required the skills necessary to identify and catalogue recovered objects that would go to the provincial and national museums of Iraq. The Carabinieri even offered instruction to the Iraqis in multiple languages in order to make the courses as understandable as possible, to facilitate the Iraqis' learning.

The new Iraqi FPS also needed physical organisation and equipment, including vehicles marked with official insignias and radios so that a site guard who found himself overwhelmed could call for help. The Italians worked to build guard towers at many sites. The Carabinieri also formed a combined special investigative team with the Iraqis called the Multinational Specialised Unit, or MSU Viper 5. The unit's goals were to: prevent looting; suppress looting when discovered; maintain control over archaeological sites; reform the archaeological system so that powerful individuals could no longer benefit from the trade in antiquities; and report and document not just the sites themselves but also criminal events threatening site preservation and stewardship.

It is difficult to imagine a more qualified and comprehensive archaeological site protection training and implementation programme. However, some of the key officers involved expressed concern over how many of the Iraqi site guards with whom they had worked had survived their assignments after the departure of the multinational forces. Following the Nasiriyah bombing, the site guard training programme moved to Amman, Jordan, where TPC officers, at the request of UNESCO, trained at least 53 members of the Iraqi Facility Protection Service (FPS), the special Iraqi force for protecting archaeological sites. Based on his experiences of the site guard programme in Iraq, at least one Carabinieri officer has raised serious questions about foreign intervention in the site protection process at the local level. He wonders how many graduates of courses he participated in as a faculty member have been killed while attempting to protect archaeological sites. In fact, one class of graduates of the Amman programme were ambushed

FIG 12.4.   LARSA, IRAQ, 2009. A UNIFORMED IRAQI GUARD POSES WITH TWO MEMBERS OF A LOCAL
BEDOUIN FAMILY WHO LIVE NEAR THE ARCHAEOLOGICAL SITE.

and killed on their way back to their assignments in Iraq (Ragusa 2012, *pers comm*). Sustainable
site protection programmes work only in situations where the rule of law at the local level has
stabilised to the point where the most heavily armed people are no longer necessarily the people
in power. Furthermore, there must be local consensus that the site should be protected. It is
unconscionable to put well-trained, armed site guards who are implementing a state-of-the-art
programme out in the desert on their own to protect a site where there exists a vast local majority
or powerful local criminal interest in looting for profit or in site destruction for economic development. The Carabinieri has learned that it does not want to place valuable, trained individuals
in harm's way when there may be no realistic hope of meaningful site protection given the wide
range of potential local situations in crisis areas.

The Carabinieri's accomplishments in Iraq were outstanding, establishing a prototype for the
development and implementation of an archaeological site protection programme for host nation
personnel under the most extreme and challenging conditions imaginable. One measure of its
accomplishment is that the author (Rush) encountered well-trained, professional site guards in
uniform at the Mesopotamian City of Larsa in 2009 (see Fig 12.4). This model can be used by
other military units in other areas of the world as a basis to develop similar programmes. The Iraqis
were so appreciative of and impressed by the Italian mission that they opened and named a gallery
in the provincial museum at Nasiriyah in honour of the Carabinieri and its efforts.

CULTURAL PROPERTY PROTECTION IN KOSOVO AND THE FORMER YUGOSLAVIA

In 2003 the Italian press began to publicise the fact that Muslim extremists were destroying Eastern Orthodox churches in Kosovo. As of spring 2003, the Italian media reported that 122 churches had been destroyed, some after NATO forces had established responsibility for stability in the local areas immediately surrounding them. The Italians, of Task Force Sauro under the command of General Fabio Mini, announced that they would not leave the Monastery of Decani unprotected. The Italian press describes this 13th-century monastery as insanely beautiful, with well-preserved frescoed walls. In their contemporary accounts of the situation, journalists have also expressed the view that if the Italians were to fail to protect the monastery, the Italian people would share culpability for its destruction (Veca 2003). The monastery complex includes four churches and its monks offered refuge to all people, regardless of ethnicity, during the violence of 1998–1999. The monks of Decani publicly credit and thank the Italians for saving the monastery, which is now listed as a UNESCO World Heritage Site. A Chief Humanitarian Officer (CHO) serving in Bosnia also commended the Italians, explaining that whenever he was involved in a heritage-related mission he always consulted Italian troops as they never needed an explanation of what had to be done or why it was important (Higgins 2010, *pers comm*).

When a valuable piece of cultural heritage is in jeopardy, it is crucial to record every possible detail. For example, in Kosovo, where Serbian Orthodox sacred sites such as the monasteries are still at risk, the Italian press reported on a Carabinieri mission headed by TPC Lieutenant Fabio Ficuciello in May 2003. His mission was to 'monitor the Kosovar landscape and to document the condition of cultural and artistic property in the area' (Veca 2003). He included film footage in his documentary material that was submitted to the Commanding General of the force (ibid). The documentation of cultural property at risk offers another level of protection. When a religious structure in a remote rural location is documented through photographs, detailed description and inventory of its contents, its destruction shifts from being a simple act of violence and loss to a crime that can be prosecuted in national or international courts of law. Documentation offers the power of 'before and after' images as well as material that can be used to publicise destruction and to encourage calls for justice in international fora. Clearly, this type of protection is abstract and only a mild form of deterrence, but it is valuable nevertheless.

The successful protection of the Decani monastery has also contributed to stability and recovery in this district of Kosovo. As of 2010, Italian forces were continuing to protect the monastery and at least one visitor described the valley where it is located as peaceful and the relationship of the community with the monastery as positive. The tomb of Stefan Decanski, who ordered the construction of the monastery, beginning in 1327, is believed by all in the area to possess healing powers and the monks welcome anyone who wishes to enter regardless of their ethnicity or religious affiliation. This example offers a lesson for the military audience undertaking complex stability missions in areas of ethnic conflict where a valued cultural property can serve as a locus for unification and community recovery.

THE CARABINIERI TPC AND ITALIAN FOREIGN RELATIONS: CENTRAL AND SOUTH AMERICA

An organisation with the capabilities and skills of the Carabinieri TPC becomes a valuable tool in terms of building positive foundations for future Italian foreign relations. Officers of the TPC routinely provide training for police officers, archaeological site guards and customs personnel from any country that requests their expertise. Some of the international training sessions are offered under the aegis of UNESCO with courses designed for high-level officials, lawyers, diplomats and museum officials. Training sessions conducted by the Carabinieri TPC have been offered throughout South and Central America, including in Ecuador, Colombia, Paraguay, Bolivia, Uruguay, Chile, Argentina, Peru and Guatemala. The Captain of the Firenze TPC unit mentioned with pride the participation of his officers in Guatemalan training (Costantini 2011, *pers comm*). During sessions delivered in 2006, the Florence officers specialised in teaching techniques for inventory, cataloguing and documentation to Guatemalan police and museum professionals.

Following the successful repatriation to Italy of objects from famous US museums, a series of countries have requested Carabinieri expertise. It is no coincidence that, after working with the Italians, the government of Peru successfully negotiated repatriation of the Machu Pichu collection from Yale University to Universidad Nacional de San Antonio Abad del Cusco. In addition, the Italians' momentum and success invigorated the Peruvian repatriation effort (Chechi *et al* 2011; Aiken 2006).

Another critical organisation that supports cultural heritage training in Latin America through Italian partnership is the Istituto Italo-Latino Americano (IILA) (Donia 2009, 173). The IILA was created in 1966 in the context of a convention held in Rome between Italy and 20 Latin American countries (Farnesina 2013). The purpose of the IILA is to:

- develop and coordinate research and documentation regarding the problems, achievements and prospects of its Member Countries in cultural, scientific, economic, technical and social contexts;
- disseminate the results of the above research and documentation among its Member Countries;
- identify, also in the light of the above results, concrete possibilities for exchange, mutual assistance and common or concerted action in the above-mentioned sectors.

Since 2001, the IILA has recognised the value of cultural heritage as a tool for economic development and, with financial support from Italy, has run an 'Integrated Programme of Technical Assistance and Training for the strengthening of the institutional system of education, management and protection of cultural heritage in Latin America' (Donia 2009), which they refer to as 'the Programme'. The Programme is implemented through a portfolio of agreements with a series of Italian institutions that include the Carabinieri TPC. The cooperation scheme also encourages Latin American countries with more experience in the heritage protection sector to partner with and mentor countries with less experience. As the Programme has developed to provide greater capacity building for the fight against illicit trafficking in antiquities it has focused on offering fellowships in Italy through the Ministry of Culture, including fellowships with the TPC, providing technical assistance to heritage professionals and law enforcement, sponsoring regional and sub-regional meetings, seminars and courses and publishing a book in Spanish titled *Lucha contra el trafico de los bienes culturales* ('The Fight against Illicit Traffic in Cultural Property').

One example of the Programme in action is the partnership that exists between Paraguay and Italy for building a more robust defence against illicit trafficking (Donia 2009, 175). In 2008 the new government in Paraguay initiated a programme to protect Paraguayan antiquities against looting and illicit trafficking. With coaching from the IILA, the project began by comparing existing Paraguayan cultural property legislation with Italian cultural property law, which resulted in the drafting of reformed legislation. This legislation led to additional statutes including a law that created a 'National Committee for fighting against illicit traffic of cultural property' (Donia 2009) and a Public Ministry Unit specialising in Cultural Heritage. The process of successfully passing these legislative reforms required lobbying and efforts to increase public awareness and understanding of the issue.

At the same time, in addition to the legislative initiatives, the Italians worked with the Paraguayans on the cataloguing and registration of cultural heritage under the aegis of the National Secretary for Culture. The team, led by an expert from the Central Institute of the Catalogue and Documentation at the Italian Ministry of Culture (ICCD), provided guidance for organisation and methodology based on the Italians' decades of experience. The Paraguayans took advantage of the publicity related to the Italian presence in Paraguay to continue to build public support for the protection of cultural heritage and the Paraguayan Director General launched a national inventory of cultural heritage. Another country-specific initiative was the provision of specialised training for Chilean cultural heritage prosecutors. In 2009, Chile created a specialised unit of legal professionals whose purpose is to fight crime involving cultural heritage and environmental and public health.

In order to address the training needs identified during the Paraguayan partnership, in 2008 the Italians organised a two-week workshop in Rome for Latin American civil service heritage professionals titled 'The protection of cultural goods: the Italian experience'. The Carabinieri TPC conducted the first week of training and the Cultural and Landscape Regional Directorate of Lazio and Umbria organised the second week. The course was considered sufficiently beneficial as to be repeated in 2010 with the additional participation of UNESCO, UNIDROIT, the Secretariat General of INTERPOL and the United Nations Office on Drugs and Crime (UNODC).

Levels of momentum and interest were such that eight months later, in December 2010, Argentina hosted a 'Regional Workshop on legal, legislative and administrative tools for the prevention of illicit traffic and restitution of cultural goods in Latin America' (IILA 2010). The event was attended by 90 civil servants from 11 Latin American countries and Italy. The workshop generated a list of recommendations that would help the region to strengthen its efforts in countering the illicit trafficking in cultural property. Recommendations included: the promotion of continued international coordination; the elaboration of efforts for census, inventories and catalogues of cultural heritage at the national level across Latin America; the adoption of adequate national legislation; and the application of international rules and conventions. In addition, Ecuador volunteered to host an additional regional workshop focusing on administration cooperation and application of criminal proceedings for international restitution requests.

AFRICA AND THE MIDDLE EAST

Representatives of the Carabinieri TPC also held a two-week course in Vicenza, Italy, for representatives from across Africa, including the Sub-Saharan region, Eritrea, Somalia, Ethiopia, Central Africa and Zimbabwe. In addition, the Italians have a bilateral training agreement with Israel and have provided courses in Lebanon. A typical one- or two-week course by the Carabinieri TPC includes sessions introducing international and bilateral agreements that cover restitution of stolen cultural property, sometimes using the Italian-US bilateral agreement as an example; prosecution for recovery of stolen property from the magistrate's perspective; international customs laws and proceedings; methods of transportation and concealment used by smugglers of cultural property; international routes of illegal trafficking of art objects; working with customs at the international level and border police responsibilities; working with INTERPOL and Europol as a potential tool; codes of ethics for dealers who handle cultural property; the Italian model for the protection of cultural heritage; an introduction to the Carabinieri TPC; methods for protection and intervention for areas of archaeological sensitivity and sites at risk; methods for sampling, treatment and custody of archaeological finds; an archaeologist's perspective on archaeology and law enforcement; an introduction to the database with an emphasis on Object ID and the importance of sound collections documentation methods; covering proactive security for museums, churches, libraries, archives and other collections; methods of investigation for tracking and recovering stolen art objects; methods of investigation for identifying and breaking up organised criminal efforts to sell stolen cultural property; and peacekeeping missions.

In summary, and as expressed in the official tasking from UNESCO (Centre of Excellence for Stability Police Units 2009), the first week was intended to focus on international regulation and conventions regarding cultural heritage with a focus on how these laws and agreements have worked in Italian experience. The topic of greatest interest for most policing units is the subject of export and import of cultural property, with emphasis on the Italian approach to judicial and extrajudicial activities required for the successful repatriation of objects from other countries. The second week was for the discussion of crime prevention, methods of investigation, the Italian approach to law enforcement with respect to cultural property and the organisation and implementation of peacekeeping missions, such as those to Iraq.

Carabinieri officers who have taught multiple courses at the international level feel that the most productive approach is to visit the country where the students are located. Firstly, Italy can be an extraordinarily distracting place for international visitors and it may be difficult for students to concentrate on the formal sessions when there is so much to see and experience in places such as Rome or Venice, where the courses may be held. In addition, if TPC officers teach in the host nation setting, they have the opportunity to witness first-hand the types of challenges that their students face; they also may be able to visit the types of sites and collections that their host nation counterparts are tasked with protecting and recovering. Furthermore, courses held in host nation settings offer opportunities for regional participation and the course or workshop may result in the establishment of new cooperative networks and partnership programmes.

The Carabinieri TPC's participation in a 2004 UNESCO workshop held in Cape Town, South Africa, is an example of the benefits outlined above. This workshop consisted of seven sessions over the course of four days with two field trips. Seven countries sent official representatives and the workshop venue also provided the opportunity for contributions from a series of regional experts. Not only did the 32 African students in attendance benefit from the informative sessions but the workshop also resulted in discussion of shared challenges and consensus on resolutions to work together to combat the illicit trafficking of cultural property from the African continent.

POST-CONFLICT CAPACITY BUILDING

In the case of both Iraq and Kosovo the Italians have ongoing relationships with heritage institutions in both countries, long after the conclusion of peacekeeping missions. In addition to their continued presence in Kosovo, the Italians have also participated in conferences and educational sessions designed to help members of all former Yugoslavian States with the protection of their cultural heritage. In 2010 the University of Urbino hosted a conference titled 'Urbino, the Ideal City: the Promotion and Protection of Cultural Heritage', sponsored by The Ministry of Culture, the Carabinieri TPC, the Università degli Studi di Urbino Carlo Bo, the Adriatic and Ionian Initiative, ICCROM and CEDU, the Centre for Human Rights Education at the University of Genoa. The Urbino conference was considered highly significant; its participants and speakers included, amongst others: the Serbian Ambassador to Italy; the President of the Marche Region; the President of the Pesaro-Urbino province; the Mayor of Urbino; the Commander of the Carabinieri TPC; the Commander of the TPC Operative Unit in Rome; the Minister of Education for the Republic of Serbia; the Minister of EU Affairs for Italy; the Councillor to the Director General of ICCROM; Rectors of leading universities in Serbia and Albania; and the Head of the Science Department for the Albanian Ministry of Education. Conference topics included discussions of technology and training programmes for heritage preservation, the announcement of scholarships for Balkan students and the presentation of an agreement for international cooperation in the field of heritage preservation. On the second day of the conference TPC officers delivered a detailed workshop on the functions of Banca Dati *Leonardo* and how to use it. The conference continued with videos of examples of successful collaborative heritage projects and training programmes and concluded with visits to the National Museum of the Marche and the home of renowned Italian Renaissance painter Raphael (Università degli Studi di Urbino Carlo Bo 2010).

In September 2011, eight years after the first Italian TPC peacekeeping mission to Iraq, the Italians and the Iraqis signed a memorandum outlining an agreement whereby the Italians would assist in the renovation of one of the National Museum of Iraq's Assyrian exhibit halls and exhibition of Islamic material, with concomitant training of Iraqi museum staff. As of the tenth anniversary of the 2003 invasion, the Italians are still assisting with the recovery of the National Museum of Iraq in the form of helping to upgrade the entire institution (Bailey 2013, 1). The Italians had previously rehabilitated two other galleries at the National Museum and assisted with renovations in regional museums in Nasiriyah, Diwaniyah and Najaf. The Italians have also organised and hosted seminars on museum management practices for their Iraqi colleagues.

There can be no doubt that efforts that began with the Carabinieri peacekeeping initiative a decade ago continue to contribute to Italy's positive relationships with Iraq and Kosovo. The Carabinieri recognises that all such efforts contribute to positive international relations and cultural diplomacy. All of the Carabinieri's international efforts reinforce the force's belief and philosophy that cultural heritage belongs not only to its country of origin but to all people, everywhere. As the Right Honourable Sandro Bondi (2009, 11) shared his belief that protecting and sharing cultural heritage facilitates cross-cultural dialogue, he eloquently pointed out in his opening address to the G8 Conference on Illicit Trafficking that 'decontextualization of the cultural heritage leads to a loss of identity, and in concrete terms, of friendship between peoples. Italy is profoundly aware that the cultural heritage represents a fundamental feature in the identity of every country, and at the same time of belonging to a common civilization.' In keeping with this philosophy, in autumn 2014 His Excellency Omar Sultan, the Deputy Minister of Information and Culture for the Islamic Republic of Afghanistan, announced with great joy that the Italian Minister of Culture had very recently agreed to send officers of this Carabinieri TPC to Kabul to assist in the training of archaeological site guards in Afghanistan (Sultan 2014).

13

'The Italian Model'

'The Italian Model' proposes examples for every aspect of saving cultural heritage, academic partnership, law enforcement, application of international law, investigation techniques, military deployment capability, protection of archaeological sites, collections security, public outreach and successful repatriation. One needs only to look again at the statistics to see that the model is working. If we consider the 1999–2011 period, we observe a steady decline in the number of art thefts from Italy, from over 2000 in 1999 to under 1000 in 2011. Between 2004 and 2011 there was a decrease in reported episodes of illicit archaeological excavation (looting) from approximately 250 per year to approximately 50; and between 2006 and 2011 an overall increase in archaeological objects recovered, rising from 26,649 in 2006 to 35,727 in 2011. In 2008 and 2010, the Carabinieri TPC recovered over 44,000 artefacts (Marín-Aguilera 2012, 570–1).

In 2007 The Associated Press ran a story titled 'Soon, *tombaroli* will be hard to find' (David 2007). The Commander of the Carabinieri TPC told the reporter that in the late 1990s TPC officers might encounter over 1000 illicit archaeological excavations, in contrast to the 40 encountered in 2006. The successful repatriation of objects from the US to Italy has also served to warn the art market that the purchase of illegal objects from Italy is no longer without risk. Art dealers, museums and collectors are paying much more attention to the provenance documentation of objects appearing on the market, thereby making it much more difficult for the average *tombaroli* to find an enthusiastic buyer. Mr David also quotes the well-known *tombarolo* Pietro Casasanta, whose looting career was also discussed previously in Chapter 4, who provided a first-hand account of the differences in enforcement that he had experienced over time. 'Nobody cared, and there was so much money going around', he recalled. 'I always worked during the day, with the same hours as construction crews, because at night it was easier to get noticed and to make mistakes.' Mr Casasanta actually used bulldozers when looting Roman villas – his favourite type of site. When he began looting in the 1950s, he was able to sell the objects he found on market stalls in Rome that openly sold antiquities. He lamented to Mr David that, 50 years on, young people were no longer interested in learning to become *tombaroli* and that 'the whole network of merchants has disappeared'. Observations of this nature provide further support for the assertion that the Italian model is working.

ARTICULATION OF PRINCIPLES FOR THE PRESERVATION OF CULTURAL HERITAGE

Just as Western women no longer wear hats festooned with the feathers of endangered birds, the days are also gone when a major museum or collector could help themselves to the cultural patrimony of others with the expectation of nothing but adulation. As Tullio Scovazzi (2009, 27), Professor of International Law at the University of Milano-Bicocca, has pointed out, perceptible international trends are emerging in terms of ethics and principles governing the stewardship of cultural patrimony. First, he notes that it is 'no longer acceptable to exploit weakness in others for cultural gain'. In other words, conflict, war, colonial domination, foreign occupation or oppression of indigenous peoples are no longer justifications for helping oneself to the cultural property of the defeated, the victimised or the oppressed. The Italians have mastered the concept of discouraging the consumption of antiquities and stolen art by members of high society, at least in the West. As Kenneth Polk remarked at a 2002 anti-trafficking conference in Rome sponsored by MiBAC and the TPC (Polk 2002, 107–8), as with all efforts to curb smuggling and trafficking of illicit property, the most effective solutions are always at the consumption end of the market. The Carabinieri also recognised that fines and court orders would never be enough; rather, consumers of stolen objects would need to be required to relinquish the objects and would need to be embarrassed in front of their friends and colleagues if patterns of antiquity-collecting behaviour were to ever have a hope of changing.

A second principle articulated by Professor Scovazzi is a commitment to cooperation against the illegal movement of cultural property. This commitment could be described as a shared belief that communities, law enforcement agencies, cultural institutions, national governments, international agencies and interested members of the public should all work together to prevent the removal and illegal movement of cultural property away from its place of origin.

The Professor goes on to point out that the prevention of illegal movement is directly tied to recognition of the importance of cultural context. As discussed in Chapter 1 of this volume, the Italians have appreciated the significance of cultural heritage for millennia. As we move into the 21st century, more and more countries and communities are beginning to share this recognition and are becoming increasingly empowered in advocating for stewardship of their own heritage *in situ*. Some of this empowerment is as a direct result of Italian mentoring. Slowly, the right to one's heritage is emerging as a fundamental human right and is beginning to be recognised as such in international courts and as customary international law. One indication of this trend was the first ever cultural property protection course for military personnel, held at the International Institute of Humanitarian Law in San Remo, Italy, in December 2010. Needless to say, a colonel from the Carabinieri TPC served as one of the faculty members.

A greater challenge will be to increase public appreciation for *in situ* heritage protection in wealthy countries where major international collecting activities still take place. This challenge is addressed by the fourth guiding principle followed by the Italians. Cooperation at the international level should guide the settlement of disputes regarding custody and repatriation of cultural property. In an ideal world, cooperation would typify the relationship between countries of origin and countries of destination for cultural property, and methods of mediation and conciliation be applied to disputes with a goal of just resolution. The Italian approach to negotiating loan and exhibition agreements with major museums as part of the repatriation process is an illustration of the fourth principle in action.

How can the Carabinieri Model Work Internationally for Success?

There is no other force like the Carabinieri TPC in the world. With over 200 officers, a headquarters in Rome, a database containing millions of entries of stolen art and 12 regional offices, this force sets the standard for art law enforcement. The Carabinieri delivers courses for other police officers, diplomats, museum professionals and high-ranking officials all over the world. Its successful international prosecutions have completely changed the world of antiquities collecting and museum acquisitions of art and antiquities. As the Carabinieri TPC continues to improve its database, linking it to other enforcement efforts, its impact on international law enforcement and the illicit art market will continue to increase.

INTERNATIONAL TRAINING COURSES

One of the most effective measures in the development of international law enforcement cooperation is education. As discussed in the context of international relations, it is clear that the TPC has influenced the development of law enforcement initiatives for arts and antiquities programmes all over the world. In addition to country-specific outreach, Carabinieri TPC officers offer cooperative programmes and educational presentations to policing organisations such as CEPOL, the European Police College.

One example of the types of course that the officers of the Carabinieri TPC can provide to international policing organisations are the presentations on trafficking in stolen artworks presented by Carabinieri Commanders to the European Police College in 2006 and 2007 (Comando Carabinieri Tutela Patrimonio Culturale 2006; 2007). The purpose of these courses was to share experience, to develop networks and partnerships among the various European law enforcement agencies, to encourage international cooperation and to search for common solutions. The courses introduced the essential elements of the 1970 UNESCO Convention,[1] emphasising the definitions of cultural property and discussing the fact that relative importance of different types of cultural property will vary across the different regions of the world. The course also discussed the importance of documentation, not only to aid in the recovery of stolen objects but also to prove the identity of original ownership. Related to that point is the fact that the less well-known the work of art or object, the more important it is to have documentation and there is no doubt that reliable and detailed documentation facilitates international cooperation and the support of judicial authorities.

The policing course also explained the dynamics of illicit trafficking in the arts, emphasising the disparities between source countries and consuming societies, as well as the ever-increasing profits of the auction houses. It also illustrated the challenges created when changing tastes among wealthy and institutional collectors influence prices and demand; as the amounts of money paid for certain styles and types of objects and works of art soar, so do the incentives to commit crimes in order to get those pieces onto the market. The changing aspects of conflict zones also play a part. When social order disintegrates in one part of the world, unscrupulous collectors in another stand ready to purchase illegally removed objects, encouraging the looting of archaeological sites, sacred spaces and even museums, as the world has witnessed in the moonscapes of looted Iraqi archaeological sites and statues severed from their feet in the temples of Cambodia. Conditions conducive to the loss of cultural property in source countries include economic breakdown, political and social unrest, deteriorating living conditions and disregard for the law. These conditions can lead to:

---

[1] UNESCO *Convention on the Means of Prohibiting and Preventing the Illicit Import, Export and Transfer of Ownership of Cultural Property 1970*; see: http://portal.unesco.org/en/ev.php-URL_ID=13039&URL_DO=DO_TOPIC&URL_SECTION=201.html.

- a failure to keep and protect objects and archaeological sites;
- indiscriminate looting;
- churches, mosques, temples and other places of worship becoming targets for theft;
- ease of hiding, transporting and selling stolen objects.

It is possible to summarise the elements that work in favour of the criminals who are part of the illicit trafficking networks:

- the ease of crossing international borders;
- poor enforcement (due to lack of resources) of criminal sanctions for those caught stealing or smuggling works of art;
- low standards of documentation of art objects, making it difficult to track the stolen objects and equally difficult to identify the criminals;
- criminals are able to move goods at the international level far more efficiently than international law enforcement efforts operate for cooperation and exchange of information;
- a lack of professional controls over acquisition of art by museums and collectors.

Another crucial aspect of law enforcement education is the need to develop and share an understanding of the nature of the criminals involved. In the world of art crime, enforcement is made more difficult by the fact that skilled thieves and fences work to present an appearance of economic and social legitimacy where none exists. The vast sums of money involved and potential profits to be made encourage galleries, museums, wealthy private collectors, dealers and auction houses to turn a blind eye, doing business with individuals and organisations they may well know to be of questionable integrity. Experts consulted by the Carabinieri believe that, if the art market were to be suddenly cleaned up, leaving only the legal transactions, it would collapse entirely.

For an impression of the challenges that international art law enforcement faces, one need only look at cases such as the St Louis Art Museum in St Louis, Missouri, which spent thousands of dollars in US courts fighting to keep a mask that had been removed from an Egyptian storehouse and smuggled to the US for the museum's collection. In his ruling, the US judge actually referenced the fact that the mask had been stolen and smuggled out of Egypt as a reason for permitting the museum to keep the object (Gay 2012). As Scott Hodes Esq pointed out in his lecture at an NYU Art Crime Conference (Hodes 2014), hometown courts rarely find against their signature museums. It is also very easy to locate literature in which prominent museum directors, curators and donors attempt to rationalise, argue and convince themselves and others that by purchasing stolen objects they are making positive contributions to society (Cuno 2008). The Metropolitan Museum of Art in New York City has on occasion hosted tours of objects of questionable origin (SAFE 2012). It is also important to remember that as the lines between criminals and legitimate dealers, collectors and institutions become blurred, false documents for object origins, provenance, identity and ownership are created and start to accompany the artefacts and works of art.

Money laundering through the illicit trade in art and antiquities adds another dimension to critical law enforcement related to the arts. Ultimately, Carabinieri advice to international European law enforcement agencies mirrors the enforcement themes present throughout Carabinieri TPC enforcement activities:

- develop greater familiarity and a more sophisticated understanding of the methods and procedures used by different forces and specialised police, eg customs and tax enforcement personnel;
- develop international police officer exchanges;
- use the public and private databases of all countries;
- acquire and use technology for sharing information across the databases so that detailed descriptions and images of stolen objects can be easily exchanged;
- develop cooperation between public and private institutions that specialise in the protection of cultural patrimony, at both national and international levels;
- identify the routes criminals use for importing and exporting works of art from their countries and the locations where they distribute, sell and provide false documentation;
- analyse criminal events where international organisations are involved in illicit trafficking;
- localise the places used by illicit traffickers to hide objects and identify commonly used border crossings;
- conduct comparative studies of various countries' legislation concerning cultural property and restitution of recovered property to all nations of origin.

REPATRIATION

The repatriation of significant objects from major US museums to Italy has been described as a 'tectonic shift' (Berger 2009, 21) in thinking about collecting behaviour by museums of the West and the international relationships with countries rich in antiquity. The solid documentation of illegal behaviour provided by the results of the Carabinieri Medici investigation put the Italians in a position of power as they approached the US museums and collectors. The clear and public demonstration that representatives of the museums had broken the law empowered the Italians to begin negotiations for repatriation. In February 2006, The Metropolitan Museum of Art in New York signed a cultural agreement with the Ministry of Culture in Rome that included the return of artworks that the Italians had proven were stolen.

It is important to note that the Italians have led by example. The tectonic shift has also applied to Italy with the return of the Axum obelisk to Ethiopia in 2005 and reconstruction of the monument, funded by the Italians in 2008. The Italians also returned the Venus of Cyrene to the Libyan people in 2008, despite challenges to its repatriation by an Italian non-governmental organisation (Scovazzi 2009, 33).

As of autumn 2013, the partner institutions and the US continue to experience the benefits of the Italian approach to repatriation agreements and the sharing of the wealth of Italian culture. The Italians loaned Piero Della Francesca's priceless 15th-century painting 'Madonna di Senigallia' to the Museum of Fine Arts Boston and the Metropolitan Museum of Art, beginning in mid-September. The exhibition is also part of an initiative by the Italian Carabinieri TPC to publicise its global efforts in recovering stolen works of art. The Madonna di Senigallia provides an excellent illustration of the TPC's work since the painting was stolen from the Ducal Palace in Urbino and recovered by the Carabinieri, who found it in a Swiss hotel room (Edgers 2013). Since signing the repatriation agreements in 2006, the Italians have also loaned the Metropolitan the marble statue Eirene, a Roman copy of a Greek bronze depicting the personification of peace, works of art for a 2009 exhibition titled *Titian, Tintoretto, Veronese: Rivals in Renaissance Venice* and classical examples for the 2011 exhibition, *Aphrodite and the Gods of Love.*

The wider art community is developing a more sophisticated appreciation of Italian accomplishments in this arena. In 2014, the Association for Research into Crimes against Art (ARCA) selected Dr Daniela Rizzo and Mr Maurizio Pellegrini, of the Soprintendenza per i Beni Archeologici dell' Etruria Meridionale at the Villa Giulia Museum in Rome, as winners of the ARCA Art Protection and Recovery Award (Association for Research into Crimes against Art 2014). The Archaeological Superintendency for Southern Etruria is responsible for Cerveteri, Tarquinia, Vulci, Veio, Lucas Feroniae, Civitavecchia, Sutri, Toscana, Pyrgi, Volsinii and San Lorenzo Nuovo. These areas contain the treasure of the ancient Etruscans and for decades they have been subject to illicit excavations. Dr Rizzo and Mr Pellegrini set up the Ufficio Sequestri e Scavi Clandestini (Office of Confiscation and Illicit Excavations). Since 1995, this office has monitored illegal excavations and objects subject to illegal trafficking, working with the Carabinieri TPC and the Italian Prosecutors Office towards tracking and recovering looted objects. Cooperation and coordination at this level produced irrefutable evidence of theft, the purchase of stolen property and violations of customs laws and regulations. The strength of these cases not only supported vigorous legal prosecution but also put the Italians in an excellent position for negotiating the establishment of repatriation agreements that both brought the objects home and also allowed for future loans and cultural exchange.

The repatriation successes enjoyed by the Italians offer hope to other nations. For example, as Native Americans consider the return of the Euphronios krater from the Metropolitan Museum of Art to Italy, they know that there is hope of repatriation of sacred objects missing from their ceremonies, clans and families. Members of the Onondaga Nation requested that the author (Rush) ask the Carabinieri TPC to look out for sacred masks and wampum belts that may appear in European collections and markets. Aside from these personal considerations, ethically they look to assist the repatriation of objects to their rightful owners, whoever they may be.

PEACEKEEPING AND DEPLOYMENT

There is no doubt that all active military personnel – whatever country they represent and whatever their mission – should be equipped with a general awareness of cultural property protection and detailed maps providing information about, and the locations of, features of cultural significance within the host nation landscape. However, as past conflicts have unfortunately clearly demonstrated, cultural property protection and its related challenges can represent a significant component of a military mission's requirements. As a result, there are occasions when a military mission may require cultural property protection capabilities. The US military sometimes uses the term 'Bottom Line Up Front' as a way of summarising the most important points. When considering the Carabinieri as a deployment model for a mission with a significant cultural property protection component, here is the Bottom Line Up Front:

- identify individuals already in uniform who have educational and/or professional backgrounds related to archaeology, art history, museum studies, archival management, library science, architecture or historic preservation;
- provide these individuals with sufficient regional deployment training;
- coordinate with host nation professionals, representatives of the academic community and appropriate defence intelligence agencies to prepare detailed maps and background information on cultural property at risk;
- deploy the identified individuals with a clearly defined cultural property protection mission.

A NATIONAL ETHIC – AN EXAMPLE FOR THE WORLD

In spring 2014, a young man looking at a book about Gauguin noticed that the images were highly reminiscent of a painting that had been hanging on his father's kitchen wall for years. His father consulted experts about the painting that he had purchased, along with another valuable painting by Pierre Bonnard, and the TPC were called. It transpired that the paintings had been stolen in 1970 from a home in London, discarded on a train travelling from Paris to Turin, purchased by a FIAT worker from a lost property sale for 45,000 Italian lire (about US $30–35) and moved to Sicily with the worker when he retired. The Gauguin is now estimated to be worth between US $15–45 million and the Bonnard approximately US $900,000. As the paintings moved into the custody of Italian law enforcement, the process of restitution to the original owners began (*BBC News* 2014). As of December 2014 it was determined that the original owners left no heirs, and the Italian family has been permitted to keep the paintings (Albertson 2014, *pers comm*).

From a US perspective, it is important to consider all of the factors that made the identification and recovery of two such valuable artworks possible. First, the appreciation of fine art is an element of Italian culture. Second, many Italian citizens are well educated in the arts and are able to recognise the style and characteristics of famous works of art and the artists who created them. Third, once an object such as the Gauguin painting 'Fruits sur une table ou nature avec un petit chien' is found, the Italians have a law enforcement unit with access to a comprehensive database that can connect discovered items with information and documentation about stolen paintings. Last, the Italians are committed to returning stolen works of art to their rightful owners and/or nations. When asked to comment on the paintings' recovery, Dario Franceschini summed up the situation accurately and with eloquence: 'It's an incredible story, an amazing recovery. A symbol of all the work which Italian art police have put in over the years behind the scenes' (ibid). He was of course referring to the Carabinieri Tutela Patrimonio Culturale – an example to us all.

Bibliography and References

Adnkronos, 2012 *Arte, a Bologna solo domani capolavori recuperati dai Carabinieri* [online], available from: http://it.finance.yahoo.com/notizie/arte-bologna-solo-domani-capolavori-recuperati-dai-carabinieri-103000161.html [17 March 2012]

Agence France-Presse, 2013 Stolen manuscripts worth 4 mln euros recovered in Italy, *globalpost.com* [online], 19 July, available from: http://www.globalpost.com/dispatch/news/afp/130719/stolen-manuscripts-worth-4-mln-euros-recovered-italy [27 July 2013]

Agreement Between the Government of the United States of America and the Government of the Republic of Italy Concerning the Imposition of Import Restrictions on Categories of Archaeological Material Representing the Pre-Classical, Classical, and Imperial Roman Periods of Italy, 2001 [online], available from: http://eca.state.gov/files/bureau/it2001mou.pdf [20 April 2013]

Aiken, H, 2006 Inca Show Pits Yale Against Peru, *The New York Times* [online], 1 February, available from: http://www.nytimes.com/2006/02/01/arts/design/01mach.html?pagewanted=all [21 November 2012]

Alberge, D, 2010 Roman sculptures withdrawn from auction amid fears they are stolen, *The Guardian* [online], 27 April, available from: http://www.theguardian.com/artanddesign/2010/apr/27/bonhams-stolen-roman-sculptures-auction [6 April 2014]

Albertson, L, 2014 Personal communication (telephone conversation with the author (Rush)), 1 December, Washington DC

Alderman, K L, 2012 Ancient Roman Artifact Seized, *Cultural Property & Archaeology Law* [online], 24 October, available from: http://culturalpropertylaw.wordpress.com/2012/10/24/ancient-roman-artifact-seized/ [24 October 2012]

Altubi (Sheik), 2009 Personal communication (conversation with the author (L Rush)), 9 April, Uruk, Di Qar Province, Iraq

Ambu, S, 2012 Germania e USA le ultime mete dei bronzetti trafugati, *La Nuova Sardegna* [online], 17 April, available from: http://lanuovasardegna.gelocal.it/regione/2012/04/17/news/germania-e-usa-le-ultime-mete-dei-bronzetti-trafugati-1.4377557 [12 August 2014]

Ammerman, A, 2010 The first Argonauts: toward the study of the earliest seafaring in the Mediterranean, in *The Global Origins and Development of Seafaring* (eds A Anderson and K Boyle), McDonald Institute for Archaeological Research, Cambridge, 81–92

Andros, 2014 L'arte del falso – 2 di 6, *Androsophy, All About Art* [online], 16 March, available from: http://www.androsophy.net/larte-del-falso-2/ [25 May 2014]

ANSA, 2013a Library theft 'incurable wound' to Naples, judge says, *ANSA.it* [online], 10 July, available from: http://www.ansa.it/web/notizie/rubriche/english/2013/07/10/Library-theft-incurable-wound-Naples-judge-says_9003902.html [14 December 2014]

— 2013b Cc recuperano manoscritti Verga da 4 mln: Sequestrati a Roma e Pavia, denunciata anziana per ricettazione, *ANSA.it* [online], 19 July, available from: http://www.ansa.it/web/notizie/regioni/lazio/2013/07/19/Cc-recuperano-manoscritti-Verga-4-mln_9044011.html#content-corpo [27 July 2013]

Arma dei Carabinieri, 2010 *Comando Carabinieri Tutela Patrimonio Culturale di Venezia, sgominata banda specializzata nei furti di beni d'arte* [online], 20 January, available from: https://it-it.facebook.com/notes/sicurezza-pubblica/comando-carabinieri-tutela-patrimonio-culturale-di-venezia-sgominata-banda-speci/264603291090 [27 January 2014]

Art Daily, 2010 Two Ancient Statues Stolen in the 1980s From Italian Museums are Now Home, artdaily.org [online], available from: http://www.artdaily.com/section/news/index.asp?int_sec=2&int_new=42692#.USUBrKU1Z1I [20 February 2013]

asca.it, 2012 Archeologia: Carabinieri recuperano testa statua trafugata a Pompei, asca.it [online], 18 October, available from: http://www.asca.it/news-Archeologia__Carabinieri_recuperano_testa_statua_trafugata_a_Pompei-1208393.html [13 April 2013]

Association for Research into Crimes against Art (ARCA), 2014 Dr Daniela Rizzo and Mr Maurizio Pellegrini Win ARCA's 2014 Art Protection & Recovery Award, ARCA [online], 12 April, available from: http://art-crime.blogspot.co.uk/2014/04/dr-daniela-rizzo-and-mr-maurizio.html [12 April 2014]

Azzaman, A S, 2011 Italy to train Iraqi archaeologists and rehabilitate National Museum, Culture in Development [online], 23 October, available from: http://www.cultureindevelopment.nl/News/Dossier_Heritage_Iraq/1381/Italy_to_train_Iraqi_archaeologists_and_rehabilitate_National_Museum [11 November 2012]

Bailey, M, 2013 Decade of conflict takes its toll on Iraq, The Art Newspaper [online], Issue 244, 19 March, available from: http://www.theartnewspaper.com/articles/Decade%20of%20conflict%20takes%20its%20toll%20on%20Iraq/29007 [9 September 2014]

Barkham, P, 2001 Dealer convicted of fraud as the aboriginal art world fights back, The Guardian [online], 24 February, available from: http://www.theguardian.com/world/2001/feb/24/patrick-barkham [22 February 2014]

Basel Institute for Governance, 2009 Conference Programme for Governance of Cultural Property: Preservation and Recovery, 29–30 September, Basel

Basevi, E, 2001 Azienda Rilievo Alienazione Residuati, in Commissione per la ricostruzione delle vicende che hanno caratterizzato in Italia le attività di acquisizione dei beni dei cittadini ebrei da parte di organismi pubblici e privati, Rapporto generale, Istituto Poligrafico e Zecca dello Stato, Rome [online], 523–34, available from: http://www.lootedart.com/MFEU4H81573 [17 February 2014]

BBC News, 2014 Stolen Gauguin painting 'hung on factory worker's wall', BBC News [online], 2 April, available from: http://www.bbc.com/news/entertainment-arts-26848889 [21 April 2014]

Berger, D, 2009 Ministry for Cultural Heritage and Activities, Advisor to the Minister, Opening Remarks, International Meeting on Illicit Traffic of Cultural Property, 16–17 December, Ministero per i Beni e le Attività Culturali, Segretariato Generale, Gangemi Editori spa, Rome, 21–3

Berni, F, 2010 Monza, recuperata preziosa Via Crucis rubata a Vercelli, Il Cittadino, 24 November [online], available from: http://www.ilcittadinomb.it/stories/Cronaca/169733_monza_recuperata_preziosa_via_crucis_rubata_a_vercelli/ [29 October 2014]

Bianchi, A, 2010 Charges dismissed against ex-Getty curator Marion True by Italian judge, Los Angeles Times [online], 13 October, available from: http://latimesblogs.latimes.com/culture-monster/2010/10/charges-dismissed-against-getty-curator-marion-true-by-italian-judge.html [20 February 2013]

Bojano, G, 2011 Casillo chiude il <<Museo del falso>>: La decisione dopo 20 anni di attività, Corriere del Mezzogiorno.it [online], 9 March, available from: http://corrieredelmezzogiorno.corriere.it/napoli/notizie/arte_e_cultura/2011/9-marzo-2011/casillo-chiude-ilmuseo-falsola-decisione-20-anni-attivita--190185330002.shtml [16 May 2014]

BolognaToday, 2013 Acquistava opere d'arte con assegni falsi, arrestato truffatore 59enne, BolognaToday [online], 26 July, available from: http://www.bolognatoday.it/cronaca/truffatore-arresto-opere-arte-gallerie.html [28 July 2013]

Bondi, S, 2009 Opening Address, International Meeting on Illicit Traffic of Cultural Property, Rome, 16–17 December

Cannataro, F, 2013 Cosenza/Tutela Patrimonio Culturale. A buon fine l'Operazione 'Ginestra', *Rassegna Stampa Militare* [online], 19 January, available from: http://rassegnastampamilitare. com/2013/01/19/cosenza-tutela-patrimonio-culturale-a-buon-fine-loperazione-ginestra/ [21 June 2013]

Cappitelli, S, 2009 Transnational crimes in cultural property's field: problems and perspectives, *International Meeting on Illicit Traffic of Cultural Property*, Rome, 16–17 December

Carabinieri Service for the Protection of Cultural Property, 2013 *Handbook on the Protection of Ecclesiastical Cultural Property*, MiBAC and Pontificium Consilium di Cultura, Roma

Carabinieri.it, 2013 Decalogo per l'acquisto di opere d'arte contemporanee [online], available from: http://www.carabinieri.it/Internet/Cittadino/Consigli/Tematici/Beni+interesse+culturale/02_ Beni_culturali_DECALOGO.htm [December 2013]

Carabinieri TPC, 2006 *Trafficking in Stolen Artworks*, l'Unità Nazionale CEPOL, 19–23 June

— 2007 *Il Traffico Illecito dei Beni Culturali*, l'Unità Nazionale CEPOL, 8–11 May

— 2011 Arte in Ostaggio, *Bollettino delle ricerche 33*

Carroll, R, 2002 Loot (Art Theft Special Report), *The Guardian*, 4 May

Caruso, S, 2012 Inaugurazione mostra Restituzione 2001 2011, *AmanteaOnline* [online], 13 April, available from: http://www.amanteaonline.it/inaugurazione-mostra-restituzioni-2001–2011–797634. html [15 April 2012]

CC TPC, 2002 Traffico illecito del patrimonio archeologico internazionalizzazione del fenomeno e problematiche di contrasto, Atti del VII Convegno Internazionale, *MiBAC, Bollettino di Numismatica*, Supplemento al N. 38

Celentano, A, 2011 Personal communication (interview with the author (L Rush)), 7 February, Carabinieri Archaeology Unit Headquarters, Trastevere

Centre of Excellence for Stability Police Units (CoESPU), 2009 Training Workshop for Specialized Officials Involved in the Safeguard of the Cultural Heritage and the Fight against Illicit Traffic of Cultural Objects: General outline and aims, Vicenza, 15–26 June

Chechi, A, Aufseesser, L, Marc-André Renold, M-A, 2011 Case Machu Picchu Collection – Peru and Yale University, *Arthemis* [online], Art-Law Centre, University of Geneva, available from: https:// plone.unige.ch/art-adr/cases-affaires/machu-picchu-collection-2013-peru-and-yale-university/case-note-2013-machu-picchu-collection-2013-peru-and-yale-university [9 September 2014]

Il Cittadino mb, 2009 Lodola dona due creazioni ai Carabinieri del Tpc monzese, *Il Cittadino mb, Il Quotidiano online di Monza e Brianza* [online], 17 April, available from: http://ilcittadinomb.it/ stories/Homepage/lodola-dona-due-creazioniai-carabinieri-del-tpc-monzese_67006_11/ [29 June 2013]

Cohen, P, 2013 Valuable as Art, but Priceless as a Tool to Launder Money, *The New York Times* [online], 12 May, available from: http://www.nytimes.com/2013/05/13/arts/design/art-proves-attractive-refuge-for-money-launderers.html?pagewanted=all [6 July 2013]

— 2014 A Modigliani? Who Says So?, *The New York Times* [online], 2 February, available from: http:// www.nytimes.com/2014/02/03/arts/design/a-modigliani-who-says-so.html?_r=0 [7 February 2013]

Colasanti, R (Lt Colonel), 2013 Personal communication (email exchange with the author (Millington)), 31 July, with reference to TPC training document, available from: http://www.uniroma3.it/scheda-PostLauream13.php?pl=309&facolta=107 [20 January 2015]

Comando Carabinieri per la Tutela del Patrimonio Culturale, 2011 *Attività Operativa 2011*

Comando Carabinieri Tutela Patrimonio Culturale, 2006 *Comando Carabinieri Tutela Patrimonio Culturale, CEPOL Course 2006/35, Trafficking in Stolen Artworks*, 19–23 June, Rome

— 2007 *Comando Carabinieri Tutela Patrimonio Culturale, Il Traffico Illecito dei Beni Culturali*, Unità Nazionale CEPOL, 8–11 May, Rome

— 2008 *Origini, funzioni e articolazioni: Legislazione di Tutela* [online], available from: http://www.

carabinieri.it/Internet/imagestore/cittadino/informazioni/tutela/culturale/Raccolta_normativa.pdf [24 September 2014]

Comuni-Italiani.it, 2012 *Statistiche Provincia di Milano* [online], available from: http://www.comuni-italiani.it/015/statistiche/ [30 March 2014]

Corriere del Mezzogiorno, 2012 Girolamini, ritrovati 240 libri della biblioteca. Altri già finiti all'estero, *Corriere del Mezzogiorno* [online], 18 May, available from: http://corrieredelmezzogiorno.corriere.it/napoli/notizie/cronaca/2012/18-maggio-2012/ritrovati-240-libri-sottratti-biblioteca-girolamini--201242456116.shtml [9 February 2013]

Corriere del Veneto, 2013 Furti d'arte, rubate tre tele di Licata alla mostra nell'ospedale Ca' Foncello, *corrieredelveneto.it* [online], 5 August, available from: http://corrieredelveneto.corriere.it/veneto/notizie/cronaca/2013/5-agosto-2013/furti-d-arte-rubate-tre-tele-licata-mostra-ospedale-ca-foncello-2222493831646.shtml [15 August 2013]

Corriere di Bologna.it, 2012 Un falso Picasso e due Carracci rubati tra i sequestri 2011 dei Carabinieri, *Corriere di Bologna* [online], 13 February, available from: http://corrieredibologna.it/bologna/notizie/cronaca/2012/13-febbraio-2012/falso-picasso-due-carracci-rubati-sequestri-2011-carabinieri-1903264676428.shtml [14 February 2012]

Corriere di Ragusa.it, 2014 Rubata la statuetta di San Francesco da edicola votiva, *corrierediragusa.it* [online], 20 January, available from: http://www.corrierediragusa.it/articoli/cronache/modica/24986-rubata-la-statuetta-di-san-francesco-da-edicola-votiva.html [23 January 2014]

Cortellessa, L (Col), 2012 The Carabinieri TPC, paper presented at *Deloitte 5th Art & Finance Conference: The new faces of art investment*, 15 June, Basel

Cortes, A, 2002 La situazione dei siti archeologici in Spagna, *Bollettino Di Numismatica, Atti del 7° Convegno Internazionale Roma, 25–28 giugno 2001*, 315–22

Corvino, C, 2013 Italian police recover Etruscan treasures, *Reuters* [online], 27 June, available from: http://www.reuters.com/article/2013/06/27/us-italy-etruscan-idUSBRE95Q0Q120130627 [8 July 2013]

Costantini, C (Capt), 2011 Personal communication (interview with the author (Rush)), 2 March, Palazzo Pitti, Firenze TPC Headquarters

Craddock, P, 2009 *Scientific Investigation of Copies, Fakes and Forgeries*, Butterworth-Heinemann, Oxford

Cremers, T, 2008 Not everything that is legal is ethical. No museum should hold on to stolen objects, not even if they bought those as good faith buyer... *Blog* [online], 13 February, available from: http://www.museum-security.org/category/blog-world-from-related-blogs/ton-cremers/ [15 November 2012]

Croce, M, 2007 Il falso d'arte. Natura, sviluppo e legislazione, *Arma dei Carabinieri* [online], September, available from: http://www.carabinieri.it/Internet/Editoria/Rassegna+Arma/2007/3/Studi/03_Croce.htm [16 March 2014]

Cuno, J, 2008 *Who Owns Antiquity? Museums and the Battle over our Ancient Heritage*, Princeton University Press, Princeton NJ

Cura della Direzione Generale delle Arti, 1942 *La Protezione del Patrimonio Artistico Nazionale dalle Offese della Guerra Aerea*, Casa Editrice Felice Le Monnier, Firenze

D'Arco, E, 2013 Arma e Gff insieme per il patrimonio culturale italiano, *Giffoni experience* [online], available from: http://www.giffonifilmfestival.it/press/item/1572-arma-gff-insieme-per-il-patrimonio-culturale-italiano.html [28 July 2013]

DaringToDo, 2013 Carabinieri, meno furti d'arte ma più falsi sul mercato. Bilancio del Comando Tutela Patrimonio Culturale, *DaringToDo* [online], 24 April, available from: http://www.daringtodo.com/lang/it/2013/04/24/carabinieri-meno-furti-darte-ma-piu-falsi-sul-mercato-bilancio-del-comando-tutela-patrimonio-culturale/ [1 May 2013]

David, A, 2007 Crackdown Curbs Italy's 'Tomb Raiders', *The Washington Post* [online], 5 July, available from: http://www.washingtonpost.com/wp-dyn/content/article/2007/07/05/AR2007070501090. html [30 December 2014]

De Caro, 2009 *International Meeting on Illicit Traffic of Cultural Property*, Rome, 16–17 December

Di Chio, F, 2011 Banda di falsari dell'arte truffa il marchese d'Aragona, *Il Tempo.it* [online], 14 December, available from: http://www.iltempo.it/roma-capitale/2011/12/14/banda-di-falsari-dell-arte-br-truffa-il-marchese-d-aragona-1.41936 [16 May 2014]

Di Fonzo, M R, 2012 'Think you can steal our Caravaggio and get away with It? Think again.' An analysis of the Italian cultural property model, *George Washington International Law Review* 44.3, 539–71, available from: http://search.proquest.com/docview/1269653277 [27 July 2013]

Donia, G, 2009 IILA cooperation in Latin America fighting the illicit traffic of cultural property, *International Meeting on Illicit Traffic of Cultural Property*, Rome, 16–17 December

Durney, M, 2009 In Pursuit of Art Theft and WWII Treasures updated, *Art Theft Central* [online], 11 February, previously available from: http://arttheftcentral.blogspot.com/2009/02/in-pursuit-of-art-theft-and-wwiis.html [11 February 2009]

The Economist, 2012 Collectors, artists and lawyers: Fear of litigation is hobbling the art market, *The Economist*, 24 November, 69–70

Edgers, G, 2013 A museum, a heist, a rescued 'Madonna', *The Boston Globe* [online], 14 September, available from: http://www.bostonglobe.com/arts/theater-art/2013/09/14/priceless-century-italian-masterpiece-arrives-museum-fine-arts/SI829Qbga8tIyhP0owWtXL/story.html [21 April 2014]

Edsel, R, 2014 Most Wanted: Works of Art, *The Monuments Men Foundation* [online], available from: http://www.monumentsmenfoundation.org/join-the-hunt/most-wanted-works-of-art [17 February 2014]

Facci, F, 2012 Cosa fu la strage di Capaci, *Il Post* [online], 23 May, available from: http://www.ilpost.it/2012/05/23/cosa-fu-la-strage-di-capaci/ [22 November 2014]

Farnesina (Ministry of Foreign Affairs), 2013 *The Italo-Latin American Institute (IILA)* [online], available from: http://www.esteri.it/MAE/EN/Politica_Estera/Aree_Geografiche/Americhe/IstitutoItaloLatinoAmericano/ [22 April 2013]

Il Fatto Quotidiano, 2012 Caso biblioteca Girolamini, gli inquirenti: 'Gente che agiva come struttura parallela', *Il Fatto Quotidiano* [online], 24 May, available from: http://tv.ilfattoquotidiano.it/2012/05/24/biblioteca-girolamini-inquirenti-gente-agiva-come-struttura-parallela/198148/ [20 February 2013]

— 2013a Biblioteca Girolamini, Dell'Utri indagato: 'I libri mi furono regalati', *Il Fatto Quotidiano* [online], 22 February, available from: http://www.ilfattoquotidiano.it/2013/02/22/biblioteca-gerolamini-dellutri-indagato-libri-mi-furono-regalati/509156/ [12 February 2013]

— 2013b Napoli, rubati libri antichi: cinque arresti. Indagata collaboratrice di Dell'Utri, *Il Fatto Quotidiano* [online], 24 May, available from: http://www.ilfattoquotidiano.it/2012/05/24/napoli-furto-libri-antichi-cinque-arresti-indagata-collaboratrice-senatore-dellutri/240097/ [12 February 2013]

FBI, 2009 Arrivederci: Recovered Italian Artifacts Headed Home, *FBI* [online], available from: http://www.fbi.gov/news/stories/2009/june/recovered-italian-artifacts-headed-home/artifacts061109 [8 June 2013]

— 2012 Protecting Cultural Heritage from Art Theft, *FBI* [online], March, available from: http://www.fbi.gov/stats-services/publications/law-enforcement-bulletin/march-2012/protecting-cultural-heritage-from-art-theft [3 April 2013]

Felch, J, 2012 Italian court upholds claim on Getty bronze, *Los Angeles Times* [online], 4 May, available from: http://articles.latimes.com/2012/may/04/entertainment/la-et-getty-bronze-ruling-20120504 [19 February 2013]

Felch, J, and Frammolino, R, 2011 *Chasing Aphrodite: The Hunt for Looted Antiquities at the World's Richest Museum*, Houghton Mifflin Harcourt, Boston and New York

Ferri, P, 2009 The illicit traffic of cultural objects and the current changes in its evaluation, *International Meeting on Illicit Traffic of Cultural Property*, Rome, 16–17 December, 205–13

Firenze Today, 2013 Arte, in Toscana e Umbria recuperati beni per 2,8 milioni di euro, *Firenze Today* [online], 10 May, available from: http://www.firenzetoday.it/cronaca/recupero-opere-arte-rubate-toscana-2012.html [9 July 2014]

Fleming, S, 1975 *Authenticity in Art: The Scientific Detection of Forgery*, Crane Russak & Co, New York

Florida Department of State, 2014 Projects, Miami Circle [online], available from: http://info.flheritage.com/miami-circle/index.cfm [14 December 2014]

Forbes, A, 2014 Twelve Old Master Paintings Worth Millions Returned to Italian Museum, *artnetnews.com* [online], 11 June, available from: http://news.artnet.com/art-world/12-old-master-paintings-worth-millions-returned-to-italian-museum-38053 [22 June 2014]

Foresi, A, 2006 La nascita della Mafia: La privatizzazione della violenza per ottenere ordine e potere, *Politica Domani* Num 5 [online], February, available from: http://www.politicadomani.it/pdov/index.html?main=Pagine/Giornale/Num55/Nascita%20della%20Mafia.htm [12 August 2014]

Franchi, E, 2010 *I viaggi dell'Assunta*, Pisa University Press, Pisa

Fravolini, F, 2012 An exhibition exposes the Calabrian culture Refunds, *Tourism in Italy* [online], 26 June, available from: http://turismo-in.it/en/news-calabria/the-exhibition-exposes-calabrian-culture-refunds/ [13 June 2013]

Frisaldi, M, 2013 Foggia e il 'tesoro' ritrovato: recuperati 548 reperti archeologici, denunciati 21 tombaroli, *foggiatoday.it* [online], 10 July, available from: www.foggiatoday.it/cronaca/sequestro-reperti-archeologici-foggia-denunciati-tombaroli.html [27 July 2013]

Gattini, A, 1996 Restitution by Russia of Works of Art Removed from German Territory at the End of the Second World War, *European Journal of International Law* 7, 67–88

Gay, M, 2012 For the St Louis Art Museum, a Legal Victory Raises Ethical Questions, *The Atlantic* [online], 30 May, available from: http://www.theatlantic.com/national/archive/2012/05/for-the-st-louis-art-museum-a-legal-victory-raises-ethical-questions/257839/ [5 July 2013]

La Gazzetta del Mezzogiorno, 2012 La scoperta dell'artista. Statue in cartapesta rubate e poste in vendita su internet, *La Gazzetta del Mezzogiorno* [online], 6 June, available from: http://www.lagazzettadelmezzogiorno.it/notizia.php?IDNotizia=525268&IDCategoria=1 [9 June 2013]

Gerstenblith, P, 2013 Personal communication (telephone conversation with the author (Rush)), New York and Chicago, 30 April

Gill, D, 2012 Sabratha portrait head returned to Libya, *Looting Matters* [online], 27 January, available from: http://lootingmatters.blogspot.com/2012/01/sabratha-portrait-head-returned-to.html [20 February 2013]

GoCity Puglia, 2012 Rimpatriati beni archeologici trafugati in Germania, *GoCity Puglia* [online], 22 October, available from: http://puglia.go-city.it/notizie/cronaca/14887-rimpatriati-beni-archeologici-trafugati-in-germania.html [10 June 2013]

Going, J, 2011 Personal communication (conversation with the author (Rush)), American Academy in Rome, March

Granata, F, 2003 *Obiettivamente: i Carabinieri e la Sicilia nella fotografia d'Autore*, Photographic Exhibition, Museo Archeologico Regionale di Agrigento, 25 July–14 September

Grassi, G, 2009 La Natività Perduta del Caravaggio, *Scudit Scuola di Italiano* [online], 19 September, available from: http://www.scudit.net/mdmafianativita.htm [10 April 2013]

Harclerode, P, and Pittaway, B, 1999 *The Lost Masters: The Looting of Europe's Treasurehouses*, Weidenfeld and Nicolson, London

Harris, G, 2011 Football star and former Formula 1 boss caught up in fakes case, *The Art Newspaper* [online], 10 November, available from: http://www.theartnewspaper.com/articles/Football-star-and-former-Formula--boss-caught-up-in-fakes-case/25039 [20 January 2014]

Higgins, V, 2010 Personal communication (conversation with the author (L Rush), recounting conversation with CHO A Higueras), 7 April

The History Blog, 2013 Police recover huge trove of looted Etruscan artifacts, *thehistoryblog.com* [online], available from: http://www.thehistoryblog.com/archives/25896 [8 July 2013]

Hodes, S, 2014 Consignment Fraud in the USA: Art Market Susceptibility, paper presented at the *NYU SCPS Symposium: Art Crime Fakes, Forgeries, and Looted and Stolen Art*, 6 June, New York

Huffington Post, 2012 Italian police recover Roman statue stolen from Pompeii decades ago, *Huffington Post* [online], 18 October, available from: http://www.huffingtonpost.com/2012/10/18/head-of-statue-of-neros-m_n_1978335.html [14 December 2014]

ICCROM, 2013 *ICCROM courses* [online], available from: http://www.iccrom.org/courses/ [1 November 2014]

ICOM, 2013 *ICOM Missions* [online], available from: http://icom.museum/the-organisation/icom-missions/ [3 September 2014]

ICOMOS, 2013 *ICOMOS' Mission* [online], available from: http://www.icomos.org/en/about-icomos/mission-and-vision/icomos-mission [3 September 2014]

IIHL, 2010 *Programme Cultural Property Seminar Draft* [online], available from: http://www.iihl.org/iihl/Documents/Programme%20Cultural%20Property%20Seminar%20%28Draft%20as%20at%2022%20Nov%2010%29_2.pdf [1 November 2014]

IILA, 2010 Book Announcement for *Lucha contra el trafico ilicito de los bienes culturales. Los Instrumentos*, available from: http://www.gangemieditore.com/scheda_articolo.php?id_prodotto=1850 [2 November 2014]

Ilari, A, 2011 Personal communication (interview with the author (Rush)), 4 April, Regional Headquarters of Carabinieri Tutela Patrimonio Culturale, Monza

Inside Art, 2012 L'arte del falso ha un giro d'affari di 1,5 miliardi, *Inside Art* [online], 17 September, available from: http://www.insideart.eu/2012/09/17/larte-del-falso-ha-un-giro-daffari-di-15-miliardi/ [18 September 2012]

InterNapoli.it, 2013 Mostra fotografica: 30 anni di furti d'arte a Giugliano, *InterNapoli.it* [online], 8 March, available from: http://www.internapoli.it/articolo.asp?id=25923 [11 March 2013]

International Meeting on Illicit Traffic of Cultural Property, Rome, 16–17 December, 205–13

Interno18, 2011 Operazione 'RoViNa'. Sgominata gang di tombaroli, scoperto un tesoro di decine di milioni di euro, *Interno18* [online], 21 January, available from: http://interno18.it/cronaca/18199/operazione-rovina-sgominata-gang-di-tombaroli-scoperto-un-tesoro-di-decine-di-milioni [2 February 2014]

Italian Association for Italian War-Damaged Monuments, 1946 *Fifty War-Damaged Monuments of Italy*, Istituto Poligrafico dello Stato, Rome

Johnson-Kelly, L, 2013 Presentation to the Annual Meeting of the New York State Archaeological Association, Watertown NY

Kila, J, 2012 *Heritage Under Siege*, Brill, Amsterdam

Kington, T, 2012 Stolen paintings recovered in Rome 40 years after art heist, *The Guardian* [online], 9 March, available from: http://www.theguardian.com/artanddesign/2012/mar/09/stolen-paintings-rome-art-heist?newsfeed=true [6 October 2013]

Kurtz, M J, 2006 *America and the Return of Nazi Contraband: The Recovery of Europe's Cultural Treasures*, Cambridge University Press, Cambridge

Lamezia Terme, 2012 Strani furti: rubata una croce in legno e altri oggetti sacri, *Lamezia Terme* [online], 23 September, available from: http://www.lameziaterme.net/index.php?option=com_content&view=article&id=2707:strani-furti-rubata-una-croce-in-legno-e-altri-oggetti-sacri-&catid=62:cronaca&Itemid=218 [25 February 2013]

Leonardis, A, 2011 Personal communication (Tour of Messapian site with the author (Rush)), 27 July

Lepri, T, 2013 Former boss of Naples historic library confesses to multiple book thefts, *The Art News-*

paper [online], 22 March, available from: http://www.theartnewspaper.com/articles/Former-boss-of-Naples-historic-library-confesses-to-multiple-book-thefts/29126 [22 March 2013]

Lettera 43, 2013 Rubava anfore romane, arrestato ex assessore. Trafugate da nave sommersa, scoperte dopo un furto in casa, *www.lettera43.it* [online], 17 May, available from: http://www.lettera43.it/cronaca/rubava-anfore-romane-arrestato-ex-assessore_4367595575.htm [30 May 2013]

Libero Quotidiano, 2012 Cosenza: quadri trafugati trovati durante perquisizione in casa pregiudicato, *LiberoQuotidiano.it* [online], 9 May, available from: http://www.liberoquotidiano.it/news/1010432/Cosenza-quadri-trafugati-trovati-durante-perquisizione-in-casa-pregiudicato.html [10 May 2012]

Livorno Now, 2009 Modigliani's Heads: One of the Greatest Hoaxes in the History of Italian Art, *Livorno Now* [online], available from: http://www.livornonow.com/modiglianis_heads [22 February 2014]

Luke, C, and Rush, L, 2011 Personal communication (conversation with unidentified Turkish child), Sardis Spring Festival, 8 May

Manola, C, and Ragusa, A, 2012 The Carabinieri TPC, public presentation at the University of Pennsylvania Cultural Heritage Center, 8 November

Marín-Aguilera, B, 2012 Italy, a huge Open-air Museum: 'Tombaroli' at Cerveteri and Tarquinia, *Proceedings of the First International Conference on Best Practices in World Heritage: Archaeology*, 563–79

Marseglia, G, 2011 Personal communication (visit to Sicily and Palermo TPC headquarters by the author (Rush)), 22–25 March

Marsicalive, 2012 Danneggiano reperti archeologici dall'abbazia di Santa Maria della Vittoria, due denunciati, *Marsicalive* [online], 10 February, available from: http://www.marsicalive.it/?p=20606 [17 October 2013]

Il Mattino, 2012 Recuperati 95 dipinti rubati nelle chiese per un valore totale di 2 milioni, *Il Mattino* [online], 17 December, available from: http://www.ilmattino.it/napoli/citta/recuperati_95_dipinti_rubati_nelle_chiese_per_un_valore_totale_di_2_milioni/notizie/238279.shtml [17 December 2012]

McCurry, S, 2003 *IRAQ. Nasiriyah. 2003. A young marine relaxes in the cool of the Nasiriyah Museum, which exhibits replicas of ancient statues*, available from: http://www.magnumphotos.com/image/NYC65664.html [4 January 2015]

McDonnell, K, 2012 Decorating with Spolia: The American Market in Ancient Architecture, paper presented at the *Association for Research into Crimes against Art Annual Conference*, Amelia, Italy

Messaggero Veneto, 2012 Recuperate due statue rubate 34 anni fa, *Messaggero Veneto* [online], 4 August, available from: http://messaggeroveneto.gelocal.it/cronaca/2012/08/04/news/recuperate-due-statue-rubate-44-anni-fa-1.5500349 [19 February 2013]

Milano.corriere.it, 2012 Funzionario sparito con 5 milioni arrestato mentre tenta l'espatrio, *Milano.corriere.it* [online], 24 October, available from: http://milano.corriere.it/milano/notizie/cronaca/12_ottobre_24/funzionario-beni-culturali-lazio-fuggito-cinque-milioni-arrestato-carabinieri-2112399296500.shtml [30 October 2012]

Ministero dei Beni e delle Attività Culturali e del Turismo, 2009 Operazione dei Carabinieri del Nucleo Tutela Patrimonio Culturale di Venezia, *www.beniculturali.it* [online], 28 September, available from: http://www.beniculturali.it/mibac/export/MiBAC/sito-MiBAC/Contenuti/Ministero/UfficioStampa/News/visualizza_asset.html_1384679076.html [27 January 2014]

— 2012 Il Nucleo Carabinieri Tutela Patrimonio Culturale di Venezia a Guardia del Paesaggio Veronese, *www.beniculturali.it* [online], 29 August, available from: http://www.beniculturali.it/mibac/export/MiBAC/sito-MiBAC/Contenuti/MibacUnif/Comunicati/visualizza_asset.html_1691148334.html [22 January 2014]

— 2013a Recuperata a Torino, ad opera del Nucleo Tutela Patrimonio Culturale piemontese, un dipinto del pittore Marc Chagall rubato nel 2002 a bordo di uno yacht statunitense ormeggiato a Savona, *www.beniculturali.it* [online], 8 April, available from: http://www.beniculturali.it/mibac/export/ MiBAC/sito-MiBAC/Contenuti/MibacUnif/Comunicati/visualizza_asset.html_206678457.html [16 March 2014]

— 2013b Operazione 'Art Gallery', *www.beniculturali.it* [online], 19 December, available from: http:// www.beniculturali.it/mibac/export/MiBAC/sito-MiBAC/Contenuti/MibacUnif/Comunicati/visu-alizza_asset.html_240085971.html [4 April 2014]

Ministero della Difesa Italiana, 2011 *Carabinieri Foreign Courses* [online], previously available from: http://www.difesa.it/SMD/Staff/Reparti/I-reparto/foreign_courses/Documents/CARABI-NIERI%20%202011.pdf [10 January 2013]

Ministero per i Beni e le Attività Culturali (MiBAC), Comando Carabinieri Tutela Patrimonio Culturale, 2008 *Comando Carabinieri TPC, XII Corso di specializzazione 'Tutela Patrimonio Culturale'*, Roma, 5–30 May

Ministero per i Beni e le Attività Culturali, 2011 *1861–2011: 150 Anni Italia Unita*, Italia Unita 150 [online], available from: http://www.italiaunita150.it/ [23 April 2013]

— 2012 *Attività Operativa, 2012 Comando Carabinieri Tutela Patrimonio Culturale Nucleo di Bari*

Ministry of Cultural Heritage and Activities, Carabinieri Headquarters for the Protection of Cultural Heritage, 2009 *The Protection of Cultural Heritage*, Edizioni Polistampa, Firenze

Modianot-Fox, D, 2008 Showcasing Shams: At the Museum of Fakes, what's not real is still art, *Smithsonian.com* [online], 7 May, available from: http://www.smithsonianmag.com/arts-culture/ art-crimes-shams.html#ixzz2DvgiSpHs [2 December 2012]

Montanari, T, 2012 Libri, Uomini e Topi, *Il Fatto Quotidiano* [online], 30 March, available from: http://www.patrimoniosos.it/rsol.php?op=getarticle&id=94629 [14 December 2014]

Montreal Gazette, 2012 Italian police recover Roman statue stolen from Pompeii decades ago, *Montreal Gazette* [online], 21 October, available from: http://www.montrealgazette.com/Stolen+Pompeii+sta tue+recovered/7408919/story.html [23 October 2012]

Monza TPC, 2013 *Operazione Reliquia* [online], available from: http://lightstorage.ecodibergamo.it/ mediaon/cms.ecodibergamo/storage/site_media/media/old_attach/2013/03/Operazione_Reliquia. pdf?attach_m [16 March 2014]

Mossa, M, 2012 Speech given to Assemblea Generale INTERPOL, Rome, 5–8 November

Muller, I M, 2012 Catalogue entry in *Recovered Treasures; International cooperation in the fight against illicit trafficking of cultural property; successes of the Italian Carabinieri*, exhibition catalogue, Sillabe, Italy

Myreggionline, 2012 Furto d'opere d'arte, due reggiani arrestati, *myreggionline* [online], 13 March, available from: http://www.reggionline.com/?q=content/furto-dopere-darte-due-reggiani-arrestati [14 December 2014]

Newz.it, 2012 Dipinti rubati e recuperati dai Carabinieri: denunciate due persone *Newz.it* [online], 7 April, available from: http://www.newz.it/2012/04/06/cosenza-dipinti-rubati-e-recuperati-dai-carabinieri-denunciate-due-persone/142036/ [5 August 2014]

— 2013 Sequestrati e confiscati dai Carabinieri del Nucleo Tutela Patrimonio Culturale di Cosenza 13 mila documenti storici e archivistici appartenenti al demanio culturale dello Stato, *Newz.it* [online], 27 March, available from: http://www.newz.it/2013/03/27/cosenza-sequestrati-e-confis-cati-dai-carabinieri-del-nucleo-tutela-patrimonio-culturale-di-cosenza-13-mila-documenti-storici-e-archivistici-appartenenti-al-demanio-culturale-dello-stato/169832/ [27 March 2013]

Ng, D, and Felch, J, 2013 Getty Museum to return Hades terracotta head to Sicily, *Los Angeles Times* [online], 10 January, available from: http://articles.latimes.com/2013/jan/10/entertainment/la-et-cm-getty-museum-hades-sculpture-sicily-20130110 [1 May 2013]

Nicholas, L, 1995 *The Rape of Europa: The Fate of Europe's Treasures in the Third Reich and the Second World War*, Vintage, New York

Norese, G, 2007 Forgotten Sculptors: 3. Modigliani's Heads, *noresize* [online], 25 October, available from: http://noresize.blogspot.com/2007_10_01_archive.html [16 May 2014]

NPS, 2014 African Burial Ground National Monument New York [online], available from: http://www.nps.gov/afbg/index.htm [14 December 2014]

NRC Research Press, 2014 When Art and Science Collide – the masterpiece unmasked: Physicists uncover secrets hidden beneath the surface of great works of art, *NRC Research Press* [online], 5 March, available from: http://www.nrcresearchpress.com/doi/story/10.4141/news.2014.03.05.223#.U0NKwl6CY0Q [7 April 2014]

La Nuova Ferrara, 2012 Ladri in azione nella chiesetta Rubato il quadro della Madonna, *La Nuova Ferrara* [online], 18 October, available from: http://lanuovaferrara.gelocal.it/cronaca/2012/10/18/news/ladri-in-azione-nella-chiesetta-rubato-il-quadro-della-madonna-1.5881511 [2 September 2013]

Ojetti, H, 1917 *Les Monuments Italiens et la Guerre*, Alfieri & Lacroix, Milan

Ornaghi, L, 2012 Catalogue entry in *Recovered Treasures; International cooperation in the fight against illicit trafficking of cultural property; successes of the Italian Carabinieri*, exhibition catalogue, Sillabe, Italy

Papadopoulos, J, 2009 The archaeologist perspective in relationship with law enforcement and finds descriptions, presentation at *Center of Excellence for Stability Police Units CoESPU UNESCO Course*, Vicenza, June

paperblog, 2012 Censis: 'La contraffazione inquina il mercato' Senza il falso più posti di lavoro e entrate fiscali, *paperblog*: Magazine Economia [online], 26 November, available from: http://it.paperblog.com/censis-la-contraffazione-inquina-il-mercato-senza-il-falso-piu-posti-di-lavoro-e-entrate-fiscali-1530812/ [3 March 2013]

Parapetti, R, 2008 The Contribution of the Centro Scavi di Torino to the Reconstruction of Iraqi Antiquites, in *The Destruction of Cultural Heritage in Iraq* (eds P G Stone and J Farchakh Bajjaly), The Boydell Press, Rochester NY, 229–34

Parisi, G, 2012 La bellezza svenduta, *Arma Oggi* [online], 2 February, available from: http://www.carabinieri.it/Internet/Editoria/Carabiniere/2012/02-Febbraio/ArmaOggi/086–00.htm [3 July 2013]

Parry, W, 2013 Smuggled Dinosaur's Return May Boost Mongolian Paleontology, *LiveScience* [online], 17 May, available from: http://www.livescience.com/32088-smuggled-dinosaur-boosts-mongolia-paleontology.html [26 July 2013]

Patrimoniosos.it, 2011 Sicilia – Avviata un'altra procedura per porre il vincolo archeologico alla Balza Acradina, *Patrimoniosos.it* [online], 19 May, available from: http://www.patrimoniosos.it/rsol.php?op=getarticle&id=85551 [22 June 2014]

Paolucci, A, 2009 Introductory Essay, in *L' Arma per L'Arte; Antologia di Meraviglie* (ed L D Volpe), Ministero per i Beni e le Attività Culturali, Rome

Pescara, G, 2013 Carabinieri del Nucleo TPC recuperano antichi manoscritti rubati, *retroonline.it* [online], 3 May, available from: http://www.retroonline.it/2013/05/03/carabinieri-del-nucleo-tpc-recuperano-antichi-manoscritti-rubati/ [2 March 2014]

Plebani, T, 2010 La Nascita di Venezia (narrazioni, miti, leggende), *Biblioteca Nazionale Marciana* [online], 17 March, available from: http://marciana.venezia.sbn.it/la-biblioteca/i-libri-raccontano/fonti-storiche-e-materiali-di-studio/leggere-il-medioevo-venezian-1 [14 December 2014]

Polk, K, 2002 'Fermate questo terribile saccheggio': Il traffico illecito di oggetti antichi analizzato come un mercato criminale, *Bollettino di Numismatica: Supplemento Al n. 38, Traffico Illecito del Patrimonio Archeologico; Internazionalizzazione del fenomeno e problematiche di contrasto, Atti del VII Convegno Internazionale, Roma, 25–28 giugno 2001*, MiBAC, Carabinieri TPC, 97–119, available from: http://www.numismaticadellostato.it/pns-pdf/BDN/pdf/SUPPL-38.pdf [29 June 2013]

Povoledo, E, 2006 Photograph of Getty Griffins Shown at Antiquities Trial in Rome, *The New York*

Times [online], 1 June, available from: http://www.nytimes.com/2006/06/01/arts/01gett.html?_r=0 [8 July 2013]

— 2013 Italian Police Recover Trove of Etruscan Antiquities, *The New York Times* [online], 27 June, available from: http://artsbeat.blogs.nytimes.com/2013/06/27/italian-police-recover-trove-of-etruscan-antiquities/ [8 July 2013]

Prima Pagina Molise, 2012 Importante ritrovamento nel mare di Termoli: ceppo d'ancora di una nave oneraria risalente a duemila anni fa, *Prima Pagina Molise* [online], 23 June, available from: http://www.primapaginamolise.it/detail.php?news_ID=48699 [2 December 2014]

Prospero Cecere, 2011 Operazione Rovina, Traffico Internazionale di opere d'arte scoperto dai Carabinieri di Roma e di Napoli, cinque arresti. Provenivano dall'Agro Aversano, *Prospero Cecere* [online], 21 January, available from: prosperocecere.blogspot.com/2011/01/traffico-internazionale-di-opere-darte.html [2 February 2014]

Purarelli, S, 2007 Generale Giovanni Nistri: Sempre più tutelato il patrimonio culturale, *Specchio Economico* [online], available from: http://www.specchioeconomico.com/200710/nistri.html [20 February 2013]

il Quaderno.it, 2013 Istituto Telesia, ancora una lezione di legalità dei Carabinieri [online], 15 November, available from: http://www.ilquaderno.it/istituto-telesia-ancora-una-lezione-legalita-dei-carabinieri-90307.html [27 September 2014]

Quagliarella, M (Major), 2011 Personal communication (interview with the author (Rush)), Carabinieri TPC Archaeology Unit Headquarters, Trastevere, Rome, 7 February

Quotidiano.net, 2012 Nel laboratorio di restauro trovate opere d'arte rubate: una denuncia, *Quotidiano.net* [online], 27 September, available from: http://www.ilrestodelcarlino.it/macerata/cronaca/2012/09/27/778601-opere-arte-rubate-laboratorio-restauro-ricettazione.shtml [25 February 2013]

Ragusa, A, 2012 Personal communication (conversation with the author (L Rush)), 9 November, University of Pennsylvania Cultural Heritage Center

Ramirez, M, and Mitchum, R, 2009 1,600 antiquities returning to Italy: FBI sending back stolen artifacts found in Berwyn, *Chicago Tribune* [online], 9 June, available from: http://articles.chicagotribune.com/2009-06-09/news/0906080743_1_artifacts-kushner-items [8 June 2013]

Regione Sicilia, 2013 Beni Culturali Carabinieri Comunicati [online], available from: http://www.regione.sicilia.it/beniculturali/dirbenicult/carabinieri/comunicati_view.asp?editid1=118 [10 April 2013]

La Repubblica, 1984 E' Morta a Parigi Jeanne Modigliani figlia del pittore, *La Repubblica.it Archivio* [online], available from: http://ricerca.repubblica.it/repubblica/archivio/repubblica/1984/07/29/morta-parigi-jeanne-modigliani-figlia-del.html [3 March 2013]

La Repubblica Bologna.it, 2014 Carabinieri ritrovano violino da 200mila euro, *La Repubblica Bologna.it* [online], 18 January, available from: http://bologna.repubblica.it/cronaca/2014/01/18/foto/i_carabinieri_ritrovano_violino_da_200mila_euro-76271517/1/#2 [20 January 2014]

La Repubblica Milano.it, 2013 Furti in chiesa, fenomeno stabile in Lombardia ma pezzi 'meno pregiati', *La Repubblica Milano.it* [online], 17 March, available from: http://milano.repubblica.it/dettaglio-news/milano-13:04/9972 [17 March 2013]

La Repubblica Palermo, 2013 Mafia, sette anni a Dell'Utri il pg ne avrebbe chiesto l'arresto, *La Repubblica Palermo.it* [online], 25 March, available from: http://palermo.repubblica.it/cronaca/2013/03/25/news/dell_utri_condannato_a_sette_anni-55342299/ [22 November 2014]

Il Resto del Carlino, 2012 Arte, mercato nero in crescita 'Nel mirino Ebay e Subito.it', *Il Resto del Carlino – Reggio Emilia* [online], 26 April, available from: http://www.ilrestodelcarlino.it/reggio_emilia/cronaca/2012/04/26/703495-arte_mercato_nero_crescita.shtml [28 September 2014]

Rizzo, S, 2012 La necropoli saccheggiata per togliere la tutela Unesco, *corriere.it* [online], 28 February, available from: http://www.corriere.it/cronache/12_febbraio_28/necropoli-saccheggiata-rizzo_aea0c8f4–61d6–11e1–9e7f-339fb1d47269.shtml [23 August 2013]

Rosa, R, 2011 Monza, smantellato traffico di opere d'arte rubate, *mbnews* [online], 29 July, available from: http://www.mbnews.it/2011/07/monza-smantellato-traffico-di-opere-darte-rubate/ [22 November 2014]

Rossetti, P, 2009 Carabinieri TPC: in un libro la lotta ai trafficanti d'arte, *Il Cittadino* [online], 3 April, available from: http://www.ilcittadinomb.it/stories/Monza/113076/ [7 March 2014]

Rossi, F (Lt), 2011a Personal communication (conversation with the author (Rush)), 6 March

— 2011b Personal communication (conversation with the author (Rush)), 18 April, Rome

— 2012 Personal communication (email to the author (Rush)), 21 October

Ruiz, C, and Pes, J, 2014 Italy threatens to sue UK firm over ancient 'loot', *The Art Newspaper* [online], 16 January, available from: theartnewspaper.com/articles/Italy-threatens-to-sue-UK-firm-over-ancient-loot/31445 [20 January 2014]

SAFE, 2012 'Inside the Met' with Oscar Muscarella, *Safe Antiquities For Everyone* [online], available from: http://www.savingantiquities.org/events/tours/oscar-muscarella/ [5 July 2013]

Sala, F, 2013 Rubava reliquie nelle chiese di mezza Lombardia e le rivendeva on-line: due gli indagati e quasi sessanta pezzi recuperati dai Carabinieri del Nucleo Tutela Patrimonio Culturale. Un bottino da quasi 30mila euro, *Artribune* [online], 15 March, available from: http://www.artribune.com/2013/03/rubava-reliquie-nelle-chiese-di-mezza-lombardia-e-la-rivendeva-on-line-due-gli-indagati-e-quasi-sessanta-pezzi-recuperati-dai-carabinieri-del-nucleo-tutela-patrimonio-artistico-un-bottino-da-30mila/ [30 March 2014]

Sala, S, 2009 69 dipinti recuperati dai Carabinieri del Nucleo TPC di Monza, *mbnews.it* [online], 26 February, available from: http://www.mbnews.it/2009/02/69-dipinti-recuperati-dai-carabinieri-del-nucleo-tpc-di-monza/ [26 February 2009]

Salernonotizie.it, 2013 Soprintendenza e Carabinieri insieme a salvaguardia del Patrimonio Culturale [online], 26 September, available from: http://www.salernonotizie.it/notizia.asp?ID=50114 [6 October 2013]

Salvati, G, 2013 Dopo 23 anni ritrovata la tela di Matteo Preti rubata da una chiesa di Torre Annunziata, *Metropolis Web* [online], 1 March, available from: http://www.metropolisweb.it/Notizie/Torrese/Cronaca/dopo_23_anni_ritrovata_tela_matteo_preti_rubata_da_chiesa_torre_annunziata.aspx [2 February 2014]

Salvi, D, 2002 Dalla Terra e Dall'acqua: Patrimonio Sconosciuto e Relitti di alta profondità, in CC TPC, Traffico illecito del patrimonio archeologico internazionalizzazione del fenomeno e problematiche di contrasto, Atti del 7° Convegno Internazionale, *MiBAC, Bollettino di Numismatica*, Supplemento N 38, 423–7

Sansa, F, and Gatti, C, 2012 *Il Sottobosco*, Chiarelettere, Milan

Sardegna Reporter, 2011 Piano di controllo straordinario dei Carabinieri delle aree marine protette e dei siti archeologici subacquei del nord Sardegna, *Sardegna Reporter* [online], 5 October, available from: http://www.beniculturali.it/mibac/export/MiBAC/sito-MiBAC/Contenuti/MibacUnif/Comunicati/visualizza_asset.html_871676085.html [22 November 2014]

Schivo, S, 2011 Personal communication (interview with the author (L Rush)), 4 April, Carabinieri Regional Headquarters, Monza

Scott, G, 2008 Spoliation, Cultural Property, and Japan, *University of Pennsylvania Journal of International Law* 29 (4), 803–902

Scovazzi, T, 2009 New trends in the field of restitution of removed cultural properties to the states of origin, *International Meeting on Illicit Traffic of Cultural Property*, Rome, 16–17 December

Segal, D, 2012 Swiss Freeports are Home for a Growing Treasury of Art, *The New York Times* [online], 21 July, available from: http://www.nytimes.com/2012/07/22/business/swiss-freeports-are-home-for-a-growing-treasury-of-art.html?pagewanted=all&_r=0 [16 March 2013]

Settis, S, 2011 Personal communication (conversation with the author (Rush)), American Academy in Rome, 15 June

Sezgin, C, 2014 Dr Christos Tsirogiannis matches two objects up for auction in London with objects identified in the Medici and Becchina archives, *ARCA Blog* [online], 27 March, available from: http://art-crime.blogspot.com/2014/03/dr-christos-tsirogiannis-matches-two.html [7 April 2014]

Shubert, B, 2013 Money Launderers Using Art to Cover Criminality, *The Jewish Voice* [online], 22 May, available from: http://jewishvoiceny.com/index.php?option=com_content&view=article&id=4199:money-launderers-using-art-to-cover-criminality&catid=110:national&Itemid=293 [27 Nov 2013]

Siracusa News, 2012 Carabinieri Sezione Tutela Patrimonio Culturale Siracusa ritrovano prezioso reliquiario rubato in Umbria nel 1986, *Siracusa News* [online], 7 March, available from: http://www.siracusanews.it/node/27188 [30 March 2014]

St Hilaire, R, 2012 Bataar Forfeiture Case Intensifies as Motion to Dismiss is Filed and a Second Dinosaur is Seized [online], 14 October, available from: http://culturalheritagelawyer.blogspot.nl/2012/10/bataar-forfeiture-case-intensifies-as.html [20 October 2012]

La Stampa, 2012a Certificava falsi Modì: arrestato il presidente degli Archivi Modigliani, *La Stampa* [online], 18 December, available from: http://www.lastampa.it/2012/12/18/cultura/arte/certificava-falsi-modi-arrestato-il-presidente-degli-archivi-modigliani-0R0UCJpqzG8Fba0MM68nGP/pagina.html [3 March 2013]

— 2012b Modigliani, la truffa 28 anni dopo la beffa, *La Stampa* [online], 20 December, available from: http://www.lastampa.it/2012/12/20/italia/cronache/modigliani-la-truffa-anni-dopo-la-beffa-nEYd5dsFPZA3pS8qVObxgI/pagina.html [3 March 2013]

Statoquotidiano, 2011 Cerignola, incredibile ritrovamento di un agricoltore. Reperti consegnati a Cc, *Statoquotidiano.it* [online], 10 November, available from: http://www.statoquotidiano.it/10/11/2011/cerignola-incredibile-ritrovamento-di-un-agricoltore-reperti-consegnati-a-cc/60800/ [25 July 2013]

Stella, G A, 2012 Girolamini Library's Missing Books, *Corriere della Sera* [online], 17 April, available from: http://www.corriere.it/english/12_aprile_17/girolamini_506eea66–8884–11e1–989c-fd70877d52ac.shtml [12 April 2012]

Stillman, M, 2013 Two More Ensnared in Massive Library Theft… More Likely to Come, *AE Monthly, The Magazine for Book Collectors & Booksellers* [online], March, available from: http://www.americanaexchange.com/articles/1428?id=1428 [5 August 2014]

Stone, P G, and Farchakh Bajjaly, J (eds), 2008 *The Destruction of Cultural Heritage in Iraq*, The Boydell Press, Woodbridge

Sultan, O, 2014 Announcement at a meeting of the *Afghanistan Heritage Preservation Project*, University of Arizona, witnessed by author (Rush), 21 October, University of Arizona, Tucson

Surano, D, 2007 La Tutela dei Beni Culturali, *Centro Studi di Diritto delle Arti, del Turismo e del Paesaggio*, 10 June, available from: http://www.dirittodellearti.it/surano.html [23 April 2013]

Tabita, G, 2012 Furti in biblioteca, fenomeno sottaciuto, *Quotidiano di Sicilia* [online], 13 June, available from: http://www.qds.it/10023-furti-in-biblioteca-fenomeno-sottaciuto.htm [15 June 2012]

Tagliabue, J, 1995 Armed with List, Italy Pursues Artworks Looted by Nazis, *The New York Times* [online], 28 May, available from: http://www.nytimes.com/1995/05/28/world/armed-with-list-italy-pursues-artworks-looted-by-nazis.html [17 February 2014]

Tartara, P, 2008 Historical and Modern Aerial Photography for Cultural Heritage and Environmental Knowledge, in *Remote Sensing for Environmental Monitoring, GIS Applications, and Geology VIII* (eds M Ulrich, D Civco, M Ehlers, and H Kaufmann), Proceedings of SPIE vol 7110, Bellingham, Washington

tele2000.it, 2013 Arrestato FANTOMAS dal Nucleo Carabinieri Tutela Patrimonio Culturale di Ancona, *tele2000.it* [online], 12 July, available from: http://www.tele2000.it/notizie-flash/1065-arrestato-fantomas-dal-nucleo-carabinieri-tutela-patrimonio-culturale-di-ancona [2 October 2013]

Terni Magazine, 2012 Castel dell'Aquila: Cerimonia solenne per la restituzione al culto della statua lignea di grande valore artistico e popolare rubata e ritrovata dai Carabinieri, *Terni Magazine* [online], 29 July, available from: http://www.ternimagazine.it/86556/il-fatto/castel-dellaquila-cerimonia-solenne-per-la-restituzione-al-culto-della-statua-lignea-di-grande-valore-artistico-e-pop-olare-rubata-e-ritrovata-dai-carabinieri.html [27 September 2014]

thaindian.com, 2009 Ancient Treasure of Satricum was Hidden in Bookshelf in Italy, available from: http://4fun-pics.blogspot.com/2009/08/ancient-treasure-of-satricum-was-hidden.html [3 April 2013]

Tiberi, A, 2008 Il Comando Carabinieri per la Tutela del Patrimonio Culturale. Con approfondite note documentali dedicate ad aspetti e particolarità riguardanti i beni culturali, *Nuova Rassegna di Legislazione, Dottrina e Giurisprudenza*, Number 11

Tiepolo, G, 1990 Giambattista Tiepolo: Zeichnungen aus den Städtischen Museen für Kunst und Geschichte in Triest: eine Ausstellung der Niedersächsischen Landesgalerie im Forum des Landes-museums Hannover, 23 Februar bis 16 April

Tiscali, 2013 Beni culturali: Carabinieri TPC, recuperati oltre 2mila reperti a Roma, *Tiscali* [online], 23 April, available from: http://notizie.tiscali.it/feeds/13/04/23/t_16_02_ADN20130423163521.html [1 May 2013]

Todeschini, C, 2011 Personal communication (conversation with the author (Rush)), 4 July, American Academy, Rome

Todeschini, C, and Watson, P, 2003 Familiar route out of Italy for looted ivory head, *Culture without Context*, Spring edition, McDonald Institute for Archaeological Research, Cambridge UK, avail-able from: http://www2.mcdonald.cam.ac.uk/projects/iarc/culturewithoutcontext/issue12/todes-chini-watson.htm [14 December 2014]

Trentino Corriere, 2012 Francobolli falsi, denunciato ragioniere trentino, *trentinocorrierealpi* [online], 14 March, available from: http://trentinocorrierealpi.gelocal.it/cronaca/2012/03/14/news/franco-bolli-falsi-denunciato-ragioniere-trentino-5701299 [20 March 2012]

UNESCO, 1970 *Convention on the Means of Prohibiting and Preventing the Illicit Import, Export and Transfer of Ownership of Cultural Property 1970* [online], available from: http://portal.unesco.org/en/ev.php-URL_ID=13039 [23 April 2013]

United Nations, 2004 *United Nations Convention Against Transnational Organized Crime and the Protocols Thereto*, New York

Università degli Studi di Urbino Carlo Bo, 2010 *Urbino, the Ideal City: the promotion and protection of cultural heritage in international cooperation*, Conference Programme, 15–16 April, Università degli Studi di Urbino Carlo Bo, available from: http://www.uniurb.it/it/cdocs/CWEB/887-CWEB-31032010120410-cweb.pdf [6 October 2013]

Valdarnopost, 2012 Torna a Vallombrosa un prezioso volume del XVI secolo scomparso da più di 20 anni. È una 'cinquecentina' di grande valore, *Valdarnopost* [online], 13 October, available from: http://valdarnopost.it/news/torna-a-vallombrosa-un-prezioso-volume-del-xvi-secolo-scomparso-da-piu-di-20-anni-e-una-cinquecentina-di-grande-valore [5 June 2013]

Valsecchi, F M, 2002 Attività di tutela nella Sardegna archeologica, in CC TPC, Traffico illecito del patrimonio archeologico internazionalizzazione del fenomeno e problematiche di contrasto, Atti del 7° Convegno Internazionale, *MiBAC, Bollettino di Numismatica, Supplemento N 38*, 348–52

Varese News, 2012 Furti in villa sul Verbano, un arresto, *Varese News* [online], available from: http://www3.varesenews.it/varese/articolo.php?id=247111 [25 February 2013]

Veca, M L, 2003 *Il Kosovo perduto*, Edizioni interculturali, Roma

Vicentini, M, and Morozzi, L, 1995 *Treasures Untraced: An Inventory of the Italian Art Treasures Lost During the Second World War*, Istituto Poligrafico e Zecca dello Stato, Rome

Vivereancona.it, 2012 Sicurezza anti-crimine nei Musei, un seminario con i Carabinieri tutela al patriomonio, *vivereancona.it* [online], 25 April, available from: http://www.vivereancona.it/index.php?page=articolo&articolo_id=346867 [15 June 2012]

vivienna.it, 2012 Carabinieri recuperano quadro in olio su tela del XIX secolo trafugato dalla Chiesa Madre di Villarosa, *vivienna.it* [online], 31 May, available from: http://www.vivienna.it/2012/05/31/carabinieri-recuperano-quadro-in-olio-su-tela-del-xix-secolo-trafugato-dalla-chiesa-madre-di-villa-rosa/ [5 June 2012]

Von Perfall, J, 2010 Hanover Forced to Return Stolen Tiepolo, *The Art Newspaper*, October, Issue 217, 20

Watson, P, 1983 *The Caravaggio Conspiracy: A True Story of Deception, Theft and Smuggling in the Art World*, Doubleday, New York

Watson, P, and Todeschini, C, 2007 *The Medici Conspiracy: The Illicit Journey of Looted Antiquities – From Italy's Tomb Raiders to the World's Greatest Museums*, Public Affairs, New York

Willey, D, 2012 Italy tracks down copy of Da Vinci's lost masterpiece, *BBC News* [online], 1 December, available from: http://www.bbc.co.uk/news/uk-england-humber-20571213 [1 December 2012]

Williams, P, 2013 Bones of Contention: a Florida man's curious trade in Mongolian dinosaurs, *The New Yorker* [online], 28 January, available from: http://www.newyorker.com/reporting/2013/01/28/130128fa_fact_williams [26 July 2013]

Wilsey, S, 2013 Open Water, Among the Gondoliers of Venice, *The New Yorker*, 22 April, 40–7

About the Authors

Laurie Rush has a BA from Indiana University Bloomington and an MA and PhD in Anthropology from Northwestern University. She has served as Installation Archaeologist for the US Army and the 10th Mountain Division at Fort Drum, NY, for over 15 years, where she created training materials for awareness of archaeology and heritage for deploying military personnel. Recognition for Dr Rush and her programme at Fort Drum culminated with the 2010 Booth Family Rome Prize in Historic Preservation. She served as military liaison for the return of Ur to the Iraqi people in 2009, is a Board Member of the US Committee of the Blue Shield and has participated in numerous international military exercises and training events as an advocate for cultural property protection. She has been referred to in the media as a modern 'Monuments Woman'.

Luisa Benedettini Millington is an independent researcher and educator. She was born and raised in Rome, Italy, where she earned her doctoral degree in Natural Sciences from La Sapienza University in Rome. In Italy she worked for several years as a physical anthropologist on numerous archaeological excavations dating back to Imperial Roman and Etruscan ages. She also studied numerous osteological remains from Roman necropolises. At the same time, she continued to teach science and mathematics. Since relocating to Vermont, USA, she has continued with her passions of teaching and research. In 2009 she received the Chemistry Teacher of the Year Award for the State of Vermont, awarded by the NEIC (New England Institute of Chemists). She is also currently a science and mathematics teacher for Arlington Memorial High School (Arlington, Vermont), archaeology professor for the Community College of Vermont and a member of the Vermont State Standards Board for Professional Educators.

Index

Heritage Matters